NIRAD C. CHAUDHURI

THE SCHOLAR EXTRAORDINARY

NIRAD C. CHAUDHURI

THE SCHOLAR EXTRAORDINARY

edited by

R.K.DHAWAN

PRESTIGE

Published by
PRESTIGE BOOKS
3/28, East Patel Nagar
New Delhi 110 008

ISBN: 81-7551-087-0

Composed by Vivek Mathur, Delhi 110 006 Ph. 3981867
Printed at Chaman Offset Press, New Delhi 110 002

Contents

Contributors

MULK RAJ ANAND	Eminent Author Bombay
MADHUMALATI ADHIKARI	Rani Durgavati University Jabalpur
SHYAM S. AGARWALLA	Dr. Ram Manohar Lohia College Ranchi
THOMAS AUGUSTINE	St. Thomas College Palai
URBASHI BARAT	Rani Durgavati University Jabalpur
R.K. DHAWAN	Shaheed Bhagat Singh College University of Delhi
TAPAN K. GHOSH	Tarakeshwar Degree College Tarakeshwar, Hooghly
RAMA KUNDU	Burdwan University Burdwan
M.K. NAIK	Formerly at Karnataka Univ. Dharwad
BASAVARAJ S. NAIKAR	Karnataka University Dharwad
C.D. NARASIMHAIAH	Dhvanyaloka Mysore
PRAMOD KUMAR NAYAR	Kuvempu University Shimoga
INDIRA NITYANANDAM	Navgujarat Arts College Ahmedabad
PURABI PANWAR	College of Vocational Studies University of Delhi
PARVATHY R.	University of Kerala Trivandrum
P. HARI PADMA RANI	S.P. Mahila University Tirupati
MOHIT K. RAY	Burdwan University Burdwan
S.P. SWAIN	Rourkela Municipal College Rourkela

Nirad Chaudhuri: The Scholar Extraordinary

R.K. DHAWAN

Nirad C. Chaudhuri, a literary genius and scholar extraordinary, died at Oxford on 1 August 1999. His reputation as a writer was always fluctuating. However, it is commonly agreed that he was original, brilliant, but highly controversial because of his strong views on men and matters. Critics always wondered whether he would remain popular or be cast into oblivion after his demise. Like his writings his migration to the West evoked a strong response. "When Nirad C. Chaudhuri dies, you will know about his death," commented the veteran writer Khushwant Singh to a journalist just before he left the country in 1970. It was a remark by someone who was close to Niradbabu and understood him quite well. Very often Khushwant Singh discussed serious matters with the scholarly genius. He found that Niradbabu was able to "talk on any subject under the sun." Singh had heard him "discuss stars with astronomers, recite lines from an obscure fifteenth century French poet to a professor of French literature." Such was the prolific quality of his scholarship that one cannot but agree with Khushwant Singh who declared him "a scholar extraordinary" after the title of Niradbabu's own 1974 book on the legendary German writer, the great Max Mueller. His encyclopedic erudition captivated many. In an interview, Khushwant Singh recalls an incident when the enigmatic writer lectured a Nobel prize-winning writer from Iceland on Icelandic literature (*The Times of India*, 3 August 1999). A brilliant polymath with a phenomenal memory, he was distinguished as much for his robust style as for his provocative ideas. No wonder, he has been considered by some critics as India's greatest prose writer of the second half of the twentieth century.

II

Nirad Chaudhuri was born on November 23, 1897, in Kishorganj, a town in East Bengal, now in Bangladesh. His parents were partly Deists, partly Hindu monotheists, and partly rationalists. His father, a lawyer by profession, had scholarly tastes. As was usual then, he had a large family. Nirad had eight bothers and sisters. He was married into a respectable family in Shillong in 1932. However, he does not reveal much in his writings about his wife and his domestic life. He received his early education in an ordinary municipal school but was brilliant as a student. He secured first position in B.A. Hons. examination in History at Calcutta University. Being nervous by temperament, he could not complete his M.A. examination and left studies without acquiring his degree. In the following period of two decades, from 1921 to 1941, he stayed in Calcutta where he had a chequered career. He never found a stable job and served at various places. But being in a big city like Calcutta, he had an opportunity to make a name for himself in the area of journalism. He wrote both in Bengali and English.

All these years, he was fully devoted to the pursuit of learning but his first book appeared only at the age of fifty-one. In his autobiography entitled *The Autobiography of an Unknown Indian*, he pledged to write off the first fifty years of his life and begin life anew. Incidentally, it is an autobiography that has stood the test of time. It does not merely tell his life-story but projects his own inner conflicts as an Indian born and brought up in pre-Independence India and co-relates it to the conflict of the whole race. Chaudhuri was fortunate to have the book published in England in 1951. The book was a great success and he was invited to England in 1955 by the British Broadcasting Corporation. Hitherto an unknown Indian, he became known to the world through his maiden work. *The Autobiography* was well-received in the literary circles. It was something new to the readers. Chaudhuri, deeply influenced by modern science, interpreted life in the light of scientific knowledge. Showing the affinity and contrast between himself and the other great autobiographical writers like Renan, Anatole France and Tagore, Chaudhuri says that though he resembles them in his recapitulation of childhood memories, he sharply differs from them in shifting the stress from the individual to the environment. In his autobiography, he wrote about his life in great detail up to the age of twenty-two, but after that he became more interested in national than in personal history.

Though Chaudhuri has written a great deal, it is desirable to approach him through *The Autobiography of an Unknown Indian* which is not only the best-known of his works but also most informative about his life and ideas. In the very beginning of the preface, Chaudhuri declares that the avowed objective of his writing the autobiography is "to describe the conditions in which an Indian grew to manhood in the early decades of the century." For him, environment is more important than personal life. This makes the book more of a "national history than a personal history." His method is different from the conventional one in that he gives us the picture of the objective world shaping the subjective element itself. That is why he boldly reverses the usual practice of autobiographers. He first gives an account of the environment—both physical and intellectual—and then gives an account of his birth, parentage and early education. Though in form the work is autobiographical, in reality it tells the story of the growth and maturity of a scholar's mind in a hostile environment. The high seriousness of Chaudhuri's approach to life enables him to recognize the complexity of life, the interdependence of character and environment, and the simultaneous existence of contraries of life.

Whileas Chaudhuri aims to portray an objective picture of life around him, *The Autobiography* is essentially the story of the author's life till his twenty-fifth year written from the perspective of a fifty-year-old man who has organized his work around certain themes and places; his selection of material is decided from the writer's point of view. It begins with a record of life lived by people in a small town, in rural Bengal. The native town of Chaudhuri, Kishorganj in East Bengal was his birthplace. The total population of this town was sixteen thousand. It was situated on a river bank. It was a place where people had a remarkable sense of equality without making difference between high caste and low, or between the rich and the poor. It seemed to have a universal appeal.

Nirad was immensely influenced by his mother Sushila Sundari who taught him the principles of honesty, etiquettes and good manners in life. His father too inculcated virtues in him, especially the value of liberal education which would lend grace to life. Above all, he had a great liking for the English language and laid stress on its importance in one's life. Nirad imbibed all these qualities from his father who had a large library, having the works of a number of English writers. He got fully steeped into these writings, especially in the works of Wordsworth, Colly Cibber, Shakespeare, Rupert Brooke and Campbell. Also he read other significant works including Milton's works, Cunningham's *History of Sikhs*, two volumes of Burke's speeches, novels of Bankim Chandra Chatterji and political works of Michael Madhusudan Dutt.

Nirad's father and mother were bound to each other by certain common principles and standards of conduct. His mother taught the children not to be rude intentionally. She was an egoist, unlike his father who was always forgetful of self. But, like his father's unselfishness, her egoism too was of an uncommon kind. There was nothing worldly in it. She was not disposed to the world more than its due. She did not expect from it more than a square deal. Like his father, she too cared little for money, position and power. Nirad resembled her mother most, in physical and mental make-up.

Nirad Chaudhuri as a writer was immensely influenced by the great historical movements in thought, morality and religion. One such great movement, in the history of this country's literature and culture, has been the Indian Renaissance. It was a synthesis of the values and ideals of the East and West. It was a cultural movement of far-reaching importance which began in the early part of the nineteenth century and reached its climax in the following decades and the early twentieth century. In the chapter "Torch Race of the Indian Renaissance," Chaudhuri describes the rebirth of learning and the splendid flowering of Bengal literature that began with the founding of Calcutta's Hindu College in 1817.

It is a well-known fact that the eighteenth century, particularly the later half of it, was one of the darkest periods of the history of India. But the impact of English education on the nineteenth century Indian became evident in the social and cultural life. Traditionally Indians were fed on superstition and blind faith. They were, largely speaking, irrational and illogical in their approach to life. Contact with English education and culture made them conscious of their retrogressive attitude towards life, especially in their blind regard for religion and dogma. Several thinkers and writers raised their voice against the custom-old traditions and fashions. Vidyasagar raised his voice against child-marriage and polygamy. Swami Vivekanand awakened the dead consciousness of the humanity. His address at the Chicago Parliament of Religions in 1893 was monumental. It brought a great change in the attitude of the Western people towards the Hindu religion. He made a cogent and lofty exposition of Hinduism and this led to the appreciation and approval of Hinduism by the English with an open mind. Raja Ram Mohun Roy and Bankim Chandra Chatterjee attempted a reexamination and re-interpretation of Indian culture and tried to educate the people. The discovery of the glorious past of India together with a new awareness of the same led to the resurgence of nationalism and patriotism among Indians.

According to Nirad Chaudhuri, Indian Renaissance was a compromise between the orthodox conservatism and modern liberalism, a happy union of the Oriental and the Occidental. It was created in a series of waves of different compositions: literary, humanistic, religious and critical. The new movement in Bengal began with the founding of the famous Hindu College in 1817. The best exponent of Bengali humanism was Michael Madhusudan Dutt, a sound scholar and the first poet of modern Bengal. To begin with, he wrote only in English. But after a few years, when he was past thirty, he wrote in Bengali. Chaudhuri's first introduction to Bengali humanism began with his reading of the poetry of Toru Dutt and Aru Dutt, which was published in a Bengali magazine in 1901.

After Dutt, Chaudhuri tells us, it was Shakespeare which captured the imagination of Bengalis: "I do not know if any other country or people in the world has ever made one author the epitome, test and symbol of literary culture as we Bengalis did with Shakespeare in the nineteenth century."

Apart from Bengali and English literature, Sanskrit made a deep impact on the mind of Chaudhuri. It was a literature that had an important element in the humanism of modern India. Interestingly, Sanskrit that appealed to Chaudhuri and other Bengalis was not the traditional literature propagated by pundits, but it was the Sanskrit learning of the European Orientalists and their Indian disciples. Whileas Chaudhuri read all these literatures, he never got any systematic instruction in any religion. At the same time, he did acquire a religious mood. This mood came to him through regular routine of devotional singing, a routine that continued till early eighteenth year of his life. Moreover, he and other students received a thorough moral education: "Contact was the subject of explicit discussion, guidance and correction with us. We received more training in school as well as at home."

In the Preface to Book III, Chaudhuri tells us that he lived in Calcutta for thirty-two years, from 1910 to 1942. During this period, he visited his native town, Kishorganj, rarely and never after 1927. His story in Calcutta played a decisive role in moulding of his scholarly temperament; it sharpened his power of perception. He felt deeply involved in the lively and vigorous literary atmosphere of the city. During the school career, he felt excited to get acquainted with the *Encyclopaedia Britannica*, and the first article that attracted him was on days. During these years, he was initiated into scholarship. Amongst all the subjects, history fascinated him the most. He wanted to be "an epitome of universal knowledge."

During his college days, History was his special subject in the Honours course. He was much interested in the nature and methods of historical knowledge. His ambition was to become a professor of History, but it could not be realized as he failed to pass his M.A. in History owing to ill-health and mental depression. Talking about his love for the subject, he says: "In the three months of summer vacation of 1917, I read every nineteenth century and early twentieth-century classic of history and made myself perfectly familiar within the history of historical writing." He makes the best use of his knowledge of History in his *Autobiography*. Following an objective method, without prejudice or exaggeration, it demonstrates his wide knowledge and his sense of accuracy. It is creditable that he writes history with a vast encyclopedic knowledge that renders his work into a great monument of national history.

Interestingly, Chaudhuri does not abandon this mode of writing even later in life. His *Thy Hand, Great Anarch! India 1921-1952* (1987) is once again not merely the story of one man but an elaborate account of an epoch in Indian history. Chaudhuri, in the work, continues to tell the story of his life while adopting a universal perspective on India's past and present. It offers a detailed picture of the society in which Chaudhuri lived from youth to middle age along with a commentary on historical events and persons he was in touch with. It was a period—of about three decades—when India was sliding steadily into chaos. He minutely surveys the political and cultural wasteland that he thinks India is becoming. Thus he completes the story of his life in *Thy Hand, Great Anarch*, written and published much later in life. It may be called a sequel or a sort of postscript to the great autobiography.

III

It sounds almost incredible that a writer should publish a work in the 99th year of his life as Chaudhuri did. His *Three Horsemen of the New Apocalypse* (1997) is a feast for those who enjoy reading Chaudhuri's scathing commentary on our times. It is indeed a magnificent book that takes into its sweep three causative factors of the decadence that we witness today—both in Western as well as Indian societies. These three horsemen, according to Chaudhuri, are individualism, nationalism and democracy. A nation is decadent, says he, when it has lost its political and economic power as well as its cultural creativeness.

Even this last work of Chaudhuri reveals the scholar's righteous indignation at the sorry state of affairs all over. Everything he says is drawn from some depth of conviction within him. He was an institution in himself and his views were most provocative. To the extent that he claimed that he did not believe in God, in life after death, in *moksha* and did not have any religious convictions. It seems ironical that the author, though highly erratic and temperamental, was capable of great sensitivity too. His faith in human bonds was evident in his love for his wife. Indeed, he never got over the death of Amiya Chaudhuri—his wife of 62 years—in 1994. He felt greatly moved by this event and started ruminating about death and man's purpose in the grand design of this inscrutable world. He bemoaned:

> Why then did the world punish mankind with death? As individuals, men are like sacrificial lambs to the world. The

> world makes him work to its own end and then kills him like a ruthless ascetic. One could say it's God's will. In my childhood, I had heard a devotional song—"Compassionate one, why are you so cruel?" Man will always ask this disinterested question to the world, which will go unanswered. I too will die with the same question in mind.

Chaudhuri was curious, questioning, inquisitive all his life and no less near his death, at the age of 102. The 'unknown Indian' had carved out a niche for himself, and not for nothing.

Bibliography

Chaudhuri, Nirad C. "Although man's body is perishable, his mind is not. It's immortal," *Sunday*, 8-14 August 1999, p. 21.

Gupta, Kanchan. "Bugle for the Retreating Brigade," A Review of *Three Horsemen of the New Apocalypse, The Pioneer*, 9 August 1997, p. 13.

______. "Picture this, Nirad," *The Pioneer*, 22 November 1997, p. 13.

Karnani, Chetan. *Nirad C. Chaudhuri* (Boston: Twayne, 1980).

Naikar, Basavaraj S. *Critical Articles on Nirad C. Chaudhuri* (Dharwad: Divaranjan Publication, 1985).

Nelson, Emmanuel S., ed. *Writers of the Indian Diaspora: A Bio-Bibliographical Critical Source Book* (London: Greenwood Press, 1993).

Shivshankar, Rahul. "Niradbabu's writings were always a treat: Khushwant," *The Times of India*, 3 August 1999.

Sinha, Tara. *Nirad C. Chaudhuri* (Patna: Janaki Prakashan, 1981).

Vaidyanathan, T.G. "A beautiful but ineffectual angel," *The Hindu Magazine*, 15 August, 1999.

Verghese, Paul.. *Nirad C. Chaudhuri* (New Delhi: Arnold Heinemann, 1973).

An Interview with Nirad C. Chaudhuri

R. PARVATHY

It was spring as I walked up the pathway at 20, Lathbury Road, Oxford, England. The garden still had a few remaining daffodils of that season. Though the garden did not seem totally neglected, it could still have done with a little tending. It was approximately 11 O'clock in the morning on 21st April 1994. Chaudhuri opened the front door himself. He recalled immediately the letter I had written a month ago where I had mentioned the topic of my research and such like. I had no appointment and no foreknowledge of Nirad Chaudhuri being available that day. I had come on the hunch that to have a chat with Chaudhuri, all one had to do was ring the doorbell and wait to be let in. To my complete surprise, Chaudhuri himself opened the front door and after I introduced myself, let me in. He was most welcoming. I was then in the thick of doctoral research and he plunged straight into an earnest explanation of the cause of his alienation in India. As his legendary style is, he talked non-stop, going into occasional cackles of laughter, seemed to be high-strung, kept leaping out of his chair frequently to bring down books and paintings from various shelves to substantiate his claims. In the course of the long interview, he showed me pictures hanging in his room: of Benares; of the infant Shakespeare, sitting up which he laughs at. He points out various discrepancies in the picture of Benares. The trees are russet coloured, according to him they always remain green. He also showed recent photos of Kishorganj and Banigram and a facsimile of the First Folio. He showed me several books that he read as a small boy. He also showed me the original of the New Testament with him written in Greek. According to the original Greek version the story of Magdalene is omitted. It was probably a later addition. Here are some excerpts from the conversation that lasted more than two hours.

Chaudhuri: You should not have bothered to come. As for your research . . .

Parvathy: We need not talk about it. if you would rather not.

Chaudhuri: No, no. There are two things I would like to say. You have made a mistake. I am not a fit topic for research. No living author can be. Let me ask you something. Why do you do research? For two things. One, to learn the methods of research. Two, in order to acquire some information. While the first may be satisfied, the second need not be. If you work on a living author you cannot find authentic sources. Moreover, to understand my writing you have to understand Bengali, as Bankim Chandra, Vivekananda, Tagore and others have influenced me. But you certainly can write literary criticism on what I write.

Parvathy: Could you describe your idea of how best to conduct research?

Chaudhuri: Rigidity in research is absolutely essential. Compromise, and you are finished. The original manuscripts should be read. But in India it is not possible to verify the authenticity of extant texts. By authenticity I mean the original manuscripts. Al-Biruni's book on India gives many quotations from the *Gita*, which cannot be found in today's version of the same text. Why is that? It is because of a lack of rigidity in scholarship, which is essential to maintain authenticity. In my life I refused to recant my beliefs and that is why I have reached where I have. Because of that it is only a few years ago that my luck changed. I have not let my emotion cloud the truth. If I see a tiger I will not say it is something else. In India on the other hand, people believe only what they want to believe. Which is why I am alienated and it is only a few years ago that my luck changed. The Queen gave me the CBF. Do you know what I said then? "I'm glad I've been given this, because I'm a diehard imperialist" (long spell of laughter).

Parvathy: What can you say about being alienated in India? Why are you alienated in India?

Chaudhuri: Why am I alienated in India? Because I do not have one single idea that is common with the upper middle class. I can only talk with them, I am even of them. But not one single idea of theirs I share. I don't believe a single myth generated in India.

Parvathy: Could you specify on that?

Chaudhuri: I do not believe in any myth. Do you know that of the ten avatars the Hindus thought that Kalki avatar had destroyed the Huns. Yashovarman Vishnuvardan. In Jayadeva at one point Kalki is mentioned in the past tense. But later with the coming of the Muslims they changed it to the future. (He goes into a long spell of laughter) On the other hand, I am the greatest admirer of ancient Hindu civilization. And that civilization is in no way connected with the Hinduism of today. Ancient Hindu civilization had a free society; men and women met, spoke, fell in love. They had exquisite manners. One extraordinary thing these had was privacy. In a novel I read, a woman goes out, falls in love, comes back, tells her maids that she is going to her rooms and is not to be disturbed. One would think that her mother could walk in. But it is not so. In another instance, a Prince visits a girl who is at her prayers. He is asked to wait, which he does. These were the manners of the period, very European. Where has all that gone?

Parvathy: What do you think has happened?

Chaudhuri: It was my endeavour to see what was going to happen. I was able to do so because I understood the decay of the Greco-Roman civilization. Many of the things that I predicted in 1951 are coming true.

Decadence has overtaken England and India. What is decadence? Simply put, it is aging. We all age. I have no teeth. Once I had a head full of hair. Now I am bald. Is that disgusting? No. It becomes disgusting when I go to a brothel at this age and contract syphillis. That is what is happening in England now. Even in India, vulgar Europeanisation is taking place. In England, a twelve-year-old boy raped an eleven-year-old girl. In ancient India, this would not have happened. In ancient India, a man would not force himself on a woman. A woman could also walk around perfectly safe with all her jewellery.

I am going to tell you something personal. I married when I was 34. Until then I had no contact whatsoever with a woman. If you want to be equal to men, you will have to listen to dirty talk by men. This is a kind of Puritanism that has come from genuine Europeanisation. Have you been reading all those dirty stories about Clinton? Such dirty stories about the President of a country!

Parvathy: What about Nehru?

Chaudhuri: Look, there is no way to determine a man's sexual behaviour from his social behaviour. But I knew Nehru. I met him soon after his wife died. He was a broken man. There was no indication that he was having these affairs when he was alive. There was no indication whatsoever. I think all the stories are fabricated.

Parvathy: What would you say in reply to the criticism that you have to face from India?

Chaudhuri: Bengalis used to say if he is such a scholar why doesn't the Oxford University confer upon him the doctorate. Now that they have, they have nothing to say. Let me give you an example of Indian servility to the British. Indians come to Oxford to do their Ph.D. The Englishmen want money, so they take them, but they are put under blackies. I tell them, why don't you do it under blackies in India? They reply that blackies in Oxford are much better. It is this slavish mentality that I cannot tolerate. Their theses are also worthless. Good for trampling under my feet. (stamps his foot)

Let me ask you something. What is the meaning of Prakrit?

Parvathy: Primitive?

Chaudhuri: No. It means natural, the opposite of Sanskrit, which means constructed. Magadhi-Prakrit was the language that united India from Mysore to Kashmir and from Peshawar to Bengal. Why were there no Sanskrit inscriptions? Even the Queens speak in Magadhi-Prakrit. What does the word Prakrit mean? It means natural but the word in Sanskrit means constructed. My daughter-in-law, who is Thai, prays in Magadhi-Prakrit. She belongs to the Hinayana cult. Even at the time of the Buddha, Aryan gods were worshipped. Buddha was visited constantly by Indra at the Rishala cave. Brahma-Vishu-Parameshwar had not come into existence then.

Parvathy: How about your religious beliefs?

Chaudhuri: Temples in India were not originally places of worship. They were recreation centres for kings. That is why you have such sculptures. I have never been to a temple since 1920. Because I did not want to mock another's belief. There are people praying inside. If I went in, I would be mocking them.

Parvathy: How about your working pattern?

Chaudhuri: I do not write continuously. I write at random. Some paragraphs are rewritten as much as fifteen times. When it is finally finished, it won't be very different from the original.

One idiot once asked me, why didn't you write poetry. I asked him, "Is it a matter of choice?" he did not understand my answer. Is it something to be done under compulsion? I knew I wanted to be a writer. Then I concentrated all my energies to that. I did not have second thoughts. It is only the weak who have second thoughts. Not I.

Someone said to me that I would have made a great novelist. Because of my powers of observation. But I cannot write novels since I am unfamiliar with the social milieu of today. The one I am familiar with is that of the early twentieth century.

By the way, I never read without a map of the region in hand. Charlotte Bronte for instance made a few terrible blunders in her novels when she wrote about her own region.

I write in English and in Bengali. Different minds are required for both. What I write in English cannot be translated into Bengali and vice versa. I have left instructions that it should not be translated. It cannot be translated because two minds create.

Parvathy: How about your life in India?

Chaudhuri: When I was earning eight pounds a month in India, I bought a book for five pounds. The landed gentry is like that. Buy now pay later. The Bengali bhadralok is not middle class. The English equivalent to the bhadralok is the Squire. I belong to the landed gentry. I don't think like the bourgeiosie about the cost of books. I buy only the best book in hardbound.

In Calcutta, a long time ago, when I was unemployed, I was asked by a newspaper to write for them. They would give Rs. 5 for an article. I asked for ten. They refused and I refused to write for them. Now they give me Rs. 20,000 for an article.

My children did not study in either a Govt. school or in schools run by missionaries. I have nothing but contempt for both. I taught my sons. My son sat for the GCE (General Council of Education) after being taught by me. In India, in England. He scored 85% marks.

I am the perfect fusion of the Westerner and European. Will you find another Indian in England wearing dhoti and jooba? I think Edward Shils has described me aptly in his essay as a citizen of the world.

Having come to the end of the interview Chaudhuri shuffled out of the room with me, excusing himself for he was off to serve his bedridden wife her lunch.

"Defence of India": Chaudhuri's First Publication

M.K. NAIK

It is eminently symptomatic of the present state of scholarship in the field of Indian English literature that while Nirad C. Chaudhuri is universally acclaimed, both in India and the West, as one of the most outstanding of Indian masters of English prose, very few people seem to have even heard of his first significant publication—*viz*. a seventy-three page essay entitled "Defence of India or Nationalization of Indian Army" which appeared in 1935.[1] Neither of the two full-length studies of Chaudhuri published so far[2] makes even a passing reference to it, and no bibliography of Indian English literature lists it. Surprisingly enough, even an authoriative work like *A Survey of Work Done on the Military History of India*[3] makes no mention of it, though the Bibliography appended to *Survey* runs to not less than sixty-three pages and includes full-length studies as well as brief articles. Apart from a casual reference to it in Chaudhuri's *Autobiography of an Unknown Indian*,[4] the only other work to mention the essay is *Oriental Studies in India*.[5] In this note, it is proposed to introduce this essay to all those interested in Chaudhuri's writings.

Chaudhuri's argument in "Defence of India" is divided into four sections. The first section entitled "The Problem Stated" occupies nine pages and discusses three issues: "The National Demand" for the progressive Indianization of the Indian army, the "Character of the present army" and the "spirit and quality of the army." Chaudhuri begins by emphasizing the demand of the Indian National Congress to transform the whole of the defence service of India from its present (i.e. 1935) to a national footing as one of the indispensable conditions and the natural fulfilment of the ideal of *Swaraj*, because the right and capacity of defence is an integral part of self-government. Discussing the "character of the present army," he argues that the armed forces, as now constituted, are Indian in only one sense—in that their cost is borne by the peoples of India; in everything else they are non-national, though an overwhelming proportion of their personnel is furnished by India. The following factors reveal the non-national character of the Indian army: (i) It is not controlled by Indians, and the constitutional representatives of the people of India in the governmental machinery have no effective voice in its affairs. (ii) It is recruited from certain parts of India only and not from the country as a whole, e.g. large areas of Madras and Bombay Presidencies do not furnish a single soldier to it. (iii) The strict regulation of the quotas to be furnished by each district, tribe, caste or sect is another inhibiting factor. (iv) The army's whole internal organization is based on a caste system more rigid than that of even Hindu society. An elaborate system of grouping and checks and balances ensures that soldiers retain their tribal or communal loyalties without developing a national consciousness. (v) Indians in the army are practically insulated from the civil population: the result is mutual suspicion and even hatred. (vi) The army in India is partly constituted of units of the British Army and till very recently Indians were not employed in all its arms. There has been some relaxation of this policy recently, but not quite enough to enable the Indians to constitute a self-contained fighting formation, by themselves. (vii) The leadership of the Army is purely British and its ideals those of British imperialism. (viii) The function of the Army in India is imperial, not national.

As for the "Spirit and Quality of the Army," though the Indian army is a good fighting machine, it stands in a class apart from the armies of the modern civilized states in several respects: it lacks the moral asset of a national feeling and its spirit purely professional, with the result that its morale is weak to that extent. Secondly, it denies to its Indian element opportunities for leadership on the highest military plane.

In contrast with this, a national army for India "should be commanded and controlled by Indians, be recruited from all parts of the country and be animated by a national spirit. It should be a self-contained fighting machine able to do without the help and guidance of foreigners and above all, it should foster the military capacity of the whole nation and be directly related to it." (9)

In the second section, "Function" (which, like each of the remaining sections, runs to about twenty pages), Chaudhuri discusses the national and imperial function of the Indian army, and the problems concerning this. He challenges the popular view that the Army in India is merely an army of occupation designed to perpetuate India's political subjection to Great Britain. This, according to him, is an extreme view which ignores the military stakes involved. The "army of occupation" role has been obsolescent since the 1880s and after its post (World) War (I) reogranization, the Indian army became at once a reserve police force, a garrison and a field army providing for border policing, internal security and external defence. And in everyone of the functions assigned to it, it is more concerned with British than with Indian interests, though British writers naturally do not admit this, pleading that the task of defending India is extremely complex and difficult.

The function of the Indian Army is decided less by the natural military requirements of India than by those created by the British connection. The three important factors in the defence of a country are: its geographical situation; its economic needs and political aspirations and its relations with foreign powers. In every one of these respects, India holds a peculiarly favourable position. It has excellent natural defences, is capable of becoming a self-contained economic and political unit and need have no direct point of friction with any of her neighbours. The official apologist's emphasis on the possibility of an invasion by the Afghan and Pathan tribes in the North-West is misplaced in view of the realities of the twentieth-century situation; in actual fact, it is the British fear of Russia that has decided the nature and function of the Field Army of India.

As for the internal security duties of the Army, they are entirely a product of the British connection, and are designed to ensure the continuation of the British rule in India. They include the suppression of revolutionary movements and of lawlessness arising from local or widespread grievances and the prevention of communal disturbances.

The last of the imperial obligations of the Army in India is the liability for service overseas. This liability has become greater after the war, so that while the old Indian army as an autonomous force with a more or less autonomous strategic role, the army of today is an integral part of the elaborate system of imperial defence. India's armed forces will be drawn upon in every war in which Great Britain may be engaged as a matter of course and without any reference to her interests, thus reducing the function of the Indian Army to that of a detachment of the British Army.

The third section, "Man Power," deals with the composition of the Army. Here Chaudhuri brilliantly exposes the manifold evils of the unjust recruitment policies adopted by the British Government. The extremely one-sided composition of the Indian army has been sought to be explained away by the notorious theory of the "martial races" of India—a theory so "full of contradictions and biologically improbable that it carries its own refutation within itself." (30) Actually, the composition of the Indian Army has been determined by questions of political expediency and immediate needs rather than by well-thought out military policies. In this connection, Chaudhuri reviews the Indian tradition and concedes that the lopsidedness of the composition of the Indian Army is also due to certain inherent features of Indian society which furnished British policy with its starting point. Indian military life in the past was governed by two principles: specialization and heredity, which together prevented the growth of a tradition of universal military service. A contributory factor was the low political development of the country as a result of which the State and the People were never considered to be synonymous terms. War was the business of kings and professionals and not "a condition of national existence"; military power of the community. The Marathas under Shivaji and his successors, and later the Sikhs and the Jats tried to take the tradition of military service from a clannish or professional to a broader national or religious ground, but they were all broken by the British before a regular tradition of national service could grow up in India.

The effects of the British polity have prevented the natural military development of India. The British practice of maintaining a small, highly-trained professional army instead of a short-term conscripted army as in most European countries has restricted the needs of the Indian army to a fraction of the total population of the country. This irresponsible use of the man-power of the country has led both to the hardening of the caste tradition and the alteration of the distribution of the fighting castes, leading to a shrinkage of the field of recruitment.

The military energy of a nation proceeds from two psychological sources derived from two simple biological instincts—the instinct of pugnacity (which marks the professional soldier) and the instinct of defence (which the ordinary citizen possesses). The two resultant types of armies are the "Condottiere" and the "Burgher" armies, and the latter type was a product of the French Revolution which saw an amazing liberation of the latent military energies of a whole nation. While the armies of most modern states are clearly "Burgher" armies, the Indian Army remains narrowly professional, while in the past (as in the case of the Marathas, the Sikhs and the Jats), Indian armies were at their best in fighting for a righteous cause, the Indian military tradition being essentially unaggressive in character.

The decline in the military capacity of the Indian people has been further compounded by the deliberate demartialization of India by the British brought about by (i) keeping the army as distinct from the general population as possible and (ii) depriving the Indian public of the right to carry arms. Both these steps are directly opposed to the practice of governments which have a stake in the man-power of their countries. All modern states try to bridge the gulf between the army and the general public through schemes like the Territorial Army and preparatory military training in schools and colleges; in India the gulf is actually sought to be widened.

The future organizers of a national Indian army will therefore have to restore the military spirit of the people and improve the efficiency of the entire population by halting their physical deterioration, which is the result of a vicious circle of poverty, ignorance and, in some cases, baneful habits of living and unsuitable diet.

"Command and control" is the sub-title of the concluding section, which begins by pointing out that the question of Indian control of the army has either been confused with the question of Indian leadership or made dependent on it. Actually, in Great Britain ministers of war have rarely been professionals, and in fact, some of the most far-reaching innovations in organization, equipment and strategy have been due to the initiative of politicians. It is this civilian collaboration in the military sphere that is wanted in India and for this nothing more is required than a sense of defence and flair for the general principles of strategy and army organization. If this sense is not as highly developed in the politically conscious classes in India as it is among those in Europe, that is not because of any lack of basic aptitude. The way to familiarize the people and the politicians of India with the reality of defence questions is to bring them into closer relation with the problems of national security. This can only be done through the increasing association of Indians with the actual defence arrangements of the country, if not at first in an executive, at least in a consultative capacity. Unfortunately, the Act of 1935 denies the Indians even this, since, according to it the Department of Defence is under the exclusive direction and control of the Governor General. This provision is clearly designed to continue the imperial character of the Indian army.

The control of the Indian army by the imperial military authorities is maintained in various ways—first by giving no voice to the Indian people in matters of defence, and secondly, by making the Government of India responsible to Parliament and the British Government. Again, the Commander-in-Chief and the principal staff officers have the right to correspond direct with War Office in most military matters. Furthermore, the British officers of the Indian army are purely local agents of the Imperial General Staff and do not acknowledge any duty to the national defensive requirements of India.

These imperial stakes in the Army in India have inevitably hampered the process of its Indianization. The scheme of Indianization approved by the Defence Sub-committee of the first Round Table Conference labours under several limitations: (i) though, for the first time in the history of the post-Mutiny army, it seeks to create a formation of all arms composed entirely of Indians, the decision to confine Indianization to a particular formation continues the principle of segregating Indian Officers. (ii) The recent establishment of a military college in India is a welcome step but the annual in-take of the college is so low that the process of Indianization will be extremely slow. (iii) The Indianized portion of the army is sought to be condemned to an inferior status by giving the new Indian Officers a lower rate of pay and restricted powers of command.

These crippling limitations make one suspect that the entire scheme is a clever attempt to divide the army in India into two parts, one to be composed of and commanded by Indians and employed for local defence, and the other, composed of both Indian and British officers, to be reserved for imperial purposes, so that if at some future date the political control of defence has to be transferred to Indians it might be confined to the field of local defence and not disturb imperial defence arrangements.

The latest argument against quickening the pace of Indianization is that there is a lack of suitable candidates even for the limited number of annual vacancies now available. But the creation of an officer class is everywhere—even in England—and at all times a long and arduous process, and the only way to succeed in it is to set about it on right lines; but the methods adopted by the present organizers of Indian military education are hardly the right ones. First, military education should be suited to national character and should not try to uproot the cadets from their social environment. But this is exactly what the military authorities are doing in India, by trying to fashion Brown Englishmen from Indian youths. Secondly, the most suitable material for this transformation is to be found in the anglicized upper-middle class which has naturally been over-represented in the Indian military academy; but this class is frankly careerist in its orientation and its mode of living has already made it a stranger to the common people. It is manifestly incapable of providing the required leadership.

Another check on the supply of candidates to the military college is the want of the necessary background. The three stages in the education of officers are: preliminary education imparted through the general education system of the country and intended to develop physique and character; the graduating stage at a military college, and the post-graduate stage at the staff college. Present day Indian military education can hardly be said to be properly organised in this manner.

The policy of appealing to the sons of *sardars* and *zamindars* to come forward for commissions is also misconceived, for two reasons: (i) not all the *zamindars* are the natural leaders of the country (ii) the history of the Indian army after the British conquest is one of the progressive degradation of the native officer, all substantive power being in the hands of British officers. This has discouraged upper-class Indians with military ambitions and they preferred to serve the princes of the native states instead.

Chaudhuri concludes by saying that this historical process must be reversed if there is to be a revival of the military capacity of the nation. "In the higher sphere of command as in the lower sphere of man-power, the only way to create a truly national army is to wipe off the slate the developments of the last hundred and fifty years and lay the foundations afresh." (73)

"Defence of India" is, in many ways, a piece of composition typical of Chaudhuri, though as an early work it is generally free from some of nastier bees in his intellectual bonnet. As his *Autobiography* (104-8) shows, Chaudhuri's interest in military matters goes back to his boyhood. He tells us how his adoration for Napolean then was only an example of the widely shared Bengali fascination for this great military leader and that he also admired Wellington, Lord Roberts ("whom we regarded as the greatest living soldier") and Lord Kitchener. When the news arrives that the post of Commander-in-Chief is abolished in England; and an Inspector-General has been installed in his place, he is filled with "unspeakable disgust," for, this is regarded as a disgrace to England; "a Commander-in-Chief was a man next only to the Viceroy, while an Inspector was only a Police inspector and even the highest inspector was no higher than the Inspector of Schools." As a boy he also gained knowledge about the "more important European wars of the previous fifty years." This early interest in military matters was obviously strengthened when Chaudhuri became a clerk in the Military Accounts Department in 1921, though he did not continue in this post for a long time.

Chaudhuri's essay also reveals glimpses of many characteristic aspects of his literary personality with which his better known works such as *The Autobiography of an Unknown Indian* and *The*

Continent of Circe have made us familiar—*viz*. the breadth of his intellectual interests, his encyclopaedic learning, his thoroughness, his "spirit of fierce intellectual defence"[6] which makes him challenge accepted positions, his brilliant marshalling of his material and his distinctive prose style.

His argument in "Defence of India" clearly shows Chaudhuri's mastery of the subject in all its ramifications. He knows as much about the Indian military tradition through the ages as about the theory and practice of modern Western military science; and at every stage of his argument, his agile mind is constantly active in sifting available knowledge, interpreting it and relating it to a comprehensive view of the subject. His numerous references to British writers on military, historical and political matters shows his wide reading on the subject. Among the authors and works he alludes to are Sir Valentine Chirol, the reports of the Royal Commission on the Mesopotamia campaign, the Royal Commission on recruitment after the Mutiny and subcommitte No. VII, on defence, of the first Round Table Conference; Sir John Lawrence, General MacMunn, Sir Richard Temple, Lord Haldane and Sir Philip Chetwode. It is entirely typical of Chaudhuri that his essay also reveals his knowledge of ancillary subjects. While discussing the question of the physical efficiency of Indians, he refers to the report of the Royal Commission on agriculture and the Imperial Institute for Nutrition established in Japan in 1920; and in pin-pointing the deficiencies of the British recruitment policy he alludes to the blunder of the Permanent Settlement in Bengal after the British Conquest.

As the summary given above indicates, Chaudhuri's argument is extremely well-reasoned and incisive. The perceptiveness of the analysis is clear throughout, one of the best examples being his comment on the British Government's decision to make a contribution towards the cost of the army in India. He characterizes the acceptance of this contribution as "one of the signal blunders in Indian politics in recent years" (66) and points out how it has materially prejudiced the case for Indianization; because this is perhaps the first move in a long-range plane to divide the Indian army into two parts, one under Indian command and the other under British.

Scrutinizing Chaudhuri's argument from the vantage ground of today, one notes that the march of history has proved him totally wrong at one place. While discussing the natural defensive requirements of India, he argues, "the natural political and economic development of all her Asiatic neighbours is in no way affected by India. None of them have (*sic*) any direct point of friction with her which could induce them to such war and unless we ourselves excited their cupidity by a culpable display of military weakness they would probably all be perfectly ready to leave us alone." (16) The fact that within less than two decades of Independence, India developed direct points of friction with two of her neighbours and had to go to war with them thrice has entirely disproved Chaudhuri's view. But in his defence it may be pointed out that writing in 1935, not even the shrewdest of political commentators could have foreseen the sweeping changes which lay hardly a dozen or so years away then *viz.* the advent of Independence, the creation of Pakistan and the establishment of a Communist government in China.

Tautly structured and to the point, "Defence of India" has no room for digression; only one of Chaudhuri's favourite ideas (to which he recurs in his later books) therefore seems to appear here and that too very briefly: his views on the inadequacies of Indian "habits of living and unsuitable diet" to which he attributes in some measure "the physical deterioration of the masses as well as the intelligentsia in India." (49) It will be recalled that this view is reiterated with further elaboration at various places in the "Essay on the Cause of Indian History" in *The Autobiography of an Unknown Indian*, *The Continent of Circe*, *The Intellectual in India* and *To Live or Not to Live*.

Two extremely interesting features of *Defence of India* are the total absence from it of both his notorious anglophilia and his "Hindu-baiting." He is highly critical of the policies of the British Government here and it is significant that his essay was published by the All India Congress Committee. There is also not the slightest trace here of those preconceived theories, and prejudices about Hindu character and culture which gradually hardened into obstinate dogmas as Chaudhuri grew older. This is perhaps because when he wrote the essay, his own individual frustrations had not yet grown strong enough to compel him to elevate his personal pique to the level of primary principle. He had not yet become a complete "stranger to my environment,"[7] nor had he decided to turn "away from the new Hindu Yahoos."[8] Writing in 1935, he had not yet made the great discovery that the ("so- called") Gandhi cap and the ("so-called") Jawahar "waistcoat" are "two of the ugliest imaginable adjuncts from non-Hindu families of clothing, which add to the unattractiveness of the political costume."[9] The writer of "Defence of India" is certainly not the incorrigible "Hindu-baiter" that the later Chaudhuri is, while at the same time manifesting at least in some measure those gifts of thought and expression which one always associates with his name. Chaudhuri himself has emphasized the principle that "style . . . is not only the man himself, it is also the subject itself,"[10] and the rather technical nature of its subject has naturally circumscribed the stylistic excellence of "Defence of India." There is not much scope here for the varied allusion and learned quotation, periodic eloquence and striking imagery, lively anecdote and sharp irony which lighten up the pages of Chaudhuri's acknowledged masterpieces. Nevertheless, in many ways the Chaudhuri stamp is unmistakably in "Defence of India."

NOTES

1. Congress Golden Jubilee Brochure No. 8, published by The All India Congress Committee, Swaraj Bhavan, Allahabad, 1935. I found a copy of this in the library of the University of Allahabad, Allahabad.
2. Paul Verghese, *Nirad C. Chaudhuri* (New Delhi: Arnold-Heinemann, 1973). Tara Sinha, *Nirad C. Chaudhuri* (Patna, 1981).
3. S.N. Prasad, *A Survey of Work Done on the Military History of India* (Calcutta, 1976). The book is sponsored by the Indian Council of Historical Research.
4. "The Congress had in the meanwhile published an essay by me on the Indianization of the army," *The Autobiography of an Unknown Indian* (Bombay, 1951), p. 263.
5. *Oriental Studies in India*, published by the Organizing Committee, 26th International Congress of Orientalists, New Delhi, 1964. My thanks are due to Professor G.S. Dikshit for drawing my attention to this.

6. Nirad C. Chaudhuri, *I Believe*, ed. Khushwant Singh (New Delhi, n.d.), p. 27
7. *The Autobiography of an Unknown Indian*, p. 522.
8. Nirad C. Chaudhuri, *The Continent of Circe* (Bombay, 1966), p. 375.
9. Nirad C. Chaudhuri, *Culture in the Vanity Bag* (Bombay, 1976), p. 101.
10. Nirad C. Chaudhuri, *The Intellectual in India* (New Delhi, 1967), p. 79.

Jawaharlal Nehru and Nirad Chaudhuri as Writers of Autobiography

C.D. NARASIMHAIAH

'Moving Frontiers of English Studies in India' is not a fanciful title; at least it is not meant to be. We have during the past quarter of a century founded more universities and colleges than in all the three hundred years since the British came to India and yet no discipline in Indian education has had to face the kind of uncertainty English has—from the politician, the teacher and journalist in regional and national languages. And English has not merely endured in India but seems destined to prevail. Never before have so many young people in school, college and university volunteered from so many diverse backgrounds to acquire English as in the past twenty-five years as though they now realize that in the past the priest had cheated them out of their Sanskrit heritage and they should not now be cheated—this time by the politician—of their international heritage. Indeed they saw for themselves that patriots who had denounced it in Parliament and were raised to bad eminence in public life for their hatred of English were seen standing in queues before English convents to have their grandchildren admitted because—how could they help?—their sons and daughters were hard to convince!

Now the gain is not just quantitative, for with it goes a value. In spite of the fall in the average never before was English so well spoken or written by so large a number! When in the past did so many Indians teach English to English-speaking people in institutions of higher learning or publish so many scholarly books and articles on English and American literature through prestigious commercial firms and in university-sponsored periodicals? When in the past did we have so many works of fiction and poetry written in English by Indians which have invited the attention of adult readers abroad and in university departments all the world over? And at home, when before did we feel so proud of our writers in English as during these years of Indian Independence—so proud that Indian writing in English has come to be a formal academic discipline in at least twenty universities and Indian-English prose and verse are taught under General English in almost every university to the undergraduates if only through anthology pieces—both teachers and students demand them because they depict the Indian scene and *they* can respond better.

I have for my first lecture chosen to speak not on the better known novelists and poets but on Jawaharlal Nehru who—few know this, indeed, he denied it himself—inaugurated in a major way this species called Indian writing in English through some half dozen masterpieces half of which became best-sellers, a privilege conferred on an Indian author for the first time in recent history. One says so because none of our distinguished novelists[1]—Anand, Narayan, Raja Rao, Sudhin Ghose, Bhabani Bhattacharya, or Desani—had started writing when the Oxford University Press brought out in 1930 'Letters from a Father to his Daughter.' The work is such a model of good prose that the 'Letters' have frequently found their way into school textbooks. It is of these 'mountain of letters' which later became *Glimpses of World History* that Tom Wintringham wrote that if in the future Indians wanted to learn English they would do well to read Nehru rather than Gibbon or Macaulay, because here was 'better history and better English'—the reason why presumably Nehru wrote them to his young daughter whose education he could not directly supervise thanks to his frequent prison-going. That he had a fine awareness of his calling as writer is continually in evidence however much his preoccupation with politics may have obscured or distorted his literary pursuits and the distinction he achieved there. It always intrigues me . . . whether one who speaks of language as 'the poetic testament of the genius of a race and culture; of words 'as trickery things always,' and that in the final analysis 'the word is the biggest thing in the world,' and confidently asserts that in spite of all the ills that befall man and the world, 'we can always admire its beauty and through art exercise the god-like function of creation'—whether such a one is a mere politician or a journalist as he often describes himself much to the annoyance of his readers who hardly fail to notice the poetic turn of his expression, the artistic bent of his mind and the inner harmony he has ceaselessly striven to achieve through his writing.[2] It is such a one that wrote the first significant autobiography in English in India and the book went into ten reprints in the year of its publication. A "total stranger" from far off New York writes that she has made Nehru's *Autobiography* her "favourite" book. It has made her feel thoroughly "ashamed" of herself as she has "wasted so much time in the past wallowing around in a personal slough of despond and disillusionment."[3] She has been in "rebellion with plenty of hard words against practically every reality." Now after reading "this moving biography," "I want very badly to be able to hold my head high and to call myself honest. I have the incentive at last. It seems to me now that the most important thing in life is the preservation of ideals." The sentimental tone of voice must not detract from the validity of the response when one realizes that the encomium is not from a professional critic or reviewer and then, too, it was in a private letter never suspected of seeing the light of day. Another woman, Ellen Wilkinson, truly cultivated, older and better known (became Minister for Education in the Labour Government in U.K.) experiences the same 'thrill' on reading it, and one can see how powerfully the *Autobiography* affected her: "I came home from the House of Commons early to get through some urgent work. The book was waiting, and I sat down and read right through the night. I made myself some tea and drank to your memory somewhere about 5.30 a.m.!" She thinks it an "important" book and that he is "magnificently objective" where he could "have foamed with wrath."

Madame Chiang Kai-Shek, one of the most distinguished women of our time, herself a reader and writer of fine literary sensibility, thanks Nehru for his *Autobiography* which had made her "enforced stay in bed" tolerable and she feels she has listened to the "promptings" of his heart and pays it one of the finest tributes: "It is a great document—your book—for it is the record of pilgrimage of a human soul lifted above the turmoil of daily strife into a realm of intellectual and emotional world unspoiled by sentimentality but so humanly moving that it will deserve to be ranked amongst the great documents of all ages." A generous tribute, but also well deserved. And within India Rabindranath Tagore was "intensely impressed" by this "great book" through which runs "a deep current of humanity." Amrita Sher Gil, whom I have reserved to the end because of her forthrightness and precision of response, wrote: "I think I like your autobiography, because where others would have said 'The sea saw me,' you say 'I saw the sea.'"

These are first-hand responses from discriminating readers but not being academics or professional reviewers this distinguished work has not gained in academic circles the supreme recognition due to it. It is my considered opinion—I presume to think I am now speaking from my accumulated, such as it is, experience of thirty years of reading and teaching of English and American literature and, more, hoping that it has conferred on me some little merit in learning to discriminate—that is one of the greatest autobiographies, if not the most supreme among them all and must contribute in large measure to the prestige of this genre called Indian Writing in English. Look at its disarmingly modest title, *An Autobiography*, as though it were one of a hundred or thousand books of that class and might well be lost to us but for the labours of the bibliographer. On the contrary, it is good to remember that it was the work of an agitating politician whose immense political prestige put the writer out of focus and the admirer of his work on the defensive as he used expressions like 'patriot with a pen' to describe Nehru's literary interests. This is doubly unfortunate since *An Autobiography* is clearly for the discerning reader. What made it so?

Consider it in comparison with those of its genre, the celebrities of the western world, if only to be aware of the limited range of their interests compared to Nehru's *The Confessions of St. Augustine*, whose chief merit is that it is the frank confession by a saint of his past sins resembling in its scope, in contrast to the immense range of his life's work which it excludes, Gandhi's *My Experiments with Truth*; or the Autobiography of John Stuart Mill, one of nineteenth century's greatest minds known to have been made into an intellectual machine by the author's father until Wordsworth's poetry restored his balance; or the life of Gibbon, the historian of the Roman Empire whose range of interests was not even as wide as that of Mill. One has only to read these autobiographies in succession, even in parts taken at random, to convince oneself that here is an autobiography greater than many of the better known ones, incomparably so not only because the subject is Nehru—Uncle Nehru to children, Prince Charming to women, Rituraj of India to poets; young men's hero, old men's fulfilment, lieutenant to Gandhi, India's chief spokesman abroad and a legend in his own life-time everywhere long before he became Prime Minister of India—but because he was the only political leader of his time universally admired for his idealism and integrity and later inspired so many books about him all the world over by men of thought and action, not by sycophants angling for patronage of one kind or another.

These have, no doubt, contributed to contemporary interest in the man and his work. But what of the generations which did not live contemporaneously with Nehru and so could not witness in action what W.B. Yeats elsewhere called the "perfection of the life" or "perfection of the work." Precisely here *An Autobiography* is found to be of inestimable value because it offers into the "life" and "work" by making available to the reader a rare dimension of the one of the most notable figures of modern history. One recalls D.H. Lawrence's salutary advice not to "trust the artist," he is a damned liar, but to "trust the tale," because he must have felt that art-speech is the only speech available to detect the subtlest lie, the smallest discrepancy between thought and action, intention and articulation. It is this aspect which is my present concern. Nehru himself speaks of the paradox that he was: he was born brahmin, and pleaded for tolerance in matters of religion and yet he records what must only be an honest admission of the facts of life: "whatever I say or do I know a Brahman I was born and Brahman I shall remain"—which may well discomfit his admirers who wish to see in him the perfect man, who exists nowhere. But watch how subtly some of the shades are woven into the labyrinth of his being which he unravels slowly to the reader:

> The women of the family indulged in various ceremonies and *pujas* from time to time and I rather enjoyed them, though

> I tried to imitate to some extent the casual attitude of the grown-up men of the family. Sometimes I accompanied my mother or aunt to the Ganges for a dip, sometimes we visited temples in Allahabad itself or in Benares or elsewhere or went to see a *sanyasi* reputed to be very holy. But all this left little impression on my mind.[4]

Note the ambivalence of thought in the juxtaposition of the attitudes of 'yes' and 'no' especially in the first sentence where the strong word "indulged" suggests his disapproval of ceremonies followed by a sneaking liking for them conveyed in "I rather enjoyed them"; and this reinforced by the frank admission: "though I tried to imitate to some extent the casual attitude of the grown-ups of the family" which even carries a touch of self-reproach, for he could see in retrospect the grown-ups themselves brought to bear a casualness on the manifestations of religion which as an adult, he 'later' may have considered irresponsible or immature. And finally his own denial when he remarks, "All this left little impression on me," which anticipates the Will written in his last years (1954) where he records that his ashes should be thrown into the Ganga not because of any religious reasons but because he played on its banks as a boy and the Ganga is the river of India symbolising the continuity of Indian culture and in praising which, despite his protests, he feels and thinks like a Brahmin, for one wonders if a Muslim or Christian in Nehru's position would have asked for such a gesture. After all, culture is manifest generally in what we say or do unconsciously, for when culture becomes conscious of itself it defeats its own end. But the contradictions underline the nature of Nehru's complex personality and precisely there lies his appeal for the intellectual especially.

The autobiography abounds with such insights and these are available to us in terms of art and it is as a work of art that we should look at it regardless of Nehru's eminence as public figure or greatness as man. That it is a distinguished *work of art* receives support from what Nehru says in the preface: "I began the task (of writing) in a mood of self-questioning and, to a large extent, this persisted throughout. I was not writing deliberately for an audience, but (honesty will not let him discount the evident possibility) if I thought of an audience, it was one of my own countrymen and country-women differently or with a different emphasis."

It is a very Indian autobiography not because the names of persons and places are Indian or it treats of the Indian scene but because the sensibility is essentially Indian and this in spite of the fact Nehru's English is closer to British English than the English of our foremost novelists. And this is strikingly there in the opening sentence itself: "An only son of prosperous parents is apt to be spoilt especially so in India." Consider how different, how very Indian, is this concern from what is generally considered the Western view of life as may be seen in the following example, which is also the opening sentence of a notable, representative English novel (*Pride and Prejudice*) where the emphasis is on marriage, wealth, status and so forth while the Nehru sentence progress from the material to the moral and spiritual—the anxiety expressed is clearly that in comparison with Jane Austen's: "It is a truth universally acknowledged that a single man in possession of a good fortune must be in want of a wife."

There is a point in comparing the first sentence of Nehru's *Autobiography* with that of a fictional work, because for all their differing sensibilities while his autobiography is not fiction or fictionalized, it has ample fictional potential in the progress of the narrative, in the creation of the elements of expectation, surprise and suspense, portrayal of character, presentation of situations and implicit comment on the socio-political scene. Note how the opening sentence, fraught with ominous forebodings is reinforced by the next sentence and the reader's interest is held intact. "And when that son happens to have been an only child for the first eleven years of his existence there is little hope for him to escape this spoiling."

One of the besetting dangers of an autobiography is the tendency of the writer to project his ego. But no one was more conscious of it than Nehru himself: the epigraph from Abraham Cowley should confirm it. Nehru's aristocratic birth coupled with his English upbringing at Harrow and Cambridge were both guarantee of his impeccable propriety in speech and gesture which forbids either the articulation, or even the feeling, or self-esteem. There was besides, no need for exhibitionism since those he came in contact with so readily conceded to him more than his cultivated mind would have wished for, because of the obvious advantages of birth, social standing and the intellectual gifts he enjoyed over millions of people of his day. See how briefly and unostentatiously he can refer to some of the important events concerning himself: "Governesses or private tutors were supposed to be in charge of my education." Or the reference to his birth relegated to a footnote though a whole country so lovingly looked forward to the day, year after year and continues to celebrate without promptings from any official quarter: "I was born in Allahabad on the 14th November 1889, or according to the Samvat calendar, Margshirsh Badi 7, 1946." (5) Or that his marriage took place on the *Vasanta Panchami* day which heralds the coming of spring in India. (37) But what he highlights is what the reader can respond to, would respond to, *whoever* is the subject, because of the author's exploiting the essential human foibles. On birthdays, he says: "I felt the hero of the occasion. My chief grievance was that my birthdays came so rarely. Indeed I tried to start an agitation for more frequent birthdays." (9) Soon a sad note to deflate the dwelling on himself and the comment, being the benefit of hindsight, is truly becoming of his adult years: "I did not realize then that a time would come when birthdays would become unpleasant reminders of advancing age." (9)

It has been pointed out especially by young American readers of Nehru's autobiography that he deliberately suppressed his love life. Perhaps true, because the autobiography is written by one who virtually lived in the marketplace when he did not go to prison but also because his Indian sensibility may have found support in the Victorian ethos in which he grew up as a boy. He does say, however, that at fourteen he became conscious of the other sex and that at Kashmiri parties pretty girls were not wanting and a touch and a sight 'thrilled' him. Later at Cambridge he admits his friends discussed sex but it didn't go far—he didn't like the usual ways adopted in matters of sex and even considered them vulgar. But there is no lack of admiration, tenderness and concern for his wife. He needed her and the very thought of her when he was in jail was fortifying: "whatever happened, I felt, we had one another." (514)

But he must have had friends among women who stayed with family. It is such a friend who once asked him if he was not pleased with all that hero-worship. But no one knew better that it did go to his 'head a little'—for he was no saint or inhuman monster—and he 'became a shade dictatorial' but soon his 'constant habit of introspection saved' him. He denies that his sacrifice and suffering were at the bottom of his popularity, for hundreds and thousands in his own day in India have suffered infinitely more even 'to the point of the last sacrifice.' In fact he informs he even felt ashamed of his 'easy-going and comfortable life and our petty politics of the city which ignored the vast multitude.' It is not even his intellectual gifts which made for his popularity, because he is convinced they were 'not abundant' and in any case they didn't make for popularity. He asks if the people did not admire some image of him which circumstances helped to project rather than his real self. Indeed, he is curious as to how the Indian people will treat him when the mask falls off. And yet if any public figure in India did not in those days wear a mask, was not so much as suspected of wearing one—he was the most transparent of them all—it was Nehru. He remarks that the solemnity of some national figures in public places made him feel like standing on his head on the dais with his tongue stuck out. For all his upbringing and education at Harrow and Cambridge he was so moved to compassion that he liked to identify himself with the masses of India. He even felt 'attracted' to the idea of the Government confiscating his ancestral house, Ananda Bhawan, for non-payment of tax as that would put him on par with the millions of India, for it was better to be 'accursed' with them than be 'saved' alone. Thus while he does not evade the question of his popularity he does not directly answer it either. And the answer to it should be found in the entire book, for it is a combination of qualities that obviously made for his legendary popularity. Primarily it is a ruthless self-examination that brought him closer to the people and even let him be absorbed into their affections; and it is this which one witnesses throughout the Autobiography.

If Nehru cultivated quite systematically the habit of examining himself he spared no less those whom he loved and admired. He 'admired' his father 'tremendously'; and there was in him, we are told, 'a magnificence and a grand manner which is sadly to seek in this world of today' but the artist soon takes over from the son when Nehru writes: 'I suppose I am partial to him but I miss his noble presence.' And he adds: 'Great as he was in many ways in my eyes, I felt that he was lacking in spirituality' (15) or: 'If there was a bourgeois democracy my father would have been the pillar of that constitution.' And: 'Consciously imperious he evoked great loyalty as well as bitter opposition.' (130)

Is it the universally admired Gandhi? '. . . in spite of his unimpressive features, loin-cloth and bare body there was a royalty and a kingliness in him which compelled a willing obeissance from others.' And Nehru portrays the whole man: not only the man who became a symbol in his life-time but also the Gandhi who had his share of weaknesses. And yet the picture is such that Gandhi himself might well have been induced to introspect:

> *Consciously and deliberately* meek and humble, yet he was full of power and authority and *he knew it*, and at times he was *imperious* enough, issuing commands which had to be *obeyed*. His calm, deep eyes would hold one and gently probe into the depths; his voice clear and limpid, would purr its way into the heart and evoke an emotional response. Whether his audience consisted of one person or a thousand, the charm and magnetism of the man passed on to it, and each one had a feeling of communion with the speaker. This feeling had *little to do with the mind*, though the appeal to the mind was not wholly ignored. But mind and reason definitely *had second place*. (129-30, Italics mine)

An admirably dispassionate picture of Gandhi by one of his closest associates, hard to believe in the Indian context, especially in the twenties.

Elsewhere he complains against Gandhi for not training the nation to *think* and asks whether the way of faith is the right one in running the affairs of a nation: 'Are the best of us so perfect as to be trusted that way? Even Plato's philosopher-kings would not have borne the burden nobly.' But his emotional attachment to Gandhi still continues. One of the best things in the *Autobi-*

ography is the presentation of the Nehru-Gandhi relationship often on the brink of a break-down, (based on genuine differences) but sure of its ultimate endurance because the links had been forged and the association was disinterested, having been forged for a cause. When Gandhi goes on fast this is how Nehru reacts in fear, anxiety and confusion and love:

> If Bapu died! what would India be like then and how would politics run? There seemed to be a dreary and dismal future ahead and despair seized my heart when I thought of it . . . confusion reigned my head and anger and hopelessness and love for one who was the cause of this upheaval. (370-71)

Here is the text of a telegram Nehru sent to Gandhi when he asked for his opinion before he went on a fast: "What can I say about matters I do not understand? I feel lost in a stranger country where you are the only familiar landmark and I try to grope my way in dark but I stumble. Whatever happens my love and thought is with you." (373) All this in a telegram which, nevertheless, does not fail to reflect the texture of his being. There is obviously a high degree of maturity in their relationship and Nehru shows a full appreciation of the consequences of his resignation from the Congress Working Committee, for he didn't like to precipitate a crisis. This is how he looks at it: "And even if we disagreed with him what could we do? Throw him over? Break from him? Announce our disagreement? That might bring some personal satisfaction to an individual but it made no difference to the final decision." (257)

It is these torments of the mind which he lays bare with the restraint of an artist that make for the success of the autobiography. And yet there is no attempt on the author's part to paint himself as a picture of poise and self-control always. For that would be to falsify his feelings and incidentally miss the chances of success for the work of art. Once when he was in gaol he received news of his mother being beaten by the police and her fainting on the road with blood flowing from her skull. He says: "I wonder how I would have behaved if I had been there. How far would my non-violence have carried me. Not very far, I fear, for that sight would have made me forget the long lesson I had tried to learn for more than a dozen years and I would have recked little of the consequences, personal or national." (335)

Clearly the situation is packed with potential for melodrama and exhibition of patriotic fervour. But Nehru does not strike out any heroic attitudes or declare in the manner of Ibsen's Brand that a mother was nothing before the cause dear to his soul. It is this utter integrity of the man that endears him to us and sustains our interest in his work. On another occasion we have a chance to see Nehru as friend and colleague. He gives himself to self-admonition because of what he thinks is let-down of a colleague. Gidwani, a fellow Congress worker, was imprisoned ostensibly for breaking an order. Nehru wrote to the gaol authorities that it was 'monstrous abuse of executive authority.' That is as far as Nehru went on that occasion and he regrets he couldn't go farther, though he felt inclined to demand that the same treatment be meted out to him as well. And he writes reproaching himself for his behaviour: "Loyalty to a colleague seemed to demand it. But many friends thought otherwise and dissuaded me. I took shelter behind the advice of friends, and made of it a pretext to cover my own weakness. For after all it is my weakness and disinclination to go to Nabha Gaol again that kept me away, and I have always felt a little ashamed of thus deserting a colleague." (116) Now the trenchant judgment: "As often with us all, discretion was preferred to valour" and if, as we see, the ignition of a cliche is a sign of a first-hand response there is reason to believe that Nehru was truly stricken with remorse for playing safe. His distinction lies in not justifying it by ingenious means. One has reasons to believe that Nehru might well have been a successful novelist if he had taken to fiction writing, for what comes out here is his capacity to *enact* not only the workings of the mind but even their hidden recesses, the motive springs of thought. Read his account of M.N. Roy: It seems M.N. Roy, a great name in Leftist politics in the twenties and thirties on Nehru's own admission, had written a great deal in condemnation of Nehru's politics and even 'hurt' him a little. But in spite of this, Nehru tells us, he felt 'attracted to Roy's remarkable intellectual capacity' but more, which is the hallmark of his culture, he was moved to compassion for Roy because of the ultimate loneliness of the intellectual. He says: "Roy seemed such a lonely figure deserted by everybody; the British Government was after him, nationalist India was not interested in him; and those who called themselves Communists in India condemned him as a traitor to the cause." (268)

Look how he can paint marvellous portraits: one has in mind particularly the portrayal of Raja Mahendra Pratap as Nehru saw him in Switzerland:

> his composite attire suitable on the highlands of Tibet or in the Siberian plains, his Russian boots, his numerous large pockets all bulging with photographs and papers, innumerable documents and pictures, because (here is the thrust) he had lost a box containing valuable papers and so he considered it safer to carry his papers on his person. He was still a delightful optimist, living completely in the air and was the founder of 'Happiness Society' whose motto was 'Be Happy' and which met with success in Latvia (or is it Lithuania?) (150)

The naivete of this visionary who founded a society to carry the trite message of 'Be Happy' and the inconsequential nature of his success as suggested by the calculated choice of Latvia and Lithuania as if to shrug his shoulders and exclaim: Does it matter where he met with success, in little known Latvia or less known Lithuania?

But playfulness can make room for bitter sarcasm bordering on crushing attack if principles are violated. The Moderates led by Srinivasa Sastri, who gets the brunt of it, wanted to avoid radicalism of the Congress and wanted the British Government to introduce reforms gradually—they recommended restraint. Nehru wondered if behind the restraint there was anything to hold back and quotes the verses of Roy Campbel written on South African novelists:

> They praise the firm restraint with which you write
> I'm with you there, of course:
> They use the snaffle and the curb all right,
> But where's the bloody horse?

It is not only Moderates but even his own partymen called forth a devastating attack when they showed a thick skin. This is when Congressmen got into offices of profit and prestige and were keen to keep them at all costs:

> But bees on flowers alighting, cease their hum—
> So setting upon places, Whigs grow dumb!

The lines are from Thomas Moore but he could endorse them from his own experience, for he knew the behaviour of birds and beasts not as a natural scientist, but as one who loved to watch their ways and share the pleasure as an imaginative experience. One has in mind the chapter on Animals in Prison where Nehru speaks of wasps and hornets, those eerie things, then the big bats in the air, the flying-foxes. He could inscape the squirrel by the choice word 'venturesomeness' and in illustration talk about a squirrel which, while he sat reading without moving for considerable periods, would 'climb up my leg and sit on my knee and have a look round. And then it would look into my eyes and realize that I was not a tree or whatever it had taken me for. Fear would disable it for a moment and then it would scamper away.' We are informed of how a little one would sometimes fall down and he would go to its succor with a fountain-pen filler for a feeding bottle. If it was not a squirrel it was a puppy which fell ill with a violent distemper which he nursed with great care and would sometimes get up a dozen times in the course of the night to look after her. Is it a mere monkey? He can tell with great gusto the breathless tale of a monkey jumping into the heart of a crowd encircling its baby which made the brave jailors and convict overseers with big sticks flee for life, when it rescued its little one.

He can talk of parrots with no less fascination because he is amused at the lot of the poor male even in the animal world. It seems there were 'fierce quarrels between two male parrots over a lady parrot who sat calmly by waiting for the result of the encounter and ready to grant her favours to the winner.'

This tender-hearted man can nevertheless view animals in intellectual abstraction, such is his unified sensibility, when he reflects on how different countries have adopted different animals as symbols of their ambition or character—the eagle of the United States of America and of Germany, the lion and bull dog of England, the fighting cock of France, the bear of Old Russia. He asks: "How far do these patron animals mould national character? Nor is it surprising (he comments with obvious pride) that the Hindu should be mild and non-violent, for his patron animal is the cow."

But it is the registration of his emotion and feeling for nature that he can rise to heights of poetic prose—his academic training in botany left the aesthetic component untouched. Nature soothes him and exhilarates and the experience is first-hand, hence the evocation is original, not bookish. Nature pulsates with life in these pages and enlivens and relieves the monotony of political and social upheaval. Once he is going along the winding road in the Himalayas and as the car speeds the panorama unfolds itself:

> Higher and higher we went, the gorges deepened, the peaks lost themselves in the clouds, the vegetation changed till the firs and pines covered the hill sides. A turn of the road would bring to our eyes suddenly a new expanse of hills and valleys with a little river gurgling in the depths below. (568)

Look how the stability of the Himalayas can impress him:

> Calm and inscrutable they seemed with all the wisdom of past ages, mighty sentinels over the vast Indian plain. The very sight of them cooled the fever in the brain and the petty conflicts and intrigues, the lusts and falsehoods of the plains and the city, seemed trivial and far away before their eternal ways. (569)

The Himalayas are hardly mountains but mighty sentinels and as symbols of the immemorial wisdom of India they scorn the intrigues of the plains. When he says 'their solidity and imperturbability looked down upon me with the wisdom of a million years and mocked at my varying humours soothing my fevered mind' the reader's participation (or is it surrender?) is complete. Or read his account of the Spring in Dehra Dun:

> Spring was very pleasant in Dehra, and it was a far longer one than in the plains below. The winter had denuded almost all the trees of their leaves and they stood naked and bare. Even four magnificent peepal trees, which stood in front of the gaol gate, much to my surprise, dropped nearly all their leaves. Gaunt and cheerless they stood there, till the spring air warmed them up again and sent a message of life to their innermost cells. Suddenly there was a stir both in the peepals and the other trees, and an air of mystery surrounded them as of secret operations going on behind the scenes; and I would be startled to find little bits of green peeping out all over them and their russet-coloured leaves glisten in the sun. (354)

Nature has held the greatest fascination for poets in India from Valmiki and Kalidasa to their descendants today, but not without deteriorating quite often into ornamental descriptions without function in the context. Nehru can get away with successive paragraphs at a stretch and make them all convincing to the reader when he excuses himself: 'prevented from indulging in normal activities we became more observant of nature's ways.' Not plausible but very convincing in the circumstances. For, prison life which can deaden most sensitive natures seems to have afforded an exceptional opportunity for Nehru to watch landscapes, insects, birds and beasts and how they minister to his need or mould his character.

I should like to look at a whole chapter entitled 'Naini Prison' to elucidate his amazingly observant eye and feeling heart as well as his remarkable capacity to capture them without rhetoric or sentimentality, but a sense of humour closely allied to pathos. Consider the range and variety of observations and the reactions they generate: the architecture of the prison (its 'circular' rather than 'rectangular' shape, adding to the sense of oppression, like being in the bottom of a well; his cell called *kuttaghar*, 15 ft. high, drab and ugly building with narrow cells); his bed 'heavily chained up lest I might get up, and walk away'; the 'nocturnal chorus of convict overseers with its varying keys till they sounded like the moaning of a distant wind'; that little 'tent of blue which prisoners call the sky' he could watch, with a wistful eye; and the Pole Star peeping over the wall—'surrounded by a revolving sky, it seemed to be a symbol of cheerful constancy and perseverance.' 'Stone walls do not a prison make nor iron bars a cage' was to Nehru no longer a poetic fancy, but the product of a lived and felt experience.

He can turn his eye from himself to the other prisoners around, the 'lifers'—the way they 'brood and wrap themselves in angry thoughts of fear and revenge and hatred, forget the good of the world . . . till gradually even hatred loses its edge and life becomes a soulless thing.' Military leaders write their memoirs and I have glanced through the pages of Churchill's War Memoirs but have not seen anywhere anything comparable to moving observations like the following: "From time to time the prisoner's body is weighed and measured. But how is one to weigh the mind and the spirit which wilt and stunt themselves and wither away?"

Or his conversation with the 'lifers' who ask him 'What of us, lifers? Will Swanson take us out of this hell?' for the date of release of one of them was 1996! He goes into the causes of crime and quotes from a book on Sing Sing Prison in New York. His distress on seeing a large number of bright-looking lads; then the transfer of prisoners from prison to prison leaving no trace of them until they had lost complete touch with their families; the difference a word of sympathy or encouragement would make, for their faces light up with joy and gratitude and the final observation that 'there is more charity inside the gaol than outside it' because when one "habitual" prisoner, a blind man, was going out into a friendless world after a long period of imprisonment the fellow prisoners came forward to help him: one with a shirt, another with some other piece of clothing, a third with his new pair of chappals which he had shown with pride that morning.

And this doesn't exhaust Nehru's reactions to prison life. Indeed there is enough material for an impressive essay in the autobiography on the subject. When summons came for him to go to prison he would view it with incredible detachment and pat comes a quotation from Shakespeare:

Absent thee from felicity a while
And for a season draw thy breath in sorrow

When Nehru quotes, and he quotes copiously, the quotation is there as much to clinch a whole argument as to—I shall not say find emotional relief from the pressures that assail him but—to gain a psychic distance from his personal predicament by contemplating it with artistic detachment. This is almost always true with Nehru, but let me just give one more example in support of my elucidation. He is writing about the famous Delhi Pact. Gandhiji had committed himself to the Viceroy and Nehru felt unhinged. He asks: "Was it for this that our people had behaved so gallantly for a year? Were all our brave words and deeds to end in this? The Independence resolution of the Congress, the pledge of January 26, so often repeated?" (258) At the end of this anguished, because insistent, questioning comes a resignation of spirit from which issue forth words like the following: "So I lay and pondered on that March night, and in my heart there was a great emptiness as of something precious gone, almost beyond recall." (259) It is this woe-begone and crushed state that summons up the lines of T.S. Eliot:

> This is the way the world ends,
> Not with a bang, but a whimper

lines with which most professors of English in India would not have been familiar with in the mid-thirties, such was our Romantic upbringing, but Nehru knew the poet, the poem, the lines and the occasion which would suit them so well that his own experience and the poet's expression fuse with such authenticity that they hardly sound like a quotation.

But this is not how the entire book is written. There are quite a few examples of dull reportage as in the chapters on the Kisans, the Agrarian troubles, No Tax Campaigns in the United Provinces, and the internal problems of India which, however important to Nehru, his political associates and others interested at the time, are very unlikely to evoke enthusiasm from the readers of today and readers outside India. But they can be cut out without impairing the flow of the narrative, the main tenor of argument or the total structure of the book. In any case those few chapters do not detract from the overwhelming favourable impression of the book on the reader who must learn in the course of reading it what sections to skip. The total impression therefore is that it is a brave book, that is, the record of a brave man who has suffered much and even carries a note of subdued but confident triumph of the spirit when at the end of the book he says:

> I have become a queer mixture of the East and West, out of place everywhere, at home nowhere. Perhaps my thoughts and approach to life are more akin to what is called Western than Eastern, but India clings to me, as she does to all her children, in innumerable ways; and behind me lie, somewhere in the subconscious, racial memories of a hundred, or whatever the number may be, generations of Brahmans. I cannot get rid of either that past inheritance or my recent acquisitions. They are both part of me, and, though they help me in both the East and the West, they also create in me a feeling of spiritual loneliness not only in public activities but in life itself. I am a stranger and alien in the West. I cannot be of it. But in my own country also, sometimes, I have an exile's feeling.
>
> The distant mountains seem easy of access and climbing, the top beckons, but, as one approaches, difficulties appear, and the higher one goes the more laborious becomes the journey and the summit recedes into the clouds. Yet the climbing is worth the effort and has its own joy and satisfaction. Perhaps it is the struggle that gives value to life, not so much the ultimate result. (596)

Here surely is the secret of the autobiography's appeal for us—the animating idealism and the extraordinary disinterestedness of a life devoted to action, action always allied to thought. The idiom is of the West but the sensibility which suffuses and charges it is Indian.

Let us now pass from this classic of modern India to Nirad Chaudhuri's *Autobiography of an Unknown Indian*. It was thought desirable to consider Nirad Chaudhuri in conjunction with Nehru both because of the enormous publicity Chaudhuri has received in the West, surpassing Nehru's reputation as a man of letters, and the opportunity it provides for comparison of the two kinds of Indian writing: one pulsating with human warmth, the other, abstract, ponderous and academic; one meant for Indians, another for an English-speaking world abroad. In a preface remarkable for its—unintended—repudiation of his own claim to be considered a man of letters, Chaudhuri says that his 'main intention is historical' and the book is 'contribution to contemporary history.' Elsewhere he says it is 'more of an *exercise* in descriptive ethnology than autobiography.' One would have preferred to dismiss this 'exercise in descriptive ethnology' but the fact is he prefers to call it 'Autobiography of an Unknown Indian' to catch the ear and eye of his western readers who had by then been familiar with at least two famous Indian autobiographies, of Gandhi and Nehru. Chaudhuri is insistent that it is primarily a contribution to contemporary history and since he offers, in his own words, 'unfamiliar point of view' and 'interpretation of history' he thought the reader was 'entitled to information about the character and idiosyncrasies of the author' as 'a background to the viewpoints of the man who must be so different from others.'

Chaudhuri posits that it is the work of one who 'after passing the age of fifty' is faced with the compulsion to write off all the years 'I have lived and begin life anew.' One would have thought that a man's life is of interest to his fellowmen precisely in proportion to the way he has gone through life in the face of defeat and disaster and his readiness to accept that past so as to alter its meaning for the present, certainly not 'write off.' It is interesting that Chaudhuri should begin the book on such a cynical note while Nehru should end the account of his travails by endorsing a conviction of Socrates that it is 'a bad thing to desert one's past.' But Chaudhuri's values are built, for all his protests, on success and failure as the world views them. The books that came out of his pen since the *Autobiography*, every one of them, must bear witness to what I say, I mean, in the choice of subject and treatment of the material.

Anyhow, ironically, the past which he wishes to write off is precisely the one he seems to value most as seen from the flamboyant dedication of the book—Kipling spoke in terms of the Empire for reasons far nobler than is pretended in Chaudhuri's dedication:

'To the memory of the British Empire'

'Because all that was good and living within us was made, shaped, and quickened by the same British rule.' But contradictions[5] don't seem to trouble Chaudhuri; indeed he seems to luxuriate in them as he knows they generate controversy and keep his name alive before the public. The epigraph further confirms the contradiction: "Here lies the happy man who was an islet of sensibility, surrounded by the cool sense of his wife, friends and children." The rest of the book is an elaboration of the attitudinizing so evident in the calculated choice of the title, the dedication, the preface characterized by the cultural cringe of an author who writes, of all things, an autobiography, not as others have done to see themselves naked, but with the conscious object of reaching the English-speaking world; indeed, everything is geared to that end. But what surprises one is that the English-speaking world should be taken in by such schoolboy-bravado as the following:

> In the first place, my personal development has in no wise been typical of a modern Indian of the twentieth century. It is certainly exceptional, and may, even be unique. But I do not believe that on this account the value of my narrative as historical testimony is impaired. Rather the independence of environment which I have always been driven to assert by an irrepressible impulse within me has given me a preternatural sensitiveness to it. In relation to the earth. It can never rise so high as to be able to sever the terrestrial connexion, but its flight helps it to obtain a better view of the lie of the land.

The pomp and circumstance of the claim is soon offset by a looseness of thinking: 'In a country like India, so vast and so populous the individuals who form the exceptions may well run into millions.' Imagine millions of exceptional individuals in any country especially in one like India which the author sets out to denounce as the most abominable under the sun.[6] And in the very next sentence we are asked to believe these millions of exceptional beings are but 'negligible when against the hundreds of millions.'

I find it hard to bring myself to like a major part of the book. But so as not to rob you of your share of the amusement, let me offer a brief elucidation of the characteristic Chaudhuri style of writing.

The 'unknown Indian' misses no chance to magnify things that have any relation to him whether it is the house he lived in, his mode of living, the fairs he visited, the festivals he celebrated, the books and paintings he owned and admired and the tastes he cultivated. Snobbery is writ large on every page. Chaudhuri devotes (in the Jaico paperback edition on which I spent my hard-earned Rs. 6) 47 1/2 pages to 'My Birth Place,' 30 pages to 'My Ancestral Village' and 22 to 'My Mother's Village' and 10 pages to reprinting what he claims as his undergraduate essay. In the Chapter on 'My Birth Place,' the author's residence, a typical Chaudhuri presentation, gets 8 pages: It was built in 1903, another was added in 1907, and both were sold in 1910. Then its description: the inner courtyard, and the big hut ('hut' obviously betrays snobbery—inverted snobbery, that is) on the western side and therefore called the West Hut which he informs was 'originally the North Hut' in the smaller house in which they lived till 1903. The West Hut presupposes the East Hut, and he must talk about it because it was also called the 'Vegetarian Hut' since widowed aunts—widows, he informs, were vegetarian—used to come and stay there. Some more details of the family before he resumes his description of the house in which he lived: "His first sister's marriage took place in 1916." (137) "His Mother visited Shillong thrice between 1895 and 1900." (93) "The most interesting ceremony in respect of an expectant mother I ever saw was in Bangaram in 1923." (137) "And the same ceremony in 1943 for the young wife of my first brother in my own house in Delhi." (137) "One of the two coloured pictures of a battleship" he saw in his school textbook was of the 1895 Majestic class or might have been even of 1901 Formidable class. (112) He goes on to give more details: "Mr. Churchill's picture in the uniform of the Lord Warden and Admiral appeared in the *Illustrated London News* for 24th August in 1946." (120) "Mr. Nathan, the Divisional Commissioner arrived in Kishorganj in 1907." (118) "Gandhi praised Nehru as the Harrow and Cambridge undergraduate and Barrister on 2nd June 1947." (117) Chaudhuri even advances an argument for including these details in the body of the text, not in footnotes, it may be remembered: "I do not want to prejudice anything I have to say in this book by making generalizations without adducing a sufficient volume of evidence to support them."

Then the catalogue of things: furniture, books, dolls, trunks. His father being a 'pioneer,' we are told, added a table, a drawing mirror, a glass fronted cupboard, and the racks with open shelves. Again: for the West Hut his father had imported from Dacca (note the word 'imported' in respect of a city in the same province as his own home town), the American bent-wood chairs 'bentoo or 'lady' chairs. 'On a pair of stay antlers above the front door of the West Hut rested a coloured reproduction of Raphael's Madonna.' Then there were panoramic pictures of the Boer War, one depicting the 'Battle of Paardebers,' the other 'the triumphal entry into Praetoria.'

He seeks to placate his Western reader not merely by a pompous display of the very English possessions in his house but by the pervasive European frame of reference in idiom (of a dead age, that is), allusion, analogy and standard of valuation. Is it colonial cringe or genuine admiration? Consider the following examples: 'The girls chanted hymns to the sun and the moon which could be called a crude and rudimentary version of the canticles of St. Francis.' (17) The wooden box in their house was 'rather like a Tudor or Jacobean chest.' (24) His family didn't share 'the Athenian contempt for those who pursued their private avocations.' (39) 'The playing of the trio of the third movement of Mozart's symphony gave him violent distaste.' (62) 'The Bengali mother kept thinking of her daughter with the infatuation rivalling, if not surpassing that of Madame de Sevigne for her cold and shrewish daughter' (70)—Is Madame de Sevigne such a by-word for motherly love throughout the world? 'In the kitchen the rice at times required the jaws of the Heidelberg man *for proper* mastication.' (74) '*The children* could have dug up the floor like the woolf in Webster's poem' (13); 'Gandhi's morality is servile, not like that of the horsemen of the Parthenon.' His 'young nephew rushed out to the rescue of the cow like Napoleon on the bridge at Arcola.' Consider, above all, the following as a test of the authenticity of

Chaudhuri's reactions: The decay of the Roman Empire held him 'spellbound'; he was 'elated by the reconquest of Italy and Africa'; 'dazed by the onslaught of the Islamic hordes.' Why? He has his reasons ready: 'The disappearance of the Roman Empire was not simply the death of an empire but the death of a world order and of universal civilization.' (478)

The statesmen of the world, those makers of history themselves are not guilty of such gravity of tone or concern which borders on bathos. What does he think of the disappearance of the splendour that was India? He says that made him susceptible to the odour of decay in a civilization and made him 'sift the atmosphere of contemporary India with an air of uneasy exploration.' And this because of the decline of the British Empire in India, for his only interest is in the India created by the British rule.

His attitudinizing, despite his protests that he has 'been cured of my Byronic posturing of earlier days' as he grew older (514) is very much in evidence, it goes without saying. He speaks as though he is at the most conscious point of the world's sorrow in history as well as contemporary life and on him depend the destinies of nations: 'What and how many crashes in human affairs and worse still, what a creeping paralysis in the lives of nations have I seen and am seeing.' (479) Or: 'The truth is that while I was being carried along by the momentum of our history, most of my countrymen were being dragged backwards by its inertia.' Is it his erudition? He claims: 'I could pass from physics to Sanskrit Literature or from novels to astronomy with an agility which seemed like volatility to those who did not know me well.' (337) Or 'These are matters of history. I refer to them because my personal testimony would go a long way towards supporting the consensus of opinion among my countrymen about the Englishman in India in the days of his power,' for, 'The British Empire in India has perished without my ever coming into personal contact with Englishmen.' (376-77) He reproduces an essay of his allegedly undergraduate years and writes in justification that he 'didn't then think so well of the essay.' But reading it thirty years later it demonstrates 'my capacity to formulate for myself independently of personal example or guidance an attitude towards life.'

What superb confidence—or is it senility?— in one who calls

himself a writer, historian, intellectual that he should permit himself to say his 'conclusions remain valid for all time' (513) because 'intellectual Prometheanism' is his chief merit.

One is not taking a risk in challenging his admirers to produce from the autobiography any well-remembered chapter, section, or even a few pages of continuous writing which can be called distinguished prose. I had at one time thought that the 'Torch of Indian Renaissance' was a possible exception but I realise on re-reading, it is distinguished for its intelligent analysis, not as a piece of imaginative writing, while at least a dozen chapters from Nehru's *Autobiography* have from time to time deservedly found their way into modern anthologies of prose. And yet Chaudhuri has the gumption to say: 'Like these great writers' and he lists Aksakov, Renan, Anatole France, Hudson and Tagore, 'I too began to be reminiscent of my childhood when I had long passed my youth.' How does he reminisce? One example will do:

> I was born on Tuesday, Agrahaya 9, in the year 1304 of the Bengali era (which corresponds to 23rd November 1897) at 6 a.m. local time. I have no birth certificate in the Western fashion and . . . no horoscope either in the Eastern fashion.

The presentations take the form of: 'I summarize below the results . . . ' (36); 'It is this house which I am going to describe now,' (20) 'There was a story behind this building and it is this.' (22)

Chaudhuri's chief merit is in loading the narrative with chunks of information some of which can lay claim to being knowledge— lay claim to, because his knowledge does not come through the senses much less as Henry James would have liked, 'through the conduits of the imagination.' When one thinks he is close to achieving enactment in writing, it turns out to be pompous parading of his learning. He says somewhere that he saw a young man, rising from a kneeling position with a rifle in his hand. And this is how he proceeds to identify him: "He could not have been a British Regular for he wore a slouched hat and a bandolier. He must have been a Boer or perhaps a man of the British Mounted Infantry." And yet he wants us to believe that he 'contemplated' him 'by the hour.' The sad fact is that contemplation has brought nothing to the surface, for we can remember no one Chaudhuri has portrayed, not even his father, mother, or grandmother, for they could have been any father, any mother, or grandmother. They are not individualized, or they have nothing of interest to other human beings. His father was 'the only Bengali father I have seen who adhered consistently to giving freedom to children.' His 'mother's face rippled to the emotions as waters to wind' (159); her features gave an impression of 'unsparing alertness and inexpressible animation'; 'even at her worst she never went anywhere near the normal behaviour of Indian mothers on seeing accidents befalling their children!' 'Yet no mother was capable of more attendance on her children in sickness.' (160)

With all this, here is an autobiography which in academic circles in the West (and among metropolitan groups in India, too) is better known than Nehru's, or Gandhi's or many subsequent ones like *The Punjabi Century* by Tandon—a very disturbing trend in criticism which the Indian student of English Studies cannot afford to be complacent about but must help to counteract, the reason why an attempt is made here to focus attention on Chaudhuri. Far from counteracting, the middle brow magazines have lionized Nirad Chaudhuri and let him thrive on controversies. But these are magazines which take their cue from English and American reviewers, even on Indian books.[7] I cannot resist here the temptation to cite the salutary lament of Chaudhuri himself over much Indian writing published in England:

> Some unfortunate and misguided Indians actuated by the desire to secure easy publication in Britain or America try to see India as if they were Western journalists. This in certain cases seems the immediate purpose because Western publications are very shy of authentic India. But almost always this shortcut produces shoddy and counterfeit books. No Indian who is true to his country will write this kind of book.

Seldom had an author so truly summed up his own motivation for writing a book, his publishers, the way their psychology works and the final outcome.

NOTES

1. Dhan Gopal Mukerjee was no doubt a distinguished writer of English prose in the period in question but he was no novelist and his stories and biographies were hardly noticed in this country.
2. See my *Jawaharlal Nehru, A Study of his Writings and Speeches,* Preface.
3. For this as well as the next few quotations, see *A Bunch of Old Letters* (Asia, 1960).
4. Jawaharlal Nehru, *An Autobiography* (India: Allied), p. 8.
5. 'Heaven preserve me from the dishonesty, so general among Indians of attributing this conflict (between the Hindus and Muslims) to British rule however much the foreign rulers might have profited by it.' (p. 234) Only two paragraphs later with a rare honesty, rare in Chaudhuri, he remarks that 'British rule itself was a factor which discouraged the cultivation of Islamic culture and sympathies by the Hindus.' (p. 236)
6. Read his *Continent of Circe* (London: Faber & Faber) and *Clive of India* (London, 1975).
7. See for example the comments on Chaudhuri's *Autobiography.* 'The personal story of an exceptional India.' *Library Journal.*

   'At times many of the long, detailed biographical passages are tough sledding, but the whole is reminiscent of a work like Vincent Sheean's Personal History and does contain some pithy material. Limited audience.' *Kirkus.*

   "An extraordinarily penetrating and analytical—though somewhat academic—study of the complex of social, political, racial and religious stresses of modern India." J.W. Rogers, *Library Journal, Manchester Guardian.*

   "His book is well written and presents a cultivated, sensitive modern Indian personality rarely available for Occidentals to meet." W.N. Brown, *Nation.*

   'Chaudhuri scorns as "superannuated folly" the notion that Hindu civilization can be revived and believes that if India is to become more than an "archaeological site" it will have to set about creating "an Indian version of European civilization in our own interest, for our private use and in order to keep ourselves within the pale of civilized life." These views and the sweeping indictments which precede them will probably obscure for most readers many of the harsh truths that fill this work of confession and self-flagellation. They make Chaudhuri as hard to take as some of his counterparts whose excesses run to narcissism and sentimental self-deception. But for the serious reader they should open lines of questioning and inquiry we will do well to explore.' H.R. Isaacs, *N.Y. Herald, Tribune BKR.*

It is a pleasure to remark here that Chaudhuri has made ample amends for his poor and irresponsible writing by contributing an excellent work of scholarship in his recent book on Max Mueller, *Scholar Extraordinary.* However Chaudhuri himself asserted in a Television interview at Leeds that of all his books the *Autobiography* would live as long as the English language.

The Autobiographies of Nehru and Chaudhuri: A Comparative Study

BASAVARAJ S. NAIKAR

Autobiographies all over the world and especially in India are extensively read and enjoyed, but paradoxically enough, they have received very scant critical attention, let alone comparative treatment. The critical negligence is probably based upon the misconception that the art of autobiography is very easy to practise or that it is not at all an art but a bold enumeration of drab events, facts, dates and places. Gone are the days of such critical negligence and indifference. Now when the world is fast moving from parochialism to internationalism in every field, it is high time for the student of literature to study the works of art not only intensively but comparatively also. The comparative approach to literature enables us to widen the critical horizon and develop the concept of world literature. As R.G. Moulton has aptly suggested, the comparative study of literature should ultimately lead to the study of world literature and liberate the minds of people from literary parochialism.[1] The comparative study of authors belonging to different nations should be preceded by that of authors belonging to the same country, preferably coming from two different parts of the country belonging to two different professions. The comparative study, needless to say, aims at establishing the universality and oneness of human experience through the depiction of the diverse particularities of it. Hence an attempt is made here in that direction.

Jawaharlal Nehru and Nirad Chaudhuri are incontrovertibly two significant Indian English writers. A comparative study of the autobiographies of these two writers belonging to two different, in fact, diametrically opposed backgrounds will, no doubt, be as delightful as profitable. Though both of them practise the same genre, they sharply differ from each other in the manner of presentation and focus. A study of the similarity between the two will inevitably show their dissimilarity and establish their distinct identities.

Both Nehru and Chaudhuri are known as good autobiographers. The autobiography is the story of an individual written by himself. But writing about oneself is not as easy as it is thought to be. In fact 'writing about oneself' is as difficult as 'knowing oneself' which is the most difficult thing in the world, according to Aristotle. 'Writing about oneself' is nothing but 'knowing oneself' and at its best helps one to have 'self-realization,' and at its worst, makes one indulge in self-deception. The art of autobiography is, therefore, a very hard job to perform. Every autobiographer will have some knowledge of the theory of the genre of which he is a practitioner. The knowledge of such a theory—implicit or explicit—presupposes an awareness of the experience of thrill and torture in the *ecriture* of an autobiography. The autobiographer may either begin with a theory of his own about his art or evolve one out of his actual *ecriture*. It is a matter of pleasure for the reader to notice that both Nehru and Chaudhuri have formulated their own theories about the art of autobiography. The theoretical differences between the two naturally create the presentational differences also. They throw light upon the two radically different personalities moulded by two different atmospheres. They differ from each other in their tastes, preoccupations, professions, family backgrounds, economic status, temperaments and world-views. Nehru, for example, is aware of the difficulty of writing the autobiography. In fact he begins his autobiography with a question from Abraham Cowley which expresses the difficulty of practising the art of autobiography. Says Cowley, "It is a hard and nice subject for a man to write of himself: it grates his own heart to say anything of disparagement, and the reader's ears to hear anything of praise of him."[2]

But Chaudhuri does not discuss or quote a passage regarding the theory of autobiography, though he implies it in his clarification about himself. Both Nehru and Chaudhuri know the nature and scope of their autobiographies. Strictly speaking, the autobiography should be confined to the revelation of the individual life of man.

But the autobiographies of Nehru and Chaudhuri differ from the conventional norm, in that they go beyond the individual and reveal the wider units of community and nation. For example, Nehru's autobiography crosses the limits of personal story and extends to the entire nation. That is why in it the personal history and national history are inseparable. The width of the scope of the autobiography depends upon the author's stature and temperament. Nehru was not an ordinary man. By virtue of his participation in the national struggle he came to symbolize the mighty issues of the great country. He became a spokesman of the national hopes and aspirations, attitudes and ideals. To read Nehru's autobiography is to read the autobiography of a turbulent nation. Nehru himself is not unaware of this relation between the two. In his preface, he says, "Essentially an autobiography is a personal document and therefore it reflects personal views and reactions. But the persons who wrote it became merged, to a large extent, in the larger movement and therefore represents, in a large measure, the feelings of many others." (v) Autobiography, in such a context, naturally assumes national significance and epic proportions.

Similarly Chaudhuri's *Autobiography of an Unknown Indian* (1973) also transcends the limits of the personal story and becomes history of the Bengali race and its encounter with other races like the Muslim and the British. In it, Chaudhuri wants to offer an ethnological description of the Bengali culture. That explains the reason for Chaudhuri's designation of it as 'descriptive ethnology.' Since these three cultures are not isolated accidents but the result of historical movements of the world like Indo-Aryan, Indo-Turkish and Indo-British movements, Chaudhuri's intention is to show how individual is the product of environment which is itself decided by historical forces of the world. Thus Chaudhuri's aim is not to give a picture of the isolated individual but to place him in the cultural context which is conditioned by the historical forces. Chaudhuri does not want to create a romantic interest in himself by describing the nostalgic memories of his childhood and youth. But his purpose in writing his autobiography is more serious and hence philosophical than romantic. He hopes to make his autobiography a guarantee against the imminent danger of the extinction of the world. Says Chaudhuri, "Men do not become aware of the precise quality of their early years until late in life. Askanov, Renan, Anatole France, Hudson, Tagore, all wrote their autobiographical masterpieces when they were advanced in years—in fact, advanced considerably into, and sometimes beyond, what Dante has called it *mezzo del commin di nostra vita*. Like these great writers I too began to be reminiscent of my childhood when I had long passed my youth. But I am not like them, calling up its memories and recording them either as things interesting in themselves or as a foil to my later life. It is not the aim of this book to create that kind of romantic interest or contrast. There is no room in it, since it is more of an exercise in descriptive ethnology than autobiography, for presenting childhood against the background of age, for presenting it as submerged city of Ys or as the times when the intimations of immortality lay about us. If there is to be any vanished or vanishing Atlantis to speak of in this book, it should and would be all our life lived till yesterday. All that we learnt, all that we have acquired, and all that we have prized is threatened with extinction. We do not know how the end will come, whether through a cataclysmic holocaust or slow, putrid decay. But regarding the eventual extinction there does not seem to be any uncertainty."[3] Chaudhuri further says in the preface, "The story I want to tell is the story of the struggle of a civilization with a hostile environment, in which the destiny of British rule in India became necessarily involved. My main intention is thus historical and since I have written the account with the utmost honesty and accuracy of which I am capable, the intention in my mind has become mingled with the aspiration that the book may be regarded as a contribution to contemporary history." (ix)

Thus both Nehru and Chaudhuri are serious in their approach to life, however different their ways may be from each other. Whereas Nehru's autobiography tends to be national in its nature and scope, Chaudhuri's is historical, scientific and microscopic. Both the works are unusual in the sense that they refuse to treat the individual as an isolated entity. It is precisely for this reason that the American edition of Nehru's autobiography was called *Towards Freedom*. Both the autobiographies testify to the truth that the experience recorded by their authors are meaningful and significant not only to them but to their fellowmen as well. Though

Nehru and Chaudhuri belonged to different stratas of society, their experiences were of equal significance for them. Otherwise they would not have attempted to organize them in the form of autobiographies. Whereas Nehru was an aristocrat of Kashmir, Chaudhuri is a man from the poor class of Bengal. Whereas Nehru was a great man in the political and bureaucratic sense, Chaudhuri is an ordinary and obscure man serving in the AIR of Delhi. Whereas Nehru was an international figure before he wrote his autobiography, Chaudhuri is an 'unknown' Indian unnoticed by the world until he wrote his autobiography. Whereas Nehru had the privilege of being educated at Harrow and Cambridge, Chaudhuri was educated at Bengali schools and University. Thus Nehru and Chaudhuri come from diametrically opposed backgrounds. The comparative analysis as follows will help us to have a better understanding of both the writers and their literary achievements. Nehru and Chaudhuri record the growth of their consciousness which was supported by environmental conditions. Whereas Nehru was born in a poor family of Bengal and brought up in a country atmosphere, Nehru was born with a silver spoon in his mouth and tutored by British teachers like F.T. Brooks. The youth-experiences of Nehru and Chaudhuri are also different from each other. Whereas Nehru being educated at Harrow and Cambridge viewed the Indian problems from outside the country, Chaudhuri was educated at Calcutta and looked at the Indian problems from inside the country. Thus, though both of them underwent their youthful experiences, they differed from each other as far as their perspectives were concerned.

Similarly, Nehru and Chaudhuri spent their middle ages in different atmospheres. Nehru spent his entire time in participation in the political events of India thereby evoking political consciousness in his countrymen and ideologically fighting against the British imperialism in India. Chaudhuri spent his time in the minute observation of the Bengali life which was influenced by Muslim and British cultures. The details such as these testify to the fact that their experiences were quite rich though the range, the intensity, the when and the how of the same differed from each other. Because of the very nature of Nehru's personality which was indistinguishable from the Indian political life, his autobiography assumes national importance and epic proportions. It can easily be considered as an epic with Jawaharlal as its hero who is concerned with the mighty issues of the vast country like India. He becomes a symbol of Indian hopes, challenges, ambitions and ideals. He, therefore, goes on expatiating on his country with heroic ebullience and romantic enthusiasm. But Chaudhuri's condition is diametrically opposed to Nehru's in the sense that his concerns are local, ethnological, microscopic and concrete. Whereas Nehru's autobiography offers an epic i.e. panoramic vision of Indian political life, Chaudhuri's autobiography offers a 'close up' picture of the diversity of Bengali life. Because of this very reason, Nehru's work is marked by broad outlines and vague and romantic vistas, Chaudhuri's work is marked by minute, concrete and almost naturalistic and photographic details of life. Whereas Nehru's view may be compared to an aerial view, Chaudhuri's may be compared to a land-traveller's one.

Autobiographies, unmistakably, offer a picture of the authors' personalities. In spite of being national and ethnological respectively, the autobiographies of Nehru and Chaudhuri cannot be mistaken for textbooks on history and anthropology, because, it must be remembered, they were written from the 'individual points of view' and therefore, reveal the personalities through the revelation of their environments. Good autobiographies always provide the best raw-material for psychologists especially for psychoanalysis. Nehru appears to have a paradoxical personality. C.D. Narasimhaiah has pointed them out and discussed them elaborately in his book on Nehru. Nehru's shyness, difference, cyrenaicism gave place to courage, confidence, hardihood and adventurousness. But loneliness and introversion happened to be the permanent features of his personality. Since Nehru was a man of paradox, contradictions and ambivalence could be very common with him. But Chaudhuri's personality differs from Nehru's very radically. Extroversion, keen sense of observation, scientific approach, objectivity, detachment, scholarly attitude, encyclopedic range of thinking, inter-disciplinary synthesis, and remarkable originality happen to be the dominant features of Chaudhuri's personality. These features cannot be discussed in detail within the scope of this article.

Now a contrastive analysis may be attempted with regard to the techniques of the two autobiographies. Though both the works are of nearly the same size, they sharply differ in their quality and impression. Though Nehru's autobiography resembles an epic as far as its national width and atmosphere are concerned, it lacks the variety and richness of Chaudhuri's autobiography which offers us the socio-psychological, religious, political, ethnic and other aspects of life. K. Raghavendra Rao is right when he says: "His *Autobiography of an Unknown Indian* is a unique work, an it defies classification. It is at once autobiography, history, sociology, anthropology, indology, political analysis—in short, it is refreshing and many-pronged attack on that nebulous phenomenon called British Empire in India."[4] Thus Chaudhuri's autobiography has not only the encyclopaedic range and variety but depth also. Whereas Nehru's work has one dominant atmosphere i.e., of Indian political life, Chaudhuri's work has a much varied and mixed atmosphere.

Nehru delineates his initiation into the Indian politics, his participation in the Congress activities, his contact with the Kisans and other masses of India, his support of the Gandhian movements, his disappointment with the inefficiency, nepotism, corruption, opportunism and narrow-mindedness of the Indian politicians, including liberals and Congress members, his opposition to the British imperialism, his constant struggle for the independence of India, and his dream of an international family, are no doubt, of enormous significance not only to himself but to his countrymen also. But all these details form part of the single and dominant political atmosphere. Of course, there are occasional deviations into religion but they do not occupy proportionately vast space in the autobiography. But Chaudhuri's autobiography contains a very diverse kind of picture of Bengali life. It delineates the geographical peculiarity of Bengal like the trees, rivers and vegetation; the special life like the joint-family system and the stock figures belonging to it; the ethnic life including their fairs and festivals of Kali, Durga, Kartik, Ganesh; the fine-arts like music, literature, dance and drama; religious life including superstitions and buffalo-sacrifices; the political consciousness of people intensified by proseletysers like Swami Vivekananda; the economic discrepancies in Bengali life and the Bengalis's cultural confrontation with the Muslim and the British. Thus Chaudhuri's work is multi-dimensional and intensive in its nature. The autobiographies of Nehru and

Chaudhuri are radically different from each other. Whereas Nehru's is like a solo performance, Chaudhuri's is like an orchestra. In other words, Nehru's work has a monolithic unity whereas Chaudhuri's work has the mosaic variety.

Nehru and Chaudhuri differ from each other in the manner of presentation of their experiences also. The overall impression made by Nehru's autobiography is romantic. Since Nehru was an idealist and a dreamer, he created a romantic halo around himself and idealized his country. In spite of his anger at and criticism of the Indian politicians and social evils, he gives a romantic elevation to his discussion of these issues. The India described by Nehru remains Nehru's India and not others's. Says Nehru, "And yet India with all her poverty and degradation had enough of nobility and greatness about her, and though she was overburdened with ancient tradition and present misery, and her eyelids were a little weary she had a beauty wrought from within upon the flesh, the deposit little cell by cell, of strange thoughts and fantastic reveries and exquisite persons. Behind and within her battered body, one could still glimpse a majesty of soul. Through long ages, she had travelled and gathered much wisdom on the way, and trafficked with strangers and added them to their own big family, and witnessed days of glory and of decay, and suffered humiliation and terrible sorrow, and seen many a strange sight; but throughout her long journey she had clung to her immemorial culture, drawn strength and vitality from it, and shared it with other lands. Like a pendulum she had swung up and down; she had ventured with the daring of her thought to reach up to the heavens and unravel their mystery, and she had also had bitter experience of the pit of hell. Despite the woeful accumulations of superstitions and degrading custom that had clung to her and borne her down, she had never wholly forgotten the inspiration that some of the wisest of her children, at the dawn of history, had given her in the Upanishads." (429) The glorification of India and her ideals is quite evident here. This is caused as much by his romantic temperament as by his patriotism. Many critics have felt this quality in Nehru. V.N. Chibber is right when he says, "Like Yeats, Nehru mythologized his generation. And his career has almost become a saint's story."[5] But Chaudhuri provides a complete contrast to Nehru. Chaudhuri is a realist and pragmatist who believed in scientific determinism. Because of his scientific temperament, Chaudhuri observes the life around him in a minute fashion and records it meticulously and the result is realistic and almost naturalistic picture of the atmosphere. Because of Chaudhuri's dispassionate description of the scenery and people, he succeeds in providing an almost photographic kind of picture and evokes the local colour of Bengal.

Unlike Nehru, Chaudhuri has a tendency to concretize the things and situations by providing maximum possible number of details. Far from giving a vague and general picture of life like Nehru, Chaudhuri offers a precise description of the particulars of experience. Chaudhuri will be very cautious not to betray his personal feelings and emotions in the description if not in the selection of things, persons and situations. His description of the semi-urbanised condition of Kishorgunj can be seen for illustration. "Had there been aeroplanes in our boyhood the term would have had the same appearance to our eyes, when looked at from a height, say, of five hundred feet, as a patch of white and brown mushrooms in the grass below must have to a little bird perched on a tree. The white corrugated iron-roofs were indeed too hard for the surrounding landscape, but this unattractive material had in my childhood just begun to oust the thatch. The brown mat walls, however, matched with the trees and the soil. Altogether, the town did not mark too hard a block on the soft countryside. Besides, the huts were flimsy. They creaked at almost every wind and one strong cyclone was enough to obliterate the distinction between country and town. I myself, arriving home one dark night from Calcutta after the great cyclone of 1919, had very great difficulty in finding the town among the fallen trees." (36) Thus Chaudhuri's description tends to be realistic, concrete, minute and photographic. One more allied feature of their autobiographies is that whereas Nehru's prose culminates in poetic heights more often than Chaudhuri's which, because of its scientific precision and abundance of details, tends to be drab. This is caused by the temperamental differences between Nehru and Chaudhuri. Whereas Nehru had a poetic sensibility which expressed itself in the elaborate style of writing, Chaudhuri had a strong, rationalistic mind which expressed itself in the scientifically precise language. Nehru's romantic ebullience can easily be contrasted with Chaudhuri's anti-romantic exactitude and precision. If one can use the cinematic metaphor, one can say though very loosely, that Nehru's work resembles a commercial film which selects the beautiful, eliminates or slurs over the ugly, exaggerates the colours and provides the idealized picture of life. Chaudhuri's work resembles an art-film which shows the ugly along with the beautiful, the cacophonous along with the melodious, the harsh with the tender without glorifying them.

The language employed by Nehru and Chaudhuri is also to be noted. Because of the temperamental difference between the two, the language used by them is different from each other. Nehru's prose is very elaborate, very often general and sometimes very poetic. But Chaudhuri's prose is cut-and-dry, precise, scientific, minute and concrete in its nature. But both the writers employ metaphorical language. Nehru's similes and metaphors are borrowed mainly from political and literary realm, whereas Chaudhuri's are drawn mainly from history and other sciences. Referring to Madan Mohan Malviya, Nehru says, "Both by his age and his long public record he is the Nestor of Indian politics, but a Nestor who seems a little out of date, and very much out of touch, with the modern world." (158) Similarly about the indifference of English rulers in India, he says, "Like Rip Van Winkle they sleep, even though walking, on Simla hill." (609) Chaudhuri's examples may be seen in the following sentences. Referring to Calcutta, Chaudhuri says, "The experience of this great city helped me to bring up certain feelings of ours about the town from the subconscious to the conscious level and I summarize below the results of this archaeological excavation in the domain of civic psychology." (36) Similarly, Chaudhuri refers to the modern humanity, "In fact, I think the humbler we are the more completely are we made up of the material deposited by historical movements like the expansion of the peoples known as the Aryans: the rise of Buddhism, Christianity, and Islam, the Renaissance, the Reformation and the French Revolution; the propagation of liberalism, Socialism, and Communism, *We are the sedimentary rocks formed out of these original igneous formations.*" (184, italics mine)

Quotations are a common feature of both the autobiographies. But the fields from which they are selected are different from each other. By and large, Nehru's quotations are relatively simple and drawn especially from poetry and testify to Nehru's wide reading of literature. But Chaudhuri's quotations are drawn not merely from literature, but from music, philosophy and similar sciences, and not merely from English, but from different languages like Bengali, Sanskrit, French and Italian. This habit, obviously, testifies to Chaudhuri's encyclopedic range of scholarship.

The alien language i.e. English which is employed by both the writers is also to be noted. Though both of them have used the 'imperially endowed' language, they differ from each other in its use. Nehru had learnt the English language through the Englishmen like F.T. Brooks, was educated at Harrow and Cambridge, and had a facility of language envied by the Britishers themselves, partly because of his romantic temperament and partly because of the influence of Persian and Urdu on his mind. His language, therefore, had a romantic elevation and elaboration about it. His elaborate style had abundant scope for generalizations and abstractions. Referring to the British Government in India then, Nehru says, "Law and order, we are told, are among the proud achievements of British rule in India. My own instincts are entirely in favour of them. I like discipline in life, and dislike anarchy and disorder and inefficiency. But bitter experience had made me doubt the value of the law and order that states and governments impose on a people. Sometimes the price one pays for them is excessive, and the law is but the will of the dominant faction and the order is the reflex of an all-pervading fear. Sometimes, indeed, the so-called law and order might be more justly called the absence of law and order. Any achievement that is based on widespread fear can hardly be a desirable one, and an 'order' that has for its basis the coercive apparatus of the state, and cannot exist without it, is more like a military occupation than civil rule." (482-83) But Chaudhuri's career was different from that of Nehru. Chaudhuri was educated not by British teachers but by Indian teachers, in Bengali institutions. Self-made man as Chaudhuri is, he learnt English by dint of sheer hard work and reached a stage when his language came to be appreciated by the English people themselves whose country he had not been able to see until his fifty-fourth year. Therefore, Chaudhuri's language is studied, precise and concrete. Because of his scholarly approach to the problems of life, his prose appears to be a bit heavy. But it should be remembered that for a man like him to attain that kind of mastery over the language without being taught in the real sense by any teacher is itself an achievement. Educational psychologists know this problem pretty well. *The Glasgow Herald* puts it thus, "This is an extraordinary book. It is written by a Hindu of East Bengal who has never been in Europe, yet with a command of English that is not exceeded by Mr. Nehru himself. . . . No other Indian self-portrait can compare, for interest or challenge, with this product of a tortured and assertive spirit." A paradox regarding Nehru and Chaudhuri and their relation to the British Empire may be pointed out. Though a product of British education, Nehru never liked the British imperialism. On the contrary, though Chaudhuri did not have a chance to see the British country until his fifty-fourth year, he grew up to be an Anglophile. In fact he dedicates his autobiography to the memory of British rule in India.

Pen-pictures are common to the autobiographies of Nehru and Chaudhuri. Nehru offers the pen-pictures of many of the people he met in India and abroad, like, for example, Shyamaji Krishnavarma, Gokhale, R.M. Roy etc. Similarly Chaudhuri provides very beautiful pen-pictures of his father and mother. But there is one difference between the two. Whereas Nehru's pen-portraits are romantic and capture the significant traits of a particular character, Chaudhuri's pen-portraits are scientifically realistic in the sense that he describes both the physical and the psychological traits of a character. A couple of examples will clarify this. Nehru's pen-portrait of Shyamaji Krishnavarma can be seen: "There was Shyamaji Krishnavarma living with his ailing wife high up on the top floor of a house in Geneva. The aged couple lived by themselves with no whole-time servants, and their rooms were musty and suffocating, and everything had a thick layer of dust. Shyamaji had plenty of money, but he did not believe in spending it. He would even save a few cents by walking instead of taking the tram. He was suspicious of all comers, presuming them, until the contrary was proved, to be either British agents or after his money. His pockets bulged with ancient copies of his old paper, the *Indian Sociologist*, and he would pull them out and point with some excitement to some article he had written a dozen years previously. His talk was of the old days, of Indian House at Hampstead, of the various persons that the British Government had sent to spy on him, and how he had spotted them and outwitted them. The walls of his rooms were covered with shelves full of old books, dust-laden and neglected, looking down sorrowfully on the intruder. Books and papers also littered the floor; they seemed to have remained so for days and weeks, and months past. Over the whole place there hung an atmosphere of gloom, an air of decay; life seemed to be an unwelcome stranger there, and one walked through the dark and silent corridors, one almost expected to come across, round the corner, the shadow of death. With relief one came out of that flat and breathed the air outside." (149) It can easily be noted that Nehru has captured the essential feature of Krishnavarma's personality i.e., his peculiar obsession. Nehru does not care to describe his physiognomy, the details of the house in which he lived and the society from which he came.

Here is a pen-portrait by Nirad Chaudhuri about his father, "He was of middle height, judged by Bengali standards, that is to say, just under five feet six inches. But he had broad and square shoulders, a deep chest and very muscular arms, so that he gave an impression of great physical strength besides actually possessing it. His body had none of those curves which in India are as much a part of masculine grace as of feminine. More especially, seen in the profile, his figure presented neither the S-shaped nor the barrel-shaped outline, which are two of the commonest anatomical configurations to be found among us. . . . He was very bony, his wrist and hips were narrow, and thus there was a preponderance of nearly straight lines in his figure. . . . In dress he was simple to the point of being shabby. . . . He was not given to criticizing or condemning others." (144-45) Chaudhuri's scientific i.e., ethnological approach to life enabled him always to describe the physical features first and then point out the psychological traits and views and offer his own opinion about the characters. Thus Chaudhuri's pen-portraits gain in vividness.

Autobiography offers a great scope for an author to reveal his world-view or philosophy of life. In other forms of literature, the author may not be able to do so in a systematic fashion or do it at all as he is used to masking his real self through the fictive garb. But in the autobiography, he can and should do it because he has a chance to 'be himself' in it. The autobiographies of Bertrand Russell or Mahatma Gandhi easily provide ample evidence of this. Nehru and Chaudhuri, serious as they are by nature, have not neglected this aspect. The idea of Nehru's philosophy becomes very clear to every reader. Nehru's humanism which was related to his idealism and patriotism which was part of his internationalism is evident in his autobiography. Says Nehru, "we record our grateful appreciation of the fact that all the major and minor communities and classes in India have joined together in the great struggle and given of their best to the cause; particularly the minority communities—Muslims, Sikhs, Parsis, Christians and others who, by their valour and loyal devotion to the cause of the common motherland, have helped in building up a united and indissoluble nation, certain of victory, and resolved to achieve and maintain the independence of India, and to use this new freedom to raise the shackles from, and to remove the inequalities among, all classes of the people of India, and thus also to serve the larger cause of humanity." (616) Thus though national independence of India was the great cause for which Nehru fought so hard, he never believed in parochialism. He believed that nationalism was part of internationalism. Nehru did not care either for ritualistic or for metaphysical aspect of religion. But he pleaded for the religion of humanity.

Similarly Chaudhuri also gives expression to his world-view in his work. Many readers, especially Indians, accuse Chaudhuri of being a cynic and a pessimist. But one should remember that to call somebody a cynic or a pessimist is not to understand him. In such a situation the autobiographer is forced to clarify his stand and enable the reader to see him from the right perspective. Chaudhuri does it superbly in the following passage: "But in the last five or six years, through another miracle, I have been enabled to put an end to this duality and found peace in a new form of monism. I have come to see that I and the universe are inseparable, because I am only a particle of the universe and remain so in every manifestation of my existence—intellectual, moral and spiritual, as well as physical. Thus on the one hand I have been disenthralled by knowledge. On the other I have believed in order to understand,

and have been rewarded with joy. I have found that to sit by the rivers of Babylon is not necessarily to weep in Hebraic sorrow. Today, borne on a great flood of faith, hope, and joy in the midst of infinite degradation, I felt that I shall be content to be nothing for ever after death in the ecstasy of having lived and been alive for a moment. I have made the discovery that the last act is glorious however squalid the play may be in all the rest." (527) The passage testifies to Chaudhuri's philosophy of monism and his belief in the principle of joy of life and nullifies the unsympathetic critics' accusation of Chaudhuri's so-called skepticism. Thus both Nehru and Chaudhuri express their world-views explicitly in their own typical manners.

Both the autobiographies have certain deficiencies. An autobiography should, as far as possible, give us an all-round picture of an individual. In one's life, one's youth is as much important as one's childhood. Sometimes youth is more important than childhood because in youth one is likely to undergo many crises. Since sex plays an important role in one's youth, amorous life including sexual problems, obsessions, adventures, frustrations, and fulfillments should have a place in the autobiography. But in the autobiographies of Nehru and Chaudhuri, these experiences are conspicuous by their absence. Rousseau describes what he experienced in the company of a prostitute. Cellini and Bertrand Russell describe their illicit relationship with maid-servants. Dom Moraes mentions how his grandmother had an illegal relation with a servant. Sasthi Brata is an expert in the descriptions of matings legal and illegal, homosexual and heterosexual. Such confidential details are not to be sensed, let alone described, in the autobiographies of Nehru and Chaudhuri. It is not at all compulsory for them to describe such situations if they *do not* have them. But they should if they *have* them. The absence of such details in the works of Nehru and Chaudhuri is ascribable either to lack of such experiences or lack of time or patience or willingness. But in the case of Indian writers it is more often due to unwillingness to do so on inhibitive and puritanical grounds. At least Nehru mentions his marriage, but Chaudhuri does not do that also. Both are one in maintaining absolute silence about the matrimonial problems and pleasures they had. It only proves that they have not liberated themselves from subconscious puritanism.

A bit of negative comparison will reveal the peculiarities of each autobiography. Chaudhuri's work does not have the kind of self-analysis and self-examination that Nehru's has. Chaudhuri analyses the Bengali society rather than himself because according to him environment precedes the individual. Nehru explodes the myths built around his father, Gandhi and himself. But Chaudhuri has no reason or occasion to do so. Whereas Nehru romanticizes India, Chaudhuri photographs it realistically. Nehru appears less sincere than Chaudhuri. Unlike Nehru who is bothered about the entire nation, Chaudhuri is interested only in the mini-world called Bengal. Similarly unlike Chaudhuri, Nehru does not create the local colour and exotic atmosphere. Nehru, unlike Chaudhuri, does not offer the picture of the multiple layers of life. Unlike Chaudhuri, Nehru is not a conscious craftsman of the art because he wrote it in a hurry and that too in a prison.

Thus a comparative study of the autobiographies of an internationally known Indian like Nehru and not very 'unknown' Indian like Chaudhuri throws light upon the achievements in the art of autobiography by two Indian writers coming from two different parts of the same country.

NOTES

1. *The Modern Study of Literature* (Chicago: The University of Chicago Press, 1928), p. 77.
2. Jawaharlal Nehru, *An Autobiography* (New Delhi: Allied, 1962), p. 1.
3. Nirad C. Chaudhuri, *The Autobiography of an Unknown Indian*, (Bombay: Jaico, 1973), p. 131.
4. *Critical Essays on Indian Writing in English*, ed. M.K. Naik et al.
5. *Jawaharlal Nehru: A Man of Letters* (New Delhi: Vikas, 1970), p. 109.

The Autobiography of an Unknown Indian: A Critique

S.P. SWAIN

A monument to "the creative clash of two civilizations,"[1] *The Autobiography* tells the story of the early period of Nirad Chaudhuri's life, of the condition "in which an Indian grew to manhood in the early decades of this century."[2] It is in the nature of an intellectual acrobatics interpreting Indian history from a non-conformist standpoint. Chaudhuri exhibits his critical acumen and insight by his elucidatory and subjective approach to the problems of Indian history, society, politics and culture. He says: "The story I want to tell is the story of the struggle of a civilization with a hostile environment, in which the destiny of British rule in India became necessarily involved. My main intention is thus historical . . . the book may be regarded as a contribution to contemporary history." (vii) Highly informative and reflective, *The Autobiography* is an Indian's self-portrait, mirroring the tortured and asserting spirit of a scholar extraordinary: "I never developed a true religious and spiritual life. . . . I had no religious culture." (215) But it is more of a national than personal history.

The Autobiography gives us a coherent and imaginatively unified picture of India's past history since all the chapters focus on our socio-cultural aspects. Chaudhuri says that it is our "unity in diversity" which has urged the British to look at Indians with esteem and regard. Chaudhuri says that ours is a civilization with past achievements and we are a single community despite being endowed with a multi-racial and multi-lingual culture. As human beings, they transcend these narrow conscriptions and barriers: "the Indian people crossed the line which divides primitive peoples from civilized peoples. They could now be said to belong to the same species as the Homo sapiens historicus of Europe." (442) In this connection, Srinivasa Iyengar observes: "Chaudhuri's real aim is to write history, and the autobiographical exercise is merely a means to get the history started. Early in his college days he had fallen in love with history."[3]

The Autobiography is not only Chaudhuri's verdict on the British Raj but it is also a virulent criticism of the Indians being poor imitators of the Western materialist culture. It delineates through concrete images the alien society's superior material culture that transforms us into what Naipaul would have called 'mimic men.' The author cites an instance of the steam-powered vessel of Mr. Stapleton on its maiden arrival near Kishorganj:

> As the house-boat stood moored a little stand-offishly, we . . . gaped at it in wonder. It seemed to be a palace in comparison not only with the other boats but also with our houses. But in spite of its beautiful lines, its red, white and green paint, and its essentially aquatic presence it was not . . . quite in keeping with the surroundings. (5)

Cultural collision between the natives and aliens occurred even at the mundane level of existence. In 1916, Chaudhuri reports that the boys of the matriculation class bowed down to locomotives as if to gods. We are also apprised of the English steel trunks which Chaudhuri's father purchased two or three a year. Even the Catalogues of British Department stores were regularly perused in the Chaudhuri household for the items that might improve domestic convenience. Chaudhuri's interaction with the West was chiefly concerned with the spiritual realm of existence: "My Westernization is of the older pattern, concerned more with the mind than material things."[4] The West had a tremendous impact on his mind. He acutely felt it like the other Indians of the time but these occidental influences were "felt mainly in the higher centres of consciousness and manifested themselves in the sphere of culture."[5] Chaudhuri says that the British Empire conferred subjecthood on us and at the same time it withheld citizenship. Cultural contact was sensibly felt by him. It was a psychic and an imaginative experience. In the Prefatory Note (Book I, Early Environment), Chaudhuri says:

> My first account will thus be of the little country town in which I was born and lived till my twelfth year; my second, of my ancestral village; and my third, of the village of my mother's folk. These three accounts will make up the first three chapters of this book; but as England, evoked by imagination and enjoyed emotionally, has been as great an influence on me as any of the three places sensibly experienced.

In Chapter IV of Book I, he has very deftly and superbly captured the spell of England. He says, "the chiaroscuro of our knowledge of England was extremely sensational . . . so that what we knew gripped us with immeasurably greater power." (101) In this context, Raghavendra Rao observes: "Chaudhuri had also built up the physical image of England as a place, churning out a whole mytho-geography out of books read and pictures seen. The England thus conjured up was 'a country which possessed not only beautiful spots but also place names which sounded beautiful.' England was always seen as a sea-girt."[6]

Chaudhuri refers to Shakespeare, Webster, Charles Lamb and even to the characters of Jane Austen. His approach to the English works of men of letters is elucidatory and comparative. Speaking of Shakespeare's Julius Caesar, he says:

> Our familiarity with the name of Julius Caesar was only a byproduct of our knowledge of Shakespeare, and the first idea we formed of the great Roman was in the image of Mr. Rames Roy, a top-form boy of Kishorganj High School, who in a black English suit had taken the part of Caesar in a performance of Act III, Scene I, given by the senior students. (103)

Again about the *Iliad* and the *Ramayana*, he says that it was the obvious parallelism which deceives us: "In both cases there was an abducted woman. Sita in the *Ramayana* and Helen in the *Iliad*. In both cases there were two rescuing brothers, Rama and Lakshmana in the Indian epic and Menelaus and Agamemnon in the Greek." (103) Speaking of John Milton's magnanimous personality, Chaudhuri says:

> Milton stood before us in solitary and somewhat awe-inspiring grandeur. His claims upon us were manifold. In the first place, he was the author of the bright volume in the glass-fronted cupboard. Secondly, he was the model of Michael Madhusudan Dutt. Thirdly, he was the writer of a most striking line which my father was fond of repeating and which ran as follows: 'Better to reign in hell than serve in heaven.' Lastly, it appeared he had something to do with the execution of Charles I, who had tried to deprive the English people of their liberties. (104)

But Chaudhuri's lucid prose at times degenerates into bold and airy exaggerations exhibiting his parochial sentiment, when he says: "If any whole-hearted Bonapartists were to be found anywhere in the world at the end of the nineteenth century and the beginning of the twentieth they were to be found in Bengal." (105) He further makes a verbal display of his deep-seated love for the Bengalis' intellectual and literary calibre: "I do not know if any other country or people in the world has ever made one author the epitome, test, and symbol of literary culture as we Bengalis did with Shakespeare in the nineteenth century. . . . It was a cult which we had made typically Bengali." (197) He goes to the extent of contrasting a Tudor chest, with the native wooden box made by the native craftsman.

Chaudhuri talks about our curiously mixed feelings of love and hate towards the English people. Articulating his ambivalent attitude towards the English in his critique of a war in which England was a participant, he observes: "One half of us automatically shared in the English triumph, while the other and the patriotic half wanted the enemies of England to win." (108) Nirad Chaudhuri, the historian, gives an account of European history as a symbol of man's struggle for freedom: "European history was a series of struggles for freedom, as a result of which the ambit of a beneficent and fertilizing freedom had been enlarged in ever widening circles in the course of modern history." (111)

Look at the caustic remarks of Niradbabu, the anti-Indian, on an Indian's lack of balance, proportion and psychic equilibrium. He says that an Indian is impulsive by nature:

> to ask an Indian to be balanced among a number of things, each good in its way, is to ask him, not to be effective in his varied loyalties, but to be futile in all of them. He has neither the vitality nor the will-power which springs from that vitality to observe proportion in his pursuits. He is and can be driven only by his impulses and emotions, fixed into impulsive and emotional habits, and these impulses and emotions cannot be checked in their natural course without bringing about . . . . an atrophy of the whole motive power of effort. (222)

The most unique, single discursive work, *The Autobiography,* is concerned with Chaudhuri's fascination with himself. "Here," says William Walsh, "Chaudhuri sees himself as an object in a landscape or as an impulse in a more inclusive and controlling rhythm, and the whole presentation of the self is impressively tranquil and objective." (45)

Chaudhuri's intellectual self was shaped and moulded by the classical ideals of Greece and Rome. Reading of the classical texts brought him enlightenment and through these textbooks he acquired "a feeling of oneness with Athens." (477) Despite his closeness with the Athenian culture and the classical texts, Chaudhuri humbly confesses that he "never became a scholar." (336) "A small read," says Niradbabu, "stirred my imagination so deeply in my early college days that they may be reckoned as very powerful influences on my intellectual growth." (340)

About the role of the historian, Chaudhuri says that he is an impartial judge of men and events. He is a man speaking to man. Ideas which are truths in religion and politics are forces in history and the task of a historian is to reflect these ideas and facts with utmost sincerity, fidelity and detachment:

> The historian must be content to state facts as they happened, or to use a modern phrase, to show a development without

> intruding his opinions and predilections into the narrative. His position is not among the fellowmen of whom he is writing. He does not share their joys and passions nor mingles in their affairs. His position is that of a spectator who stands on a balcony and watches a crowd street under him. (353)

To Chaudhuri "objectivity is a distinct advance in the direction of the historical point of view" and that the "fundamental idea of history is the idea of change." (354)

Dedicated to "The Memory of the British Empire in India," *The Autobiography* describes all that was noble and ideal within us being moulded and transformed by the British rule in India. The view of history that Chaudhuri projects is highly unorthodox. He says at the end of "An Essay on the Course of Indian History" that "from the personal standpoint, the historical thesis has emancipated him from a malaise that has haunted me throughout my life." (526) Speaking of his alienated plight during his educational career, he further says, "During the years of my education I was becoming a stranger to my environment . . . in the next ten years I was oppressed by a feeling of antagonism to the environment." (526) Despite having aped all the appurtenances of Westernization, India has remained a static entity. Hence Chaudhuri bemoans the Indian endeavour to carve out a modern culture out of a East-West cultural synthesis. There was an all out effort by Indian intellectuals for taking in the West. Michael Madhusudan Dutt, Raja Ram Mohun Roy and Bankim Chandra were the pioneers in bringing about an East-West cultural tryst. But extreme Westernization in some cases led to nativization, as with Michael Madhusudan Dutt who having begun his literary career being inspired by Western literature had at length to return to his native Bengal. Not only that, even he had to return to his native language after carrying out his literary pursuits in the English language. His "early poetry was written in English, but after once going over to Bengali he never came back to English for literary expression." (196) Bankim Chandra, too, wrote his very first novel in English, but "came over to Bengali permanently after that youthful misfire." (196) Chaudhuri sarcastically points out that the English were more hostile than the most bigoted Hindu orthodox to the modern Indian culture based on an

East-West cultural fusion. As pointed out by the critics, Chaudhuri cannot be dubbed as an anti-Indian for he "entertained no ambition of hobnobbing" with the English in India: "As long as I lived in Calcutta," says Chaudhuri, "I wore no article of English clothing and had none. In general, I disliked and despised the local English." (376) Chaudhuri was never an adherent of the British Empire, its ideas and ideals. He was out and out an Indian, a true Bengali babu:

> The British Empire in India has perished without my ever coming into intimate personal contact with Englishmen. . . . I do not regret it for with all the Anglicism of my spirit I should have felt a total stranger in the English society of Calcutta. (377)

Nirad Chaudhuri, the Anglophile, had a special fascination for the beauty associated with English life. Such a beautiful life had left an indelible romantic impression on his mind:

> However scrappy and simple our ideas of English life and society might have been, they could not exist at all without the accompaniment of some visual suggestion. Everything we read about the British Isles or in English evoked pictures of the external appearance of the country. . . . Taken together, these gave us the impression of a country of great beauty . . . a country which possessed not only beautiful spots but also place-names which sounded beautiful . . . their beauty of appearance produced a vivid effect on me. (113)

Despite such romantic fascination that the English way of life had on Chaudhuri and despite the magic spell it had cast on his psyche, Chaudhuri "could never think of England," as he "thought of Bengal and of India, as a stretch of land alone." (115) Very humorously does Chaudhuri talk about the Indianization of English text-books in order to make them easily comprehensible to the average Indian student:

> when I was young the educational authorities had had a sud-

> den inspiration that it was too much of a burden for young Indian boys to have to cope with English ideas in an English background in addition to having to master the intricacies of a foreign language. In pursuance of this theory our English text-books were being Indianized as the administration of India was Indianized later. (116)

Chaudhuri attributes the cause of the fall of the British Raj to "the bankruptcy of European civilization, its spiritual poverty, and its moral iniquity." (323) Another factor that precipitated its sudden fiasco was the inefficiency and the "declining calibre"[7] of the Viceroys sent to India:

> But India had no Viceroy of genius after Lord Curzon. Hardinge, Reading, and Willingdon were clever men, who succeeded in stealing a few marches on the nationalists. . . . They may be compared to very experienced old foxes. . . . But they were not the grand animals to scatter the pack with a roar and rush. Not for a single moment between 1905 and 1945 did the British Government in India succeed in wresting the initiative from the nationalists, although at quite a number of junctures that could easily have been done. (326)

The unique trait of Chaudhuri's critique is that he represents India as a static and moribund culture. He debunks the Hindu culture. To him, the Hindu civilization is "dead for ever, and cannot be resuscitated, and to hope to create a second civilization of the same order is for us today a superannuated piece of folly." (521) "In the eighteenth century," says Chaudhuri, "on the eve of the establishment of British rule, the Hindus had no recollection of their real past, nor any idea of the true character of the classical Sanskritic civilization. Their Hinduism was a broken-up and simplified version of the Hinduism of ancient India. It was unorganized in space and unsupported in time." (442) He further adds, almost derogatorily and disparagingly:

> Hindu society does not teach its youth to face life bravely. The phrase 'courage of life' is unintelligible to a Hindu, who

> accepts the first wail of birth as the leitmotiv of existence and manages quite successfully to lead a mock-turtle's life during the whole of it. (369)

One of the most controversial and difficult writers of the age, Chaudhuri sounds a bit anti-Indian in *The Autobiography*, especially in his criticism of Hindu culture. Hence it won't be erroneous on the part of the patriotic and orthodox Indian readers to describe the book as "The Autobiography of a Known Anti-Indian." This is not all. He even goes to the extent of saying: "Hinduism appears to be swimming against the current . . . it is retrograde and out of sympathy with reality." (439) He agrees with Alberuni that "Hindus are haughty, foolish, vain, self-conceited and stolid. They are by nature niggardly." (416) It seems Nirad Chaudhuri's love for the Hindus is only skin-deep. But such seemingly pessimistic appearance of this great man of letters is only a wild guess for he is very judicious in his critical remarks. He appears to be an anti-Hindu but in reality he is not so. He is all praise for Hinduism's moral virtues. "Hinduism," he says, "cannot justly be charged with having let down moral conduct . . . it has safeguarded the operative part of morality through a method peculiar to itself." (222)

Chaudhuri says that all endeavours of the Indians to imitate the West, and be Europeanised has been a failure and what one sees today is nothing but "an immense expanse of debased Europeanization mottled here and there with Hindu or Muslim traits." (508) This dilution is transparent in every sphere of our cultural activity. We have been barbarized. About the Western education, Chaudhuri says that it was received only outwardly and superficially. We have not imbibed the spirit of Western education in us. In spite of our aping the Western culture, we are still not modern in spirit and temper. Our "Westernization" is by and large sartorial and cosmetic. Our 'Secondrateness' had made us a poor travesty of all that is Western and European. We have missed the reality beneath the surface of our sham and hypocritical existence. This is our predicament, something uniquely conducive to our sedimented and fossilised feelings and ideas about the West. Our attempts at Westernisation are limited to the adoption of Western dress, food and manners which do not necessarily mean the acceptance of occidental ideas and values.

Chaudhuri's extremist thesis in *The Autobiography* that Indian history comprises three cycles during each of which "a strong and creative foreign influence provided the primary motive force viz., the mid-European Aryan, the Muslim and the British respectively . . . appears very much like an intellectual extension of the wish-fulfilment of a self-confessed Anglophile, alienated from his own culture."[8] The invasion of India by the Europeans, especially the British was a blessing to the Indians. It aroused in us our feelings of nationalism and made us what we are to-day. Chaudhuri seems to acquiesce with Vivekananda who said that "one of the great blessings of British rule in India was that the days of exclusive privilege and exclusive claims were gone for ever from the soil of India. . . . Even to Muhammadan rule we owe that great blessing, the destruction of exclusive privilege. . . . The Muhammadan conquest of India came as salvation to the down-trodden, to the poor." (qtd. 434) While speaking at a public meeting on religion, Vivekananda said, "Had it not been for the power of the Anglo-Saxons, we should not have met here today to discuss the influence of our Indian spiritual thought." (qtd. 434)

With a relish for the specific and a refined perception, Chaudhuri eulogises the Britisher's love for the actual, the concrete and the substantial, something which was lacking in Indian civilization which is manifest in Hinduism with its love of the illusory, the unreal, the abstract and the unsubstantial. Hinduism is not with the current, it is against the tide of life. As said earlier, it is retrograde and out of tune with reality. Chaudhuri also focuses on the influence of the English language on our men and manners. He says that the linguistic basis of modern Indian culture is made up of a combination of English, a denatured vernacular, and a mixed colloquial language. And it is this fact which testifies to the basically alien character of modern Indian culture. Even our literatures today are alien in spirit, since what we write to-day hardly has the stamp of originality. It is but an idea of an idea, an imitation of an imitation. It is an absorption of all that is alien without any assimilation. Our use of the English language and literature is just a mechanical process. This is because we "never know the Englishmen properly."

The socio-cultural and socio-historical facts of *The Autobiography* are supported by "a massive fund of anthropological and historical learning and penetrated by sensitively intelligent sociological speculation."[9] Basically melancholic and nervy, the tone of *The Autobiography* is less cordial and almost humorously solemn. The attitude that Chaudhuri exhibits is arrogant and antagonistic. His historical vision is catholic but at times it becomes myopic and hyperbolic. Hence I do not agree with William Walsh when he says that Chaudhuri is "faithfully Indian and saltily himself." (51) Walsh is certainly right when he says: "He fiercely cherishes what most people would find intolerable, the identity of the alien," and the most tragic of all, Chaudhuri makes "half the population of India foreigners in their own country." (51) Truly indeed, an Indian, especially a Hindu, after reading *The Autobiography* becomes an alien in his own soil since the cultural attire which he puts on today is a mask. It is a borrowed garment which smacks of all that is occidental, all that is second-rate and an imitation of the West.

NOTES

1. William Walsh, *Indian Literature in English* (New York: Longman, 1990), p. 52.
2. Nirad C. Chaudhuri, *The Autobiography of an Unknown Indian* (Bombay: Jaico, 1973), p. viii.
3. K.R. Srinivasa Iyengar, *Indian Writing in English* (Bombay: Asia, 1973), p. 591.
4. Nirad C. Chaudhuri, "The Western Influence on India," *The Atlantic*, March 1964, p. 71.
5. *Ibid.*, p. 72.
6. Raghavendra K. Rao, "An Epitaph for the British Raj," *Critical Essays on Indian Writing in English*, ed. Naik et al. (Madras: Macmillan, 1977), p. 395.
7. Rao, p. 398.
8. M.K. Naik, *A History of Indian English Literature* (New Delhi: Sahitya Akademi, 1992), p. 265.
9. Walsh, p. 46.

A Jaundiced Eye or Exaggeration:
An Autobiography of An Unknown Indian

MADHUMALATI ADHIKARI

It is interesting to note that Nirad C. Chaudhuri, twice in the course of the book *The Autobiography of an Unknown Indian,* refers to Calcutta and the people of Calcutta, in great detail. The first chapters of book III and book IV, titled 'Calcutta' and 'Man and Life in Calcutta' respectively, deal with description of the city life and present observations about the residents of the particular city. These two chapters concentrate on mirroring Chaudhuri's attitude towards the Bengali community and the dwellers of the city. By his own confession, he lived in Calcutta continuously from June 1910 to March 1942. A long association of thirty two years and yet, it is strange that he had not developed any sympathetic ties with Calcutta! Regarding Calcutta, his comment recorded in his autobiography (1951) is, "none the less I remained wholly unaffected by the surge of its daily life; the city as an abstract entity engrossed me, as a reality it was intolerably irksome."[1] A scrutiny of the relevant sections of the book uncovers the fact that the 'abstract entity' of Calcutta had also failed to move him. It is very perplexing to note that despite his stay in Calcutta since 1910, he "did not set eyes on Tagore till 1927." (264) He admits that though he was interested in politics, he avoided ordinary public meetings and had never felt the urge to attend the three important sessions of Calcutta held in 1917, 1920 and 1928. He had only a fleeting glimpse of Surendranath Bannerjee and C.R. Das. For many years Subhash Chandra Bose remained a total stranger to him. (265) One is really amazed to find Chaudhuri's isolation in Calcutta, the nerve centre of diverse activities. One can summarize that to a great extent it was self-sought and not imposed upon him.

Repeatedly, he decries the life and men of Calcutta. In fact, he cannot perceive anything good and beautiful in it except squalor and filth. The Muslim and the Hindu areas, according to him, both were ugly. From the house tops of these areas, "Calcutta seemed in these crowded and untidy rows to bid the most solid and the ugliest imaginable defiance of the sky." (268) The only area which suggested any architectural design, was according to him, the 'West' where one could see the well known public buildings of Esplanade and Dalhousie Square. (277) This was the British area that he found pleasing. It has to be admitted that Chaudhuri has observed the city minutely but due to some personal reason, he has focussed only on the dark details. He begins the description of the Bengali parts of Calcutta in a censorious manner:

> To this morphological dinginess the Bengali parts of Calcutta added the ebbs and flows of a functional dinginess. . . . The Bengalis wash (i.e. rinse in plain unsoaped water) their cotton *dhotis* and *saris* at home everyday. . . . The front verandah if there is any or the roof is reserved for this. . . . The houses when the washing is drying have the appearance of being draped in dirty linen. (267)

The picture drawn minutely is true but unfortunately he does not seem to understand the plight of these middle class people who face the acute problem of open space. The other side of the picture, beautiful and soothing, noticed by Tagore and Bankim Chandra Chatterji, had never attracted Chaudhuri's attention. Tagore had composed so many lyrics of love and nature from his Calcutta residence and the fiction writers had woven a magic of love and romance viewing Calcutta from the same place. Chaudhuri never felt the urge to wrap Calcutta in any mystery. It is because he disliked Calcutta with his body and soul. He never felt 'buoyed' up by the environment and failed to 'glide' naturally on it. He had to 'beat' it until 'unwillingly' it generated 'the force' to keep him 'afloat.' (278) This inherent animosity coloured his vision.

Chaudhuri's narrative includes a description of Bengali girls and their faces which, again, is disapproving. The girls with 'unusual immobile placidity' (278) engaged in collecting dry clothes from the clothes-lines either look like 'washerwomen' or appear most ordinary while bargaining for their choice goods from the 'hawkers' (293) which invariably are 'gaudy trifles.' (391) He had not witnessed any Charulata, Lavanya or Mrinal of Tagore or a Parvati of Sarat Chandra Chatterji's *Devdas* or a Durgeshnandini of Bankim Chandra Chatterji's novel of the same name. Is it a conscious omission or a matter of limited vision? In fact, during the Bengal Renaissance, many women writers like Sita Debi, Shanta Debi, Kadambari Debi, Jyotirmoyee Debi, Toru Dutt etc. were engaged with their creative worlds and were making their place in the world of Bengali literature. Toru Dutt's photograph is mentioned and nothing more. Chaudhuri hardly takes cognizance of their presence. His keen eye concentrates only on the mediocre and the ordinary. One cannot but feel that he has constructed an imaginary wall of dislike between himself and the world of Calcutta. He could only think about the dripping taps and discuss about the 'flagstone under the tap called the Foot of the tap' (392) and not the beautiful monsoon or the heart-moving vegetation of Bengal. The artistic characteristics of Calcutta were totally omitted by him.

Calcutta is known for its beautiful colonial buildings. It is natural because the British rulers had made Calcutta their capital. It boasts of some beautiful dwelling quarters constructed either by the Britishers or the native residents. Chaudhuri is critical of this arrangement also. He openly admires the English architecture but condemns the mansions as either being a modest copy of the Buckingham Palace or being cheap imitations. He fails to recognize that the imitative quality of these mansions is neither startling nor degrading in any sense because every nation, to some extent, has copied the style of the masters. He criticizes the interior decorations of these mansions. He is annoyed with the drawing rooms of the Bengalis because it has 'no place for women, they kept themselves within the Zenana.' (385) The author of the *Autobiography* seems to forget the power of the *purdah* system common in all the states of India. Most of the regions of India permitted their women folk to appear in public only on special occasions. The Indian ladies of the Anglicized families were the fortunate few who had the liberty to sit and communicate with their male counterparts. It is surprising that Chaudhuri forgets about the peculiar traditions of India.

Despite his denial, it is easy to perceive that, in this book, Chaudhuri has preference for things that are English. Regarding the standards of woman's beauty, he insists on favouring the 'English tradition of charming in women.' (378) Jamini Roy's concept of a beautiful woman, traditional in nature and quite similar to the French concept of beauty, is disapproved by the writer. Many other traditional systems like the special position of the master of the house during meals is also criticized by him. In the present-day context, the system is meaningless and also harmful but the suitability of expecting certain norms in our tradition-bound society of early twentieth century, by a discerning person like Chaudhuri, is unthinkable. His critical remarks can be defended only if we recollect that he had an unconventional upbringing in a family that followed the principle of *Brahmo Samaj*. He was prone to question the archaic system of the *Sanatana Dharma*. I do not intend to justify the artificial segregation of men, women and children advocated by the rigid care-takers of society. But I am surprised, because despite his penetrating intellect, Chaudhuri has failed to see the inevitability of the situation. How can one forget the control of these norms over the conscience of the Indian people?

The social life of Calcutta has a very typical practice; it is of meeting people in different locations for gossiping sessions. Such sessions are described in Bengali by the word '*Adda*.' (398) Chaudhuri, an active person, cannot tolerate this total waste of precious time. These meetings are conducted on the pavements. This is an easy method of doing away with daily tensions. Chaudhuri finds it highly objectionable because he thinks that these *Addas* keep the husbands, the fathers away from their wives and children. He observes, 'There is no custom among them [Bengali men of Calcutta] of a man sitting with his wife and children in the evening.' (400) One must accept the authenticity of the statement but also not forget that it was the Western civilization that had inculcated in us the need for a family communication. Even today, this modern practice is restricted to urban life only. Women and children do join the daily ritual of dining together but not in many homes can we witness genuine communication. The difference continues in the name of generation gap. Chaudhuri idolizes the English and takes great pain to establish the sacred qualities of an English family wherein justice, equality and other Victorian qualities, he thinks, come from the inner consciousness of man. 'The Victorian respectability, strict discharge of family obligation and steadiness' are some of the 'commendatory' qualities that he highlights. His comment suggests indirectly that the Bengalis of Calcutta neglect their pious duties towards their family. To condemn an entire community for non-existent shortcomings is unfair and fallacious.

Chaudhuri's notion of an interesting social life is definitely not Indian but Western: "There was very little social life among the Bengalis of Calcutta, as understood even in the more frivolous connotation of the words 'society' and '*monde*.' No afternoon or evening parties, no dinners, no at-homes and of course, no dances, enlivened their existence." (397) He either consciously overlooks the role to thousand and one, big and small religious festivals of Bengal that reinforce the foundations of social and cultural contacts or he has been deprived of joining these celebrations because of his 'outsider' status of a 'mess-dweller.' To reflect that an evening with 'no dances' is dead and dull, is nothing but a reflection of a confined self.

In India, the first four decades of this century have resounded with patriotic feelings. In this connection, Chaudhuri refers to Rammohun Roy's contribution but remains silent about the other stalwarts of the age who had dedicated their life and soul for the liberation of the motherland. He has either ignored or decried the famous revolutionaries of Bengal. In a general sense he appreciates 'the spirit of self sacrifice and dedication' but he condemns the passionate enthusiasm of the youth as 'fanaticism.' (231) It is not difficult to accept that the line between nationalism and fanaticism is very thin and often, under highly charged circumstances, necessary restraint is lost but to condemn Praphulla Chaki or Khudiram Bose of Maniktala conspiracy case for their drastic step, is a miscarriage of justice: "I could not make a hero of Praphulla Chaki, one of the young men who had killed the Kennedys and had escaped arrest. . . . Nor could I share the apotheosis of Khudiram Bose, the other young man responsible for the Muzzafarpore outrage. I felt that there was something repelling in the glorification of mere murder." (253) In other words, he had equated the revolutionaries with the terrorists. He admits that his moral attitude was nurtured by his mother's view who 'refused that the end justified the means.' (245) Who can doubt the sanctity of the idealism? But it would not be wrong to add that some terminal diseases require drastic treatment. Chaudhuri's consistent hostility towards Calcutta and the Bengalis is very apparent and may be, he has his reasons. He wonders also, if he has been too 'malicious' in spreading 'calumnies' about the city and been 'guilty of ungrateful meanness towards the great city.' (405) The reason of this unkindness may be rooted in his feeling of peripheral existence in the city.

In contrast, his descriptions of his own village life in Banagram and later his birthplace Kishorganj, are very sympathetic. The reason of this natural affinity is not far to seek. His happy memories of childhood have propelled him to appreciate the beauty of the small town and to ignore its weaknesses. He defines himself as the son of the soil. He comes from a rural 'land-owing line.' (266) He believes that 'a true rustic can never separate himself from his surroundings.' (266) This was one other reason why he never felt any close relationship with Calcutta. He had faced another problem, the problem of regional intolerance. Chaudhuri was a '*Bangal*' and was looked down upon by the natives of Calcutta. (373) The *Bangals*, the dwellers of East Bengal and now Bangladesh, were thought to be inferior in every way by the permanent residents of Calcutta. The *Bangals*, treated as refugees, were refused admission to the *sanctum sanctorum* of the community life. The class difference also must have aggravated his problems. He could not participate in the social activities because of his restrained financial condition. In *The Continent of Circe*, he refers to his weary days of poverty: "I entered the world in 1921 and for sixteen years after that suffered such poverty, want and humiliation as I cannot wish even an enemy, if I had any to be punished with."[2]

These were the difficult years of his Calcutta life and under the circumstances not the romance but the harsh facts of Calcutta must have made its presence felt to the writer. I think this is the precise reason why the descriptions of his native place have a touch of poetry and the account of his city life is replete with harsh and ugly comments. The caustic depiction undoubtedly reflects his misery and resentment against Calcutta that had refused to embrace him. Nirad C. Chaudhuri seems to be suffering from prejudice though some irrefutable grating truths about the famous city cannot be ignored altogether. Despite its weaknesses, Calcutta is not a garbage dump. It has a rich heritage of cultural life resplendent with music, theatre and a glorious history of cinema which he has overlooked because of his partial vision. Unfortunately, the adventures and the circumstances of his life had deprived him of the artistic experiences. All that museums and libraries could offer, he gathered eagerly and that is why he was well versed with Western literature and language, music, painting, sculpture, architecture etc. In comparison, he scarcely refers to Indian art, music and literature. It can be his conscious revenge on a culture that had failed to recognize his genius. His feelings of outrage restrained him from viewing Calcutta and its people positively. Khushwant Singh's comment on Nirad C. Chaudhuri is apt: 'He is provocative and at times offensively Anglophile, at the expense of his countrymen.'[3] Another intriguing statement of Chaudhuri should be considered very seriously. In an interview to the *Times* of London, he is reported to have said, 'People are about half and half, against me and for. Previously all were against me. I know I am extreme. It is like a tug-of-war. I cannot stand up straight or the other side will pull me down. But I *know* my exaggerations.'[4] It is quite possible that he never really had a jaundiced eye; it was just an exaggeration, a Swift-like mask to conceal his deep wounds and also his admiration for a city that had refused to recognize his identity.

NOTES

1. Nirad C. Chaudhuri, *The Autobiography of an Unknown Indian* (Bombay: Jaico, 1951), p. 264.
2. Qtd. Srinivasa Iyengar, *The Indian Writing in English* (New Delhi: Sterling, 1985), p. 593.
3. *Ibid.*, p. 590.
4. *Ibid.*, p. 601.

The Other Unknown Indian: The Indian Woman in *The Autobiography of an Unknown Indian*

URBASHI BARAT

In an essay on Henry James's private universe, Graham Greene makes a comment that could well have been made about Nirad C. Chaudhuri's ideas and obsessions too:

> To a biographer the early formative years of a writer must always have a special fascination: the innocent eye dwelling frankly on a new unexplored world, the vistas of future experience at the end of the laurel walk, the voices of older people, . . . the strange accidents that seem to decide not only that this child shall be a writer but what kind of a writer this child shall be.[1]

Chaudhuri's "early formative years" shaped not only the iconoclastic social ideas and the originality of his historical vision that he is so justly famous for but, also, more specifically, his understanding of and attitude to Indian womanhood. Interestingly, it is in the occasional essay and article in newspapers and magazines, and not in his more substantial books, that the Indian woman is the subject of Chaudhuri's observations; this itself should indicate what he feels about her role and function in his world. That is, she is obviously only tangential to his main theme/s, much as she was marginalized in his own childhood and youthful relationships—notwithstanding, of course, his courtly behaviour towards women later in life and all the evidence of a happy marriage as well. Paradoxically, then, with all his unconventionality, Chaudhuri is very much in the Indian-male tradition in the way he sees her. For him, as for the patriarchal world, he inhabits and examines so searchingly in all his writings, she is far more "unknown" a person than he had perceived himself to be when he had thought up his title for his first autobiography, *The Autobiography of an Unknown Indian.*

Perhaps it might be useful at this point to turn to what Chaudhuri has to say about Indian women in *To Live or Not to Live,* a collection of essays in which he "prob[es] into the sociological foundations of our social and family life. Neither can be just accepted for what they are, but must be perpetually kept moving towards an end which offers us ever greater happiness and fulfilment."[3] I refer to this anthology chiefly because it so conveniently brings together the author's obiter dicta on Indian women in his studies of contemporary Indian society (or, more accurately, Indian society in the mid-fifties to the mid-sixties). But there is also a more personal reason behind this choice: the essay on "Women in Social Life," in its original version in *The Statesman,* was my first acquaintance with Nirad Chaudhuri's writings, and I still recall the interest and approbation with which I had read his remarks on what he termed "Sexual dimorphism in Calcutta":

> This phenomenon of dimorphism is, of course, a familiar phenomenon in the animal world . . . wherever the sexes differ from each other in the animal world the male is usually more impressive than the female.
>
> But among the Bengalis in Calcutta the situation seems to have been reversed. No one, judging by external appearance, will dream of placing a Bengali man by the side of a Bengali woman in regard to smartness, handsomeness, and refinement of appearance and expression.
>
> Taking every strata of Bengali society from the wealthy down to the very poor, individual for individual, the woman in every case looks superior. (71)

This was my personal impression of not just Bengalis but of Indian men and women as a whole, and Chaudhuri's remarks revealed a startlingly fresh point of view about the relationship between the sexes at a time when feminism was no part of the Indian vocabulary.

There was the complete absence of hypocrisy and the disregard for political correctness in Chaudhuri's pronouncements on man-woman relationships that made for very pleasant reading, in particular his views on the social graces, in which he finds Indian women invariably superior to the men. These views may of course have been derived from the West—witness, for example, his attempts to introduce into everyday social intercourse the undoubtedly charming but quite foreign, Gallic, gesture of kissing a lady's hand (70)—but they were usually irresistibly attractive, and rang a sympathetic chord within the young reader chafing at traditional social restrictions. Thus, his complaints about the absence of a "personal social life" in India apart from visits from relatives, especially from elderly women whose "officiousness and curiosity" made them "an infliction and a torture" for younger women (50), or his caustic comments on the joint family, which, far from nurturing and providing emotional anchor to its members, led in fact to "the destruction of individuality and the spirit of self-help, and the erosion of good feeling among the members of a large family," (90) were very different from conventional wisdom, then and now, and certainly closer to real life. The harm that the joint family causes is evident, above all, feels Chaudhuri, in relationships between the women of the family, the mother-in-law-daughter-in-law relationship being "the fundamental aberration of Hindu life" (113)—an echo of his remark in the *Autobiography* (170). The unitary family is, paradoxically, much closer to the early Hindu notions about the family, not a Western concept, and it is far more healthy: but "the higher values of family life" can be attained only when husband and wife are equal partners, with the woman as the more important factor. (167) The contemporary version of the traditional arranged marriage among Hindus, moreover, has become "a mere commercial transaction, and a degraded commercial transaction at that," (145) unnatural, and demeaning to women in particular.

But there was also an occasional discordant note in Chaudhuri's remarks about women that seemed to suggest that he was not all that different from other male writers after all: the less-than-charitable comments on the Punjabi social ethic in "The Great City," for instance, in which the unkindest attacks are reserved for the woman (although here, too, her "air and deportment" are superior to the man's (29-30) or the elderly female relative being described as a harpy or a gorgon. (50) What we have here are ethnic and gender stereotypes unexpected in a writer who does not otherwise hesitate to be different. But what caused the greatest discomfort—and still continues to do so—was Chaudhuri's views on Indian working women, which repeated the same old male arguments about how "the married working women harm the children, unmarried working girls, themselves." (122) For him, woman's emancipation and feminism are marks of a decadent society; the Indian woman does not need economic independence because "We have *stridhan*," (125) and "All talk that the girls are taking to bread-earning to live a richer life or acquire a higher personality is undiluted bunkum." (123) Several similar observations would suggest that Chaudhuri knew very little, in fact, about the Indian woman's actual place and role in society or, indeed, about feminine nature at all. It is this, undoubtedly, that led to his attacks on the contemporary woman in "The Unitary Family," for instance. (168-70)

These apparent contradictions in Chaudhuri's statements can best be understood with reference to his *Autobiography*, for he himself has explained that his ideas are based on the views and experiences of his parents (*To Live* . . . , 85). Nirad Chaudhuri was born on 23 November 1897 in an old East Bengal zamindar family; his father left his ancestral village to set up a flourishing legal practice at Kishorganj, a small country town where his eight children were born. The family retained their close links with their roots, however, even as it began to look citywards, and to a world of Westernized education and cultural norms so remote from the village: this was characteristic of the dichotomy of the Bengali middle-class and upper-middle-class lifestyle of the time, and helps to explain in large part the views and attitude to life and society that Nirad Chaudhuri shared with so many of his contemporaries. He is, in other words, one of the last vestiges of the Indian/Bengali Renaissance which flourished from the middle of the last century to the early years of Independent India. The post-Nehru years, and the post-Indira Gandhi era in particular, has seen the collapse of that world of expansion, imagination and hope that had lit the minds of so many great intellectuals; it is no wonder that Chaudhuri should be only too aware of the decadence and corruption in art, literature, culture and social relationships that Satyajit Ray, for instance, perhaps the last flower of this great Renaissance, portrays in films like *Jana-Aranya* and *Shakha-Proshakha.*

By the time Nirad Chaudhuri's father had established himself, the family fortunes, which had been at a low ebb in the village, had been restored, so that at no time or place did the writer ever experience at first hand that penury in youth that can so often stunt intellectual growth. The Chaudhuris were in fact very proud of their lineage, as he himself suggests; indeed, as his wife has pointed out in her own charming autobiography in Bengali, *Didimar Jug o Jiban* ("The Life and Times of a Grandmother"), although in those days the Bengali married woman never adopted the surname of her husband's family, the wives of the Chaudhuri household rejected the more common appellation of "Dasi" considered suitable for Kayastha women, preferring to call themselves "Chaudhurani."[4] Chaudhuri's belief in himself and the firmness of his views, and his attitude towards women, spring equally clearly from his family background of proud men and proud and strong women, although he himself does not appear to think so.

The *Autobiography* devotes much space to Upendra Narayan and Sushila Sundari Chaudhuri, Nirad's parents. Certainly he much admired his stern, high-principled, strong-minded and very "individualist[ic]" father (141), and owed the vastness of his scholarship and the width of his mind to his father's ideas on education and freedom to think. No less important were Upendra Narayan's views on family relationships, which the adult Nirad appears to have accepted fully and whole-heartedly. As the writer has told his readers again and again, his father had deliberately broken away from the joint family norm and all that it involves to set up "a true family—composed of the father, the mother, and the children—in which each element had its due share of importance and proper status." (141) Indeed, "the status of my mother was noticed by all our relatives and neighbours." (142) While Upendra Narayan never hesitated to assume his parental responsibilities, his wife had an equal share in their children's moral and social upbringing, so that they complemented each other in their familial roles. (162) In a sense, therefore, the father was the real pioneer, the real iconoclast; the son is merely his follower.

Sushila Sundari was as strong-minded and principled as her husband, and even more strict as regards social and moral conduct. Her "fierce" honesty won her the respect of even her redoubtable mother-in-law. (165-66) She was not only an "uncompromising puritan," she was also a "reformist" in her personal life, rejecting both superstition and the accepted norms of personal attire, and was very methodical and meticulous in whatever she set out to do. (136) The ability to face facts and to analyse them objectively, the uncompromising intellectual honesty that Nirad Chaudhuri is so famous for, are undoubtedly his mother's gifts to him—the product, partly at least, of the Brahmo influence over her (Brahmo views on women's emancipation were very liberal and Westernized; the clash between the Brahmo and the orthodox Hindu ways of seeing women has often been written about in Bengali prose, the most notable example being, of course, Tagore's *Gora*)—as much as his conviction about the Indian woman's strength and her power over her family.

Interestingly, however, Chaudhuri does not acknowledge the impact of his mother on the development of his ideas. This is of course partly due to his patriarchal conditioning, as a result of which he learnt to admire his father and the liberality and unconventionality of his ideas even as he respected his mother but saw the dark spaces within her where he saw none in his father. When he remarks,

> Patriarchal society always prescribes and enforces the duty of filial piety, and one of the very first things a Hindu boy learns, or at all events used to learn, is and was the Sanskrit tag which declares: "Father is Heaven, Father is Morality, Father besides is the Highest Prayer, and if Father is pleased also are all the Gods." (143)

he does not seem to realize the implications of the absence of the mother from the prayer, or of the sexist language he employs unthinkingly. This is also borne out in the way there is no mention of his sisters—apart from the fact that they were born and were married—in his story of his youth: they had no significance for him. It is from his wife's autobiography that his readers learn anything about his two sisters, one of whom was responsible for arranging his marriage with Amiya.[5] There is generally a special closeness about the members of a unitary family that does not exist for Chaudhuri where the females are concerned; this silence is thus symptomatic of his attitude towards Indian women as a whole: a woman is important only insofar as she is a mother and performs her mother's role adequately, to his satisfaction. No wonder, then, that while he is prepared to accord her respect if ever she should impinge on the masculine consciousness, her personhood, her sense of self are irrelevant. Woman has traditionally been the Other of Indian culture, always being defined with reference to man: if Chaudhuri's autobiography is read not merely as a personal account of his early years but, as he would have it, as "a contribution to contemporary history" ("Preface," ix), Simone de Beauvoir's comments on "Otherness" clearly apply to his statements and his silences about the women in his life: "The category of the 'Other' is as primordial as consciousness itself . . . the subject can be posed only in being opposed—he sets himself up as the essential, as opposed to the other, the inessential, the object."[6] It is not surprising that in Nirad Chaudhuri's autobiography-as-history, there should be so little mention of the role of women in the freedom movement (except for a passing reference to his wife's participation on page 264) to quote Beauvoir again, "Society has always been male; political power has always been in the hands of men." (102)

The contradictions in Chaudhuri's portrayals of women are thus more apparent than real. His belief in feminine strength is based not on an understanding of the power structures in society but goes back, rather, to the mother-figures of his youth, his grandmothers who battled against overwhelming odds to bring up their children, and to his mother, who occupies an interestingly important place in his otherwise so obviously male-oriented and male-centred *Autobiography*. Sushila Sundari belonged to a family as aristocratic as her husband's,[7] but her father had died when she was very young, leaving his children in the grip of poverty and neglect. The struggles of these early years, suggests Amiya Chaudhurani, had made her mother-in-law "highly-strung" and hysterical. (125) Chaudhuri, however, ascribes her possessiveness, her "grasping emotional demands" on her husband and children—"she always wanted to feel her children as pieces of herself" (169)—to her early deprivations; he prefers to believe that her mental condition was due, instead, to her unhappy experiences with her mother-in-law, which so traumatized her that even though she had lived with her for only six and a half years and was free to lead her own life from the age of 22, she never got over them. He pays little heed to the implications of her own explanations and ideas; evidently he could never understand why she suffered so, or why she always blamed her husband for her state:

> What my mother found wanting in my father I could never discover. To all appearances there was no more devoted and loyal husband to be met with anywhere; a husband who made no demands on his wife, on the contrary was ready to answer any and every demand from her. In actual fact, he seriously weakened his splendid constitution and went very near ruining his worldly career for her sake. Yet she was always complaining of his conduct towards her. She seemed to be like the person who did not know what he wanted and was not happy because he did not have it. (170)

Sushila Sundari was in fact the archetypal "mad life" of women's writing, as Annis Pratt describes her[8]; Chaudhuri is thus not just the typical male in his response to her so-called hysteria but the typical son as well, who, as he admits, shrinks from "probing into those parts [of a parents's character, personality and life] with a reluctance which is somewhat akin to a healthy man's revulsion from incest." (143)

The Indian woman in Chaudhuri's *Autobiography* is ultimately, then, an unknown quantity. She is strong, she is powerful, she moulds men and lives, but her selfhood is irrelevant and unimportant, and the way she thinks and feels of interest only as they affect the men in her life. The worlds of men and women are clearly distinct. Later he is to complain that, in spite of "all the talk about the equal rights of women, in which some of the women are quite unnecessarily cantankerous and cacophonous,"[9] there is a lack of healthy social intercourse between men and women in contemporary society; in his *Autobiography*, however, there are no young women outside his immediate family whom he mentions even in passing, and no sense of loss at being deprived of feminine company either. In the *Autobiography*, Chaudhuri's feelings about Indian women appear most clearly in his portrayals of his mother, and to a lesser degree his grandmothers, all victims who survived through triumph over vicissitudes and who yet failed to find success and happiness; the Indian woman for him, accordingly, is an ambiguous figure, strong-minded, high-principled, but with inexplicable recesses within her that do not need exploration, elaboration or healing. She might be an important member of her immediate family circle, but has little to do in his otherwise searching analyses of Indian history and society. If only Chaudhuri had directed his searching intellect and his powers of analysis on to the other unknown Indian, his "story of the struggle of a civilization with a hostile environment" ("Preface," ix) would have been more complete.

NOTES

1. Graham Greene, "Henry James: The Private Universe," *Collected Essays* (Harmondsworth: Penguin, 1981), p. 28.
2. Nirad C. Chaudhuri, *The Autobiography of an Unknown Indian* (Bombay: Jaico, 1991).
3. Nirad C. Chaudhuri, "Introduction," *To Live or Not it Live* (New Delhi: Orient Paperbacks, 1995), p. 13.
4. Amiya Chaudhurani, *Didimar Jug o Jiban* (Calcutta: Mitra and Ghosh, 1992), p. 125.
5. *Ibid.*, p. 119.
6. Simone de Beauvoir, *The Second Sex*, trans. H.M. Parshley (Harmondsworth: Penguin, 1987), pp. 16-17.
7. Chaudhurani, p. 125.
8. Annis Pratt, *Archetypal Patterns in Women's Fiction* (Bloomington: Indiana University Press, 1981), p. 45.
9. Nirad C. Chaudhuri, "Women in Social Life," *To Live or Not to Live*, pp. 62-63.

The Image of India as Portrayed in *A Passage to England*

P. HARI PADMA RANI

Given the title *A Passage to England*, one might wonder what one could find of India in a book like this. But the title seems to take after E.M. Forster's *A Passage to India*, which was published in 1924. A major difference between the two books is that the former is written by a Britisher while the latter is by an Indian. Besides the titles, there are not many significant points of comparison between the two texts. While *A Passage to India* is a purely fictional work, *A Passage to England* is a travelogue, an account of Chaudhuri's visit to England.

The immediate question that pops in one's mind here is "If the book is an account of Chaudhuri's visit to England, where could India possibly figure in?"

One must not forget the fact that it is an Indian who is making a passage to England. Having made a passage from India to England, Chaudhuri could not but make use of the tool of extensive comparison in his account of the English life. In the hands of Chaudhuri, comparison becomes doubly functional. On the one hand, it helps define England clearly and on the other, it defines India better. Both England and India are pitted against each other. Therefore the readers will find India "walking in freely" in Chaudhuri's account of England, which makes it extremely interesting as well as enlightening. As Chaudhuri remarks:

> In this account of England, India will be found to be walking in freely. I could not define my sensations about the new

> country without placing them against those about the only country known to me. One-half of my perception of England was the perception of something not India.

Time and again in the course of the book, Chaudhuri keeps comparing the conditions in India and those in England. This gives a piquancy and edge to his writing. Very interestingly, the book begins with a remark on Indian philosophy.

There is virtually no aspect of English life which Chaudhuri does not contrast with that of Indian life. Even the colours of flowers in England are different from those of the Indian ones:

> In England, I found that colour in my country and colour there were quite different things. In our country we have many flowers with blazing colours, but these hues always seem to flow and run into surrounding atmosphere, as dyes which are not fast do in water. In England, on the other hand, I saw floral colours almost as frozen masses. (Part I, Chapter II)

Chaudhuri finds the rivers of England more interesting than those of India. He justifies his preference by saying that the rivers of England have a 'scenic complement' which none of the rivers in India has.

In England one cannot make out the social class or status to which a person belongs by merely looking at him whereas in India,

> Wherever we go, we notice two kinds of people, the ordinary folks who dress in their own way, speak their own dialects, behave in their own way, without sophistication and affectation, as against the minority who wear the older Hindu or Muslim aristocratic costumes, speak both English and the standard forms of the Indian languages and have what in the west would be called a middle class pattern of behaviour. (Part II Chapter I)

For Indians, noise is an essential condition of cheerfulness while the English people have silent habits. Life in London, even, in the most crowded streets, seems like a film of 'pre-talkie days.'

After living in the bazaars of India for years, when Chaudhuri sees a sight like this, he feels like crying out, 'the eternal silence of these infinite crowds frightens me!'

Chaudhuri rightly observes that there are no better places than buses and trains to observe the public behaviour of a nation. In India, the buses are full of conversation not only between acquaintances but also between people who have never met before. Nobody minds being used as a cushion. So far as newspaper reading is concerned, the fellow passengers never snatch away anybody's paper, but they take the pages he is not reading, in the most polite manner, and distribute them among themselves. The passengers help one another in many ways. The buses in India are in short a microcosm of Indian life.

In England, people do not disclose their position in the world. If they are authors, they do not refer to their books; if they are statesmen, they do not disclose programmes for reforming the world, whereas in our society a man is always what his designation makes him. Whenever we introduce a person, we always emphasize the official position the person holds. We also see people adding it themselves when the introducer omits to announce their designation.

Evidently Chaudhuri does not say all this in criticism of his people. He is only describing what usually happens. In India obsession with one's designation and degrees is a commonplace phenomenon. Even in a thing like a wedding card, one would not like to see one's name without his or her degree beside it.

Many a critic has accused Chaudhuri of being an Anglophile. Particular objections were raised to his delineation of India in a patronizing manner. Passages like the following in particular have raised the hackles of many an Indian nationalist critic:

> In India physical beauty is largely associated with a fair complexion or what we regard as such, and this among a people who are generally dark attracts attention immediately.
>
> (Part II Chapter I)
>
> The proportion of handsome women being somewhat low in India outside the Punjab, the women who are considered beautiful or who consider themselves beautiful are very self-con-

> scious. They never allow anybody to overlook them.
> (Part II Chapter I)
>
> The dominant class in India is very paradoxical in one thing: it will never give any well-paid job to anyone who has not been educated or trained in the west.
> (Part II Chapter VII)
>
> In our society, an official of middle-class origins not only does not carry his briefcase, he does not even take a paper to a colleague, he rings for the peon. This peon, on his part, will carry papers and files, but no packages.
> (Part II Chapter VII)
>
> The English middle class is much more simple and general than we are.
> (Part II Chapter VII)
>
> Even in the big cities, for every two persons in clean and adequate clothing there are eight in an assortment of shabby, dirty, insufficient, and tattered clothes. In the cold season, as I travel in the public transport of Delhi, I often have sitting by my side men who have wrapped themselves with dirty blankets or quilts in which to all appearance they have been sleeping for years. In the villages, it is virtually impossible to meet men in clean and adequate clothing.
> (Part III Chapter III)

Surprisingly enough, many Indian critics have taken umbrage at Chaudhuri's observations. It would be preposterous to conclude that Chaudhuri is disparaging India before England. These are the differences that would quite naturally and automatically strike any one when one is faced with two diametrically opposite cultures. What Chaudhuri says about India in all the above instances is very nearly true and one can easily see eye to eye with his views. This does not, however, mean that we have to swallow all that Chaudhuri tells us in his book. Far from that, we cannot accept certain sweeping statements he makes in the books without a pinch of salt. For instance, the following statements are unconvincing generalizations:

> Religion and civilization were still interwoven with each other in England, as indeed in the west as a whole. (Part III Chapter V)

> In England the so-called upper classes were more religious than the common people. While in India the situation is exactly the opposite. (Part III Chapter V)

One cannot swallow these statements without questioning their validity.

Critics have placed Chaudhuri cheek by jowl with V.S. Naipaul, the author of *An Area of Darkness*. Both of them have been unduly accused of giving a morbid picture of India to the world. The image of India as it is projected in Chaudhuri's *A Passage to England* is quite different from that of *An Area of Darkness*. It must be conceded that Chaudhuri's portrayal of India is, by and large, realistic though unpalatable to most nationalist Indians.

To Metaphorise—A 'Literary' Act?: Chaudhuri's *A Passage to England*

PRAMOD KUMAR NAYAR

Nirad C. Chaudhuri's *A Passage to England* (1966)[1] has been categorised as a travelogue, a "collection of a series of impressions" about his Britain visit.[2] A travelogue, like diaries or memoirs and letters, occupies a shadowy territory among the genres of literature. Theorists of literary genres have noted, with some hyperbole and a lot of cynicism, that this writing may not be categorised as literature.[3] It is thus conveniently provided residence in the suburbia of "high" literature for its journalistic affiliations.

Such an easy classification is not readily applicable to Nirad Chaudhuri. In the present essay I plan to read Chaudhuri's travelogue for its *literary* features. To this end I focus on the language, specifically, the metaphorisation, of *A Passage to England*.

To provide a tool for the analysis, I have found it useful to view metaphors under five heads: linguistic, conceptual, communicative, emotive and moral.[4]

Journalistic metaphors are more conventional, and frequently trite in their linguistic organisation. Everyday images are employed for the purpose. Literary writing however teems with unconventional metaphors which are original and striking in expression. Chaudhuri, while writing a travelogue, displays an array of metaphors, all of which are poetic and literary. We note, for instance, his description of the white cliffs of Dover that "seemed like white creases between the blue gray sheet of the channel and the mist softened green expanse of Kent." (22) Of the English towns, Chaudhuri writes: "they [the towns] convert what would otherwise have been still life . . . into a living genre picture." (47) At Canterbury cathedral, he observes a "little English boy of about six sitting on the grass and looking at me with an intense gaze, like a lion cub watching a distant zebra." (133) Cambridge is described as "not extreme in either direction, and yet was very good in the middle ranges, with, however, sufficient elbow room within that range." (120) We realise that this unusual description is of a comparison of prices in the shops of London and Cambridge! This effective use of prosopopoiea is a traditional literary device and rarely a journalistic one. Thus, linguistically, Chaudhuri's text uses striking and poetic metaphors for purposes of description.

Obviously, the images/metaphors are expressions of Chaudhuri's subjectivity. England is viewed, as the blurb of the book announces, through Chaudhuri's "shrewd, peeled gaze." Hence the travelogue is written as a piece of literature: since it proceeds, is produced out of a very personal and subjective experience. And hence the personal metaphors—a typical literary feature.

Literary metaphors are complex, abstract and rich where journalistic metaphors are usually old, concrete, simple and occasionally superficial. Conceptually, then, a literary metaphor has more complexity than a journalistic one. A literary metaphor may combine two, possibly disparate metaphors to increase its complexity. (Keatsian synaesthetic imagery or deliberately catachretic writing, exemplified in a writer like Arundhati Roy may have such a purpose). A beautiful example of such a conceptually intense imaging in *A Passage to England* occurs in Chaudhuri's description of the English houses. Talking of their vast interiors he notes that such houses are meant for a "people who had to spend long evenings indoors." Chaudhuri elaborates that on such occasions when "the mind would be *benumbed* by its own emptiness *unless it could crawl from* one object to another along a continuous chain of interest—furniture, china, glass, plate, pictures, ornaments, fireplaces, and other fixtures" (110, emphasis mine). Hence he is not surprised to find huge libraries in these houses. Chaudhuri has personified the mind, has described the largeness of the houses, has listed the usual contents, all in the space of *one* image.

Later, Chaudhuri finds that the resplendent and expensive shops in England are "continuous as the stars that shine and twinkle in the Milky way." (118) Chaudhuri's brilliantly complex metaphor serves two purposes: (a) to indicate brightness, the "splendour" of lights and festoons of the shops, like stars in the night; (b) their inaccessibility, in terms of prices, to most people (again like stars which beckon, tempt but remain unreachable). This is sheer poetic language, if a trifle over-used. Another example would be Chaudhuri's description of a Church service. He notes that the devout left the Chapel "with a grave and abstracted expression as if what they had gone through was still holding them in its grip." (184) Now, where Chaudhuri's description of Dover was beautiful and poetic, it was hardly complex. In the above quoted description, Chaudhuri has managed to evoke the sense of devotion *and* the "grip" religion has on people of such bent. The language—"grave," "what they had gone through"—suggests a possibly difficult experience. It also lends an austere air—since religion *is* a serious element of their lives. This kind of complex metaphor is surely literary in its conceptualisation.

Such conceptually complex metaphors may also be quite abstract. To revert to the above example, the notion of gravity and hints of an unremitting "grip" on peoples' minds is abstract and possibly overstated. It becomes staged discourse wherein Chaudhuri attempts to emphasise the terror that religion may induce, or thrive on. Yet the description *follows* and *precedes* a more "positive" imagifying of the Chapel, its decor and the actual service. I believe that Chaudhuri has overloaded the image in order to be emphatic. Such a complex metaphorisation however runs the risk of being obscure, or the reader missing precisely what Chaudhuri is desirous of emphasising.

This brings us to the next factor in reading metaphors. Gerard Steen points out that journalistic metaphors are meant to inform and explain while literary metaphors may be entertaining, persuasive or even confusing (208). Chaudhuri can be occasionally flippant for the sake of entertainment. His long description of the British cats is an example:

> At Canterbury . . . a cat came up and rolled on the path before me, in order to be picked up and tickled under the chin. When I do so it purred until I was ready to cry, thinking of the

> cordial state of Indo-British friendship in which I had never believed. . . . Cats are however, very good judges of the human character, and all nations get the cats they deserve. (95)

The metaphor for/of friendship is here not providing any information or explanation though it is a comic relief. Again, when Chaudhuri describes park benches in England, he comments on the European's public expressions of love. Chaudhuri writes:

> I also saw that love-making was an easily observable activity . . . all the benches [in the park] were occupied by lovers, and not one couple would make room for an aged and footsore stranger, although to all appearance they had one another to prop themselves up on and hardly needed an additional material support. They were giving a demonstration of love among the ruins. (125)

This periphrastic and wry comment, with a borrowed image from Robert Browning, is certainly hyperbole. Tara Sinha has also recognised Chaudhuri's tendency to exaggerate, with no obvious intention than to entertain. (211) Such descriptions, as the one quoted above, are communicatively worthless since they do not explain or add to our fund of knowledge gleaned from Chaudhuri.

If exaggeration and confusing metaphors haunt Chaudhuri's text, there are also beautiful and poetic ones. The emotive value of a metaphor is different for journalism and literature. Negative emotive value is attached to trite, superficial, shocking or conforming metaphors noticeable in journalism. Literary metaphors on the other hand may be informal, critical and beautiful. Chaudhuri describes the English meadow thus:

> If [the green of the grass] was set off very charmingly by the black and white or brown and white of the cattle and creamy white of the sheep and lambs, which lay like bundles of fleece on the meadows. (37)

This beautiful and tasteful description is also casual: since lamb and fleece go together. Here there is no violent coalescion of images as occurs in other passages.

The gently ironic description of the Indian worship of rivers is likewise emotively beautiful and casual. The passage is worth quoting in full:

> The secular Government of India becomes aware of the rivers when they threaten the cities with floods, or dry upto endanger the water supply . . . the people of India, more religious than their Government, remain in touch with the rivers through Hinduism. . . . The big rivers are sacred all over the country, and they were sacred even before the great gods immigrated to their banks. As a matter of fact, they migrated to take advantage of a pre-existing holiness. (41)

The casual tone or irony ("as a matter of fact," though the veracity of this "fact" cannot be established!) is however misleading. This is where we recognise the hitch regarding the "literariness" of a non-literary piece.

Gerard Steen argues that literature consists of metaphors which are touching, impartial and apolitical where journalistic metaphors are opinionated and political. (208-9) In the case of Chaudhuri, we have already noted his very subjective tone of writing. We also gather from *A Passage to England* his stance vis-a-vis India: his knowledge of India, or his contempt for the average Indian's life-style and so on. The long illustration quoted above is scathing in his vivisection of Hinduism's superstitions and the Indian government. Hence, to regard *A Passage to England* purely as an unbiased work of the "literary" imagination is difficult.

Yet, the overall effect of reading *A Passage to England* is that of a *literary* masterpiece. In comparison to, say, Chaudhuri's *Autobiography of an Unknown Indian* or *The Continent of Circe*, it is less polemical, striving to become mere "reportage." It is also better crafted and has a poetic style. Thus Chaudhuri's attempt to write in the journalistic mode is defeated by his own brilliant and *literary* prose. And, as demonstrated before, *A Passage to England* reads like any other work of fiction. All this would really warn us against the dangers of easy categorisation. Chaudhuri's work, like his own geographical, cultural and ideological location, straddles the two realms of literature and journalism. At this point, then, I readily place the two categories under erasure.

NOTES

1. Nirad C. Chaudhuri, *A Passage to England* (Delhi: Orient, 1966).
2. Tara Sinha, *Nirad C. Chaudhuri: A Sociological and Stylistic Study of His Writings during the Period 1951-72* (Patna: Janaki Prakashan, 1981).
3. See, for instance, Alastair Fowler's acceptance of the ambivalent status of the genre in his *Kinds of Literature: An Introduction to the Theory of Genres and Modes* (Oxford: Clarendon, 1987).
4. This study of the metaphor in literature has been inspired by Gerard Steen's magnificent work. See his *Understanding Metaphor in Literature: An Empirical Approach* (London: Longman, 1994).

The Intellectual in India: A Guide for Intellectuals

INDIRA NITYANANDAM

An Anglophile to the core, Nirad C. Chaudhuri has always been proud of his intellectual abilities and has placed himself apart from the general stream of Indians of his own generation. Even as a child, his preference for everything English was obvious as he considered "English poetry . . . the most wonderful reading in the world."[1] Though he was himself a product of the Indian Renaissance of the nineteenth century, he viewed with scepticism the nomenclature itself. According to him, this period could not be compared to fourteenth century Europe and hence did not merit such an honour. Looking westwards is our only hope was his strong conviction: "At this moment of our history, the instinct of life impels me to look abroad, for it is only with a renewed affiliation with the countries which stand in the mainstream of human evolution that we can hope to live. The choice before us is of revolving round ourselves to die, or of revolving round a Sun in order to live." (522) With eyes set firmly westwards, he naturally dedicates his *Autobiography* to the memory of the British Empire in India because, to him, "all that was good and living within us was made, shaped and quickened by the same British Rule." It is in the context of his total obsession with everything British that his *The Intellectual in India* (1967) has a special significance among Chaudhuri's writings. It is the first in the series "Tracts for the Times," a title borrowed from the famous tracts of the Oxford Movement in England. This monograph describes the present conditions of intellectual activity in India. To my mind, it is more Indian than the author's earlier published works because it was not written with Western readers in mind and it is the first of his works to be published in India.

Hailed as "a grand solitary" with "coruscating intelligence who remains at the top class of Indo-Anglian writers both stylistically and cerebrally," Chaudhuri reveals his scholasticism throughout this monograph. To him, "scholarship itself is the product of personal temperament and what it brings to personality is only temperament returned to temperament in the form of an embodied activity. I believe I possessed and still possess this temperament." (*Autobiography*, 336) His wide reading and encyclopaedic knowledge helped him apply the historical approach in many of his writings including his voluminous book on Hinduism published ten years later and his earlier *Autobiography* which is more a portrait of India than a self-portrait. Chaudhuri begins the tract by delineating the intellectual traditions of India—making a clear distinction between the Hindu and Islamic tradition. The third tradition is the "modern tradition" and the writer does not ascribe any credit to the Hindu tradition in fostering this modern tradition. Instead, he categorically states that "the only two men brought up in this tradition who have yet played a part in the life of modern India are Isvar Chandra Vidyasagar and Dayanand Saraswati."[2] Separate and wholly different from these two intellectual traditions, Chaudhuri places the modern tradition which "was created by the Hindus who had received a Western type of education particularly Bengali Hindus who set in motion the modern Indian cultural and intellectual movements." (8) In keeping the three schools mutually exclusive, Chaudhuri rejects the familiar assumption of Indian culture as being a huge cauldron in which all new ideas mingled with traditional ones to create an Indian tradition in which there was no scope for isolating or identifying each separate strand. Yet, he says it with such authority that he provokes us into thinking.

Indian Renaissance, which helped Indians in a reappraisal of ourselves as Indians and set in motion the stirring of pride in being Indians, is dismissed by Chaudhuri as an offshoot of Western thought. Indians, he believed, merely imitated western intellectual traditions. Statements like this have led to Khushwant Singh's conclusion that "He is provocative and at times offensively anglophile at the expense of his countrymen." Chaudhuri considers it as being merely a conventional verbal symbol "which led to an expression of applied rather than pure thought." (14) With his historical approach, the writer leads us through the religious, social, political, economic and cultural areas of study in India which revealed the growing conflict between Liberals and the Conservatives—again, he reiterates, an obvious offshoot of the influence of European thought. Everything that Chaudhuri writes is drawn from a deep sense of conviction and hence he emphasizes again and again the Indian intellectual's indebtedness to European thought. "Even the incentive to intellectual effort was furnished by the two great external factors of their existence: alien rule and the impact of Western ideas and culture." (15) Indian intellectual activity, he concluded, is thus purely derivative. Chaudhuri strikes us here as an Indian who is anti-Indian. This attitude finds expression time and again in his *Autobiography*.

During this period, the Indian intellectual belonged to a "dominant minority" which could not influence the "internal proletariat" i.e., most Indians lie beyond or below the activities of this minority. Chaudhuri considers the caste system as being responsible for fostering this distance in India. The masses continued with their age-old ideas without being affected by all the intellectual and cultural activity of this minority. Only those individuals belonging to the liberal profession and the higher rank of civil services were affected by the intellectual activity around them. With women also kept out of intellectual activity, the quantitative influence was further reduced. The distance between intellectuals of India and the west also kept widening because of a very important reason, he argues. Even when steeped in Western ideas, the Indian intellectual failed to apply the same standards of assessment to Indian writings as he did to Western writings. This naturally led to a clear distinction between European and Indian standards—the end result being a deterioration in the quality of Indian writing. It is interesting to note that Chaudhuri equates the intellectual with the writer and just makes a passing reference to the scientist particularly to Bengali scientists like J.C. Bose. The major achievement that Chaudhuri attributes to the Indian intellectual of that period is that he succeeded in integrating "intellectual activity with the day to day life of a minority and made that minority the dominant one." (34) Simultaneously, the distance between the traditional Hindu and the intelligentsia continued to widen.

Having thus described in detail the conditions of intellectual life in India at the beginning of this century, the writer follows it with a quick survey of the conditions as they existed in 1947 when the country attained independence. He is convinced that there has been a considerable intellectual decline in our educational and research fields, purely because of the imitative nature of Indian intellectuals in literary and art criticism and in philosophy and social thought as well. Chaudhuri considers Indians to be fully capable of intellectual activity but views the time as being unripe for it. He writes that the mental and cultural development of modern India was forced and consequently led to an intellectual decline. "The Indian intellectuals created what might be called a mental tour de force, an achievement comparable to those of the Indian magicians who plant a mango tree and make it grow fruit before the spectators. . . . There is no doubt that too early and an unnatural intellectual effort has had a good ideal to do with the decline of intellectual life." (43) It is in such stances that Chaudhuri strikes us as being an Indian who is totally against Indians. In an effort to provide an all-round picture of the causes for the decay of intellectual standards in India, the author analyzes the social and economic as well as political factors that have led to this decay. Pointing an accusing finger at the Hindu mind, he calls it "authoritarian and intuitionist" which made it "unintellectual and anti-intellectual." Proud of his Western learning and Western attitudes, Chaudhuri refuses to see any positive qualities in the thoroughbred Indian of his time. This led C. Paul Verghese to call him "a historian who believes in objectivity but leans heavily on subjective dogmas."[3] In the same chapter, Chaudhuri blames Western technology and modes of entertainment for taking Indians further away from all real intellectual activities. A love-hate relationship towards the homeland is obvious in many such utterances.

It is only in chapter 5 of the monograph that the author attempts a definition of the term "intellectual." Viewing it as an easy exercise, he describes an intellectual as one "who applies his intellectual faculties . . . formulates conclusions . . . and communicates his ideas to fellow-men with a view to influencing their mind, life and actions." (55) And then, he launches a detailed series of dos and donts for writers in an attempt to help them lead normal lives along with their writing. He quotes extensively from John Stuart Mill to prove the validity of his arguments e.g. "the writings by which man can live are not those that themselves live." (57) Real writing, according to Chaudhuri, can be taken up only after one enters the third ashrama—Vanprastha—as he should be able to write without worrying about having to maintain a family. This chapter ends on a very positive note: "with a little intelligence, management and above all firmness and determination the difficulties can be surmounted and the dangers avoided." (61)

In the last two chapters of the monograph, Chaudhuri provides detailed advice to prospective writers about the type of employment that they should aspire to in order to earn their livelihood and then about the gamble that is involved in getting a good publisher for one's writings. In both cases, he cites examples from his own life and experiences, thus giving the entire exercise a strong autobiographical flavour. This Anglophile is convinced that "books written in Indian languages do not make any impact that can be called intellectual." (72) Hence aspiring writers are advised to write in English with a note of caution: "Even when an Indian writes in English, to be taken seriously, he has to publish abroad. This is due to an egregious snobbery or xenolatry, but this state of affairs has to be reckoned with whatever may be the reason." (72) Finding the right publisher and a complete mastery over the English language are other requisites. Chaudhuri is highly critical of "Indians who try to see India as if they are Western journalists." (77) Strange indeed that a man who always saw India thorough Western eyes should make such a statement. Hence Verghese says, "Chaudhuri's views on India and her people may be irritating, but he compels our admiration even when he causes irritation." (10) Over the last thirty years since this monograph was published, there has certainly been a proliferation of publishing houses in India which cater to the growing number of Indians writing in English.

Nirad C. Chaudhuri's ideas "tease us into thought," into a line of thinking quite contrary to the universally accepted one. He reveals a courage of conviction even to the extent of seeming self-opinionated. He is a master craftsman with a fine feel for the English language. Many of his views are dated and are an obvious corollary to the Raj syndrome—the Brown sahib attitude to Chaudhuri's generation. The colonised is attempting to be like the coloniser in many respects. He is different from the average Indian of his times, he asserts, and is proud of that difference. Indeed, he is the "Grand Solitary" of his generation.

NOTES

1. Nirad C. Chaudhuri, *The Autobiography of an Unknown Indian* (London: Macmillan, 1951; Jaico, 1969), p. 116.
2. Nirad C. Chaudhuri, *The Intellectual in India* (New Delhi: Vir Publishers, 1967), p. 5.
3. Paul Verghese, *Nirad C. Chaudhuri* (New Delhi: Arnold-Heinemann, 1973), p. 116.

Chaudhuri's Intellectuals in *The Intellectual in India*: Ariel and Caliban

SHYAM S. AGARWALLA

Nirad C. Chaudhuri's *The Intellectual in India* is a tract "for the Times," published with an intention to "enlist the best minds of India," who "will deal with all aspects of the contemporary situation—not only to analyse the present ills and discontents and lay bare their causes, but also to suggest remedies in a positive approach to all the problems."

India is suffering from evils of casteist-intellectuals, communal-intellectuals, loyal-intellectuals, opportunist-intellectuals, political-party-intellectuals, and tradition-bound-intellectuals. An intellectual is a rational human being, free from superstition, bigotry, isms, prejudices, pride, and emotions. We know Chaudhuri's intention as he writes in the preface to his book:

> All over India those who have any intellectual ambitions and aptitudes are discouraged. Authoritarianism in politics and social life which runs deep among the Hindus, hostility or apathy to intellectual activities, the precarious economic condition of the intellectual who has most often to pell himself to make a livelihood—have all tended to make him feel frustrated if not wholly paralyzed. I want to tell him that the situation is not as bad as he imagines, and that it is largely a question of his own faith, energy and intelligence.

Chaudhuri is neither an *enfant terrible*, as some critics label him, nor an apologist. He is, I think, an angry old man, who, by dint of his erudite scholarship and prodigious memory, tries to jolt us into awareness of our shortcomings, defects, vices and virtues. He does so by applying methods of writing which is often egoistical and sublime, dark and beautiful, paternalist and childlike, prophetic and contemporaneous. He is both Ariel and Caliban. Let me elaborate the last comparison.

In a moving passage in "Caliban," Retamar locates both Caliban and Ariel in the intellectual in neo-colonialism:

> There is no real Ariel-Caliban polarity; both are slaves in the hands of Prospero, the foreign magician. Buf Caliban is rude and unconquerable master of the island, while Ariel, a creature of the air, although also a child of the isle, is the intellectual. The deformed Caliban—enslaved, robbed of his island, and taught the language by Prospero, rebukes him thus: "You taught me language, and my profit on't/ Is, I know how to curse."[1]

Some "mental-workers," like C. Paul Verghese, Chetan Karnani, A.K. Majumdar and M.K. Naik, have been less than fair to Chaudhuri. Reviewing Chaudhuri's second volume of autobiography, *Thy Hand, Great Anarch*, M.K. Naik writes: "Chaudhuri tells us that during his residence in Delhi, he was known as 'The Kuttawallah Bengali Babu' (The Bengali Babu with a dog), because he owned a golden retriever and an Alsatian in succession. This description is perhaps even more than the author realizes. There is indeed a rather superior canine housed deep down in his mind and heart—a canine, with its ears nostalgically cocked to his British 'Master's Voice.'"[2] Very good. Then, what about Salman Rushdie's books *Midnight's Children* and *The Moor's Last Sigh*? Are they flattering to M.K. Naik's subjective reasoning. Katherine Mayo's *Mother India* was dismissed by Gandhiji as a "gutter inspector's report." It was published in the late twenties of the twentieth century. A number of books and articles were published to condemn this book. In the late nineties of this century, after a gap of nearly seventy years, the feminist press, Kali for Women, has published *Selections from Mother India*, to trace the history of the imperialistic-nationlist context for the emergence of a politics of middle-class feminism, which is addressing the kinds of oppressive social practices that were highlighted in Mayo's book. M.K. Naik, a traditionalist, a "mental-worker," lives in a chauvinistic world, where even a whiff of iconoclastic air gives the shivers in the dark. No one can stop the juggernaut of iconoclasm, be it Chaudhuri or Kali for Women.

Nirad C. Chaudhuri writes about the Islamic tradition of intellectual activities. He says that the hallmark of the Muslim tradition was "the continuation of the divinely ordained Islamic way of life, and . . . a correct interpretation of the *Shariiah*, or Islamic Sacred law."[3] The poetry of Rahim and Kabir; *Akbarnama*; Abu Fazl; Ghalib, Iqbal, and Jinnah; disapprove of the conclusion of Chaudhuri's concept of an intellectual. M. Mujeeb, writing on Ghalib, a Sufiist, writes:

> The liberty to accept, modify or reject dogma on the basis of their own spiritual experience was demanded and exercised by the Sufis and has a history of its own. . . . The Sufis were at first suspected and persecuted but they established themselves through their appeal to the masses, and from the twelfth century onwards the Sufi *tariqah* and the orthodox *shariah* became two recognised ways the Muslim could follow, with the option of crossing over from one to the other as and when he liked. . . . In this way Urdu poetry, which represents the grafting of the Persian tradition on an indigenous base, brought together all those whom historical circumstances, social laws, ritualistic restraints and traditional beliefs kept apart, stimulating them to realize unity at a high intellectual and aesthetic level. And Ghalib may well claim to be the culminating point of an intellectual, aesthetic and ideologically integrative development which is of great significance in the cultural history of India.[4]

Of Iqbal and Jinnah, Chaudhuri writes, contradicting his own conclusion on page 5. He says: "Neither Iqbal nor Jinnah can be regarded as typical Indian Muslims. The story goes that after Iqbal had given a recital of his poetry at Lucknow a scion of the old Muslim royal line said waggishly with folded hands: 'Farsi to sun chuka. Abhi Urdu-me kuchh farmayé.' Iqbal is said to have gone red."[5] Iqbal and Jinnah were two intellectuals behind the creation of Pakistan. Jinnah "by his upringing . . . was not a truer Muslim than Jawaharlal Nehru was a Hindu."[6] He was a beef-eater, did not believe in abstract theology, and never went to a mosque to pray. Chaudhuri, perhaps, revises his formulation on Muslim intellectual tradition in 1993.

It is true that there is no love for intellectuals in India. Chaudhuri rightly says that Hindu society "understood worldly greatness, particularly, in its miraculous aspect, it also understood worldly greatness, but had no consciousness of anything in-between, which belonged to the spirit of man." (35) In such a society one needs courage to pursue intellectual activity for its own sake. The Western rationalism is the product of the achievement of science and technology, arising out of the Industrial Revolution. The Orientalists have laid greater emphasis on the distinctiveness of India's spiritual culture. We overlook the fact that a significant part of what is seen as 'Western' science and technology were directly influenced by contributions from elsewhere, including Indian mathematics which reached the West through the Arabs. Joseph Needham had written an authoritative account of the history of science and technology in China. No such discourse has been attempted in India. On the one hand, those who take a rather spiritual—even perhaps a religious—view of history do not have a great interest in analytical and scientific parts of India's past. On the other hand, many who oppose religious and communal politics, are particularly suspicious of what may even look like a 'glorification' of India's past. The spread of science and technology has remained in the hands of the elites in the past 52 years.

Continuing with this failure of the elites, on the one hand, and the passive role of the peasants, labourers, and artisans who constitute the vast bulk of the Indian population, on the other, we find that the latter group played a positive role. It "supported successive cultures by supplying food, land revenue, goods and services," and although "partially influenced by [those] cultures" they have made "no positive contribution to them." "The masses . . . have been the eternal Sudras, and if they continue in this state, they will not play a significant part in any future conflict of cultures in India."

(28) Chaudhuri starts with an assumption that the lack of identification between the elites and the subalterns is total. Chaudhuri fails. Gayatri Chakravorty Spivak says: "the intellectuals . . . become transparent in the relay race, for they merely report on the non-represented subject and analyze [without analyzing] the workings of [the unnamed Subject irreducibly presupposed by] power and desire. The produced transparency marks the place of "interest"; it is maintained by vehement delegation: "Now this role of referee, judge and universal witness is one which I absolutely refuse to adopt. One responsibility of the critic might be to read and write so that the impossibility of such interested individualistic refusals of the institutional privileges of power bestowed on the subject is taken seriously."[7] The subject is of the oppressed. The varieties of intellectuals, mentioned earlier, work for their selfish interests. I, therefore call them "mental-workers." Some Anglophone intellectuals like Ranjit Guha and Gayatri Chakravorty Spivak, some Indian intellectuals like Partho Chatterjee and Amartya Sen and some social scientists like Ashis Nandy, are working hard to bring the elites and the subalterns together, thus, generating lights of reason, intellect, love for science and technology, for all.

Chaudhuri naively says that "the food habits of the Indian middle middle-class and the kind of food they took, and still take, were utterly unsuited to give them the vitality and nervous energy needed for hard brainwork. The lack of adequate proteins was a particularly harmful factor. Among vegetarians the vitality was even lower still. . . . This inadequacy in food is responsible for keeping any inherent intellectual powers that Indians have at the level of mere cleverness." (44) Mahatma Gandhi, Acharya Vinoba Bhave, V.K. Krishna Menon were vegetarians. Mr. Menon was labelled a "vegetarian tiger" by the American press.

The lack of spacious place in a house, the call of "friends and relatives at any time of the day," "the general noisiness of life in India," are undoubtedly serious handicaps in the way of intellectual effort. The individualism is a modernist *mantra* very often, leading to existentialist *angst* downing an individual in the depth of isolation, loneliness, which are against the very tenets of postmodernism. In Bengali, Ashapurna Debi is a star novelist, rearing a large family. Tagore or Premchand had never lived a lonely life.

An intellectual cannot live in an ivory tower. An intellectual-in-action, like Abul Fazl, was a success in the practical world of men and affairs. One day the Khan-I-Khaanaan Mirza Abdur Rahim brought the erstwhile ruler of Sind, Mirza Jani to visit Abul Fazl, when he was the Prime Minister and Plenipotentiary *Wakeel-I-Mutluq*. Fazl did not receive him properly. A few days later he again visited Fazl. Fazl was full of courtesy. Mirza Jani was astonished at the change in the attitude of Fazl and enquired of the possible reason from Rahim. Rahim responded: "Do you remember what Abul Fazl was doing when we entered? He was reading the chronicles of the reign of his master. He was deeply embroiled in the narrative. He was hardly aware of the world around him. In the circumstances he responded as best as he could. No offence was intended as he was just not there in the text he was reading."

Nirad C. Chaudhuri does not have a kind word for writers of regional languages in India. He says:

> I have become convinced that books written in them [the Indian languages] do not make any impact which can be called intellectual. They serve as entertainment of a high or low order, but many do not do even that, being very boring. Entertainment, I would add, is a legitimate and even indispensable part of writing, but, as entertainment pure and simple, it lies outside the scope of this discussion. (72)

Here Chaudhuri is not fair to Indian regional writers. He gives ample scope to "mental-workers" like Verghese and Karnani to call his knowledge of Indian literature into question. Or, he is called an anglophile. Indeed, Chaudhuri is rather proud of his lack of reading books written by Indians. "In an age of economics," he proclaims "I am not only ignorant of the subject but even contemptuous of it."[8] A.K. Majumdar says: "Conceit and arrogance are perhaps built-in defence mechanisms of an intellectual and valuable aids to his methodology."[9] Here the Caliban in Chaudhuri gets better of the Ariel. His egoistical dark mood and temperament envelops his reasoning. His slavish praise of Prospero, and his gift of language to him, makes him sing paean for "Three Horsemen" of the English culture. Only Susie Tharu and K. Lalita's two volume *Women Writing in India* would prove Chaudhuri wrong. There is no need to discuss many serious writers in regional languages in India.

In Chapter IV, he says: "Over and above, the relative poverty of the Indian middle-class was a serious handicap in the way of intellectual effort. . . . Thus the intellectual insolvency and the economic insolvency of the middle-class have been running along parallel course during the last thirty years, each keeping pace with the other and helping each other." (46) Undoubtedly, his prophetic voice, since 1967 is still true and valid. But Chaudhuri's paternalist voice is missing. He does not show us as to how to solve this problem. Joon-Chien gives an answer in his book *Eastern Intellectuals and Western Solutions*. He says: "The intellectual tradition of the West is such that works of an applied nature with problem solving in mind do not command much of a premium. Utility is not the most prized element in the world of Western scholarship. . . . In fact it may not be far from the truth, at least from the point of developing countries in Asia."[10] Even Nirad C. Chaudhuri lashed out: "There is nothing which frightens the present Indian ruling class more than the idea of doing anything without the advice and help of white experts."[11] The award of the Nobel Prize to Dr. Amartya Sen is a belated recognition of the Western world of the usefulness of applied economics.

Indian universities are hot-beds of politics, not propitious for Intellectual effort: "The Indian academic world is laden with a deep somnolence without the justification of deep potations: it is mental vacuum, and not vintage port, which produces the abstracted air on the faces of the professor." (64) Edward Shils also saw this tendency everywhere during his visit to India: "The jealousy of an archaic head professor intimidates or obstructs the lively young man with ideas and enthusiasm, dull colleagues deaden the resonance of the atmosphere and contribute towards the slackening of standards."[12] Many promising scholars and scientists have migrated to the USA and the UK and Canada, out of frustration. Chaudhuri's beautiful analysis of the academic world in India has found echoes in Upamanyu Chatterjee's novel *English, August* and Vikram Seth's *A Suitable Boy*.

His advice to budding writers is very well said: "Even when an Indian writes in English, to be taken seriously, he has to publish abroad. This is due to an egregious snobbery or xenolatry, but the state of affairs has to be reckoned with whatever might be its reason. . . . So, it is essential from every point of view to secure the imprint of a London or New York publisher, and the higher the status of even these publishers the better for the writers." (73) Chaudhuri is correct as long as the book is in English and interests a foreign publisher. What about vernacular language books? But one thing is certain, that is, a book published in London or New York gets our attention to its merits. See the example of Arundhati Roy's novel *The God of Small Things*. Even some elite universities, like Delhi University and JNU, appoint teachers, who have a degree from Cambridge or Oxford or Harvard, and who have managed to publish an article or a book from abroad. This colonial mind-set is the bane for the subaltern class of teachers.

Wolf Biermann, a poet of the erstwhile East Germany, set in motion the disintegration of the Wall. India needs intellectuals who would inspire people to break the Wall of casteism, communalism, parochialism, regionalism, separatism and integrate Indians into bonds of brotherhood, prosperity and nationalism. Chaudhuri can preach but cannot inspire. He writes for the elites, not for the subalterns. He is a modernist writer, not a postcolonial or a postmodernist one. His intellectual is a prototype of Ariel and Caliban coalescence.

NOTES

1. Roberto Fernandez Retamar, "Caliban: Notes towards Discussion of Culture in Our America," trans. Lynn Garafola et al, in *Massachusetts Review*, 15, Winter-Spring 1979, p. 28.
2. M.K. Naik, "Pride and Prejudice Unabated," *Indian Literature*, Vol. XXXIII. No. 1, 1990 p. 138.
3. Nirad C. Chaudhuri. *The Intellectual in India* (New Delhi: Vir Publications, 1967). p. 5.
4. M. Mujeeb. *Ghalib* (New Delhi: Sahitya Akademi, 1969), pp. 30-31.

5. Nirad C. Chaudhuri, "The Hindu-Muslim Confrontation," *The Statesman Festival*, 1993, p. 71.
6. *Ibid.*
7. Gayatri Chakravorty Spivak, *A Critique of Postcolonial Reason: Towards a History of the Vanishing Present* (Calcutta: Seagull, 1999), p. 265.
8. Nirad C. Chaudhuri, *A Passage to England* (Delhi: Orient Paperbacks, 1999), p. 113.
9. A.K. Majumdar, "Portrait of an Indian Intellectual," *Quest*, Sept.-Oct. 1979, p. 22.
10. Doh Joon-Chien, *Eastern Intellectuals and Western Solutions* (New Delhi: Vikas, 1986), pp. 19-20.
11. Nirad C. Chaudhuri, *The Continent of Circe* (Bombay: Jaico, 1966), p. 22.
12. Edward Shils, *The Intellectual between Tradition and Modernity: The Indian Situation* (The Hague: Mouton, 1961), p. 50.

To Live or Not to Live: An Assessment

BASAVARAJ S. NAIKAR

No man with a keen sense of observation of life around him and a deliberate analysis of the observed phenomenon can escape the Hamletian dilemma which presupposes an awareness of the contradiction between appearance and reality, between the falsification of the traditionally sanctioned values and the simultaneous inevitability of a given phenomenon. A man who is caught in the strange context such as this cannot help responding to it in the Hamletian manner. Nirad C. Chaudhuri has the courage to see the problem in the face and try to understand and analyse it however ugly and unsolvable though it may be. There is a greater heroism in having the Hamletian knowledge of reality than in being satisfied with the ignorance of the same. As Aristotle says, it is always desirable to have the knowledge of reality although it is quite ugly and harsh. Chaudhuri who is known for his objective analysis of the Indian society is compelled to raise a Hamletian problem. *To Live or Not to Live*,[1] is an essay which shows Chaudhuri's attempt to understand and account for the peculiar problems of the Indian society which make it difficult for a sensitive man to continue to live meaningfully in that society.

Again, the book need not be mistaken for a textbook of social psychology, as it is the embodiment of Chaudhuri's personal vision which is the result of the life-long observation and which may correspond to the impersonal vision of sociologists and psychologists What makes his essay personal is the fact that his generalizations about the Indian society are based upon his personal experience with people, events and situations of the Indian society. His observations are *a fortiori* rather than *a priori* and hence assume an authenticity of individual vision as contrasted with that of scientific and hence universal vision. The ingredients of Chaudhuri's vision of life as embodied in *To Live or Not to Live* may be discussed in the following paragraphs.

Chaudhuri begins his 'informal' and 'discursive' book with a discussion of the basic question about living a meaningful life in India. Both the social and the family life fall within the large framework of human life. "That is why I have put these two aspects of living under a title which raises the general question of living soundly, living to some purpose—which alone is *living* to me, living unsoundly, being, in my view, not *living* at all. In short, I would not deal with social and family life without raising the basic question: Do we live at all?" (7) Chaudhuri thus raises the fundamental and epistemological question about life because it is the epistemology which gives a sense of direction and vocation to all the aspects of life and makes it a matter of beauty and joy for ever. Since Chaudhuri, like many other sensitive men, has felt the presence of a great lacuna between the Indian ideals and the actual Indian practice, he cannot but ask the basic question again and again. Life in India has become so paradoxical and farcical that one who wants to relate the actual values practised to the ideals professed, one is bound to have a Hamletian question as to whether to live or not to live in such a context of multiple contradictions. The Hamletian condition forced upon Chaudhuri is based upon his life-long observation and a conscious analysis of the content of that observation. The details of his experience with Indian life could be enumerated as follows.

Life in India is not to be understood as a matter of intellectual awareness. On the contrary, it is one of intellectual blindness. Chaudhuri; therefore, describes the life in India as 'uncritical living': "We live uncritically, without paying heed to Plato's famous dictum: The uncriticized (or un-examined) life is not worth living." (8) Life in India is marked by a general lack of idealism and is therefore characterized by negative qualities like eccentricity, stupid vanity, malice, spite and so on. The conspicuous gap between the tall ideals traditionally professed by the Indians and the stark materialism of their pragmatic life is bitterly noted and attacked by

Chaudhuri in the manner in which the seventeenth century England and the nineteenth century England were attacked by Milton and Charles Dickens respectively. Chaudhuri's extraordinary sensitiveness to life around him is proportionately matched by his courage to see the ugliness of life in the face and to withstand the shock that is caused by the minute analysis of reality. The overall impression of Chaudhuri about Indian life is that money plays an extraordinary role in the life of the major groups of society like the youths, the intellectuals and the politicians. Money, thus, becomes the keynote of the Indian society, of human relation, of enjoyment and of achievement. The Indians, according to Chaudhuri, can do anything and everything for money and are the potential sharks or swindlers.

The dominant feature of Indian life could be conspicuously noticed in the large cities of the country like Delhi, Calcutta, Bombay and Madras. These large cities in Chaudhuri's opinion, exhibit the main ingredients of Indian character in a major key, whereas the minor cities or towns or villages do the same in a minor key. The difference between the Indian metropolis and the Indian village is one of degree rather than of kind. The great cities exhibit certain features and qualities of Indian character which create an atmosphere of Indianness in all the fields of life. A great city is said to be a great desert where the individuality is lost in the mass life and the generalities of life look more conspicuous than the idiosyncracies. Since there is a uniformity among the great cities of India, the description or analysis of one city can as well represent that of other cities also. Chaudhuri who is exigentially compelled to stay in Delhi for a large part of his life, has obviously chosen to analyse the archetypal megalopolis of India. The first thing that strikes Chaudhuri's attention is the planning of the city of Delhi. In fact, as noticed by him, there is no organization at all in the capital city. Delhi which ought to be exemplary to other cities of India, is ironically enough, the most ill-organised city in the country. Chaudhuri rightly says that it is organised—if at all it is organised—only biologically and is like a go-getting machine, as such it has the terrifying complexity of a modern computer with its logic elements, transistor, thermistors, capacitors, resisters and so on." (20-21) Obviously Chaudhuri has implicitly shown the lack of artistry in the structure of Delhi. Even the American professor who is interviewed by Chaudhuri confesses his own puzzle about the city. Says he, "I saw something today which I cannot understand. It was all disorganization and confusion and squalor." (21) The drabness and the absence of sophistication of Delhi are aptly described by Chaudhuri who says that "Delhi was a crude descendant of Damascus, Baghdad or even the new Babylon of Nebuchadnezzar, through Pataliputra, Ujjayini and Kanyakubja and of course, Muslim Delhi." (23)

After pointing out the structure of the city of Delhi, Chaudhuri captures the essential spirit and nature of the city. Delhi enjoys a special importance in the life of India on account of the role it plays in the lives of the Indians in different fields of life. Delhi, for example, is an industrial city with all the paraphernalia and is on par with other industrial cities like Bombay, Calcutta or Madras. But what distinguishes it from other cities is its political importance. Chaudhuri has highlighted two features of Delhi which are of extraordinary importance. The bureaucratic government and the centralization of all the political administration are the striking features of the city of Delhi. It is this speciality that contradistinguishes it from the other great cities of India. Delhi, therefore, can be compared to the brain of the body of India. These two aspects are the manifestation of the great monster. Chaudhuri, as usual, employs the satirical language in describing this phenomenon. "The second force behind the growth of Delhi is a formidable Estatism, which might be called the advent of the Leviathan in this country—Ah! an incompetent Leviathan not the Hobbesian. Socialism is only a euphemism for it, or rather a cloak." (25) Then he points out the most striking features of these aspects of Delhi. The bureaucratic set up of India, of which Delhi is the seat, is represented by the clerical job for which every educated Indian, generally hankers. Thus the creation of clerical jobs was part of the expansion of the class interest of the urban land and moneyless middle class. The worst feature of this bureaucratic system is the extraordinary and artificial importance given to the man who never does the basic work and the consequent delay, check and dilution of the process of work. This principle holds water in all the bureaucratic units of Indian life. Chaudhuri, therefore, points out the conspicuous feature of this set up symbolized by the top level administration of Delhi. "The most significant expansion has taken place at the tip, in the more highly paid ranks. As a result for every clerk who does some original work there are about five stages of supervision by highly paid superiors. This also was bound to happen in the interest of the politicians. Most of them were members of the middle class who failed to get government jobs, and therefore, so far as worldly status is concerned, they regarded themselves as men who had been unfairly deprived of their legitimate inheritance. For this reason, after getting power, they do not show any disinclination to live wholly on the public revenues." (26) Thus clericalism happens to be the keynote of the Indian administration as well as a means of livelihood for the middle class people. Centralization which is the second major aspect of Delhi is again the conspicuous feature of Indian political administration. Chaudhuri's attribution of centralization to the four causes is a clear evidence of his historical sense and insight into the Indian's psychology. The centralization is caused by (1) the unwillingness of the Indian to delegate power to the others; (2) the distrust by the central government or the provincial government; (3) need for the formulation of a foreign policy paving the way for foreign help and depicts the Indian political behaviour in describing the capital city of Delhi. One can obviously see a combination of satire and description in his writing.

After providing a description of political aspects of Delhi, Chaudhuri proceeds to offer a visual picture of the great city, which testifies to his minute observation and keen perception. Like a philosopher he points out the contradictory nature of Delhi when he says that it is metropolitan as well as provincial. One can see the resident aliens who come to India from foreign countries for political and no-political visits, as well as the provincials, like Tamilians, Maharashtrians, Bengalis or Punjabis, who "never submerge their provincial identity in a pan-Indian identity, and very largely confine their social life to fellow-provincials." (37) Obviously Chaudhuri's keen observation confirms the view that Delhi, like London, is a city of contradictions. Another peculiarity of this great city, according to him, is the pervading commercial and feminine atmosphere. "Due to this routine, the external impression of human life in Delhi, is, in the first instance, all bazaar, and next all feminine. It is not the man-about-town but the woman-about-town who sets the tone of urban life, and gives to it movement, colour, and charm." (32) Another contradiction of Delhi, as pointed out by Chaudhuri, is the simultaneous presence of Islamic culture and superficial westernization. "Delhi is of the Islamic Middle East with a modern veneer. It is really Cairo of Tulunid, Mameluke, or Fatimid times, and Baghdad of Abbasid times, disguised by a superficial Westernization." (33) Similarly the splendour of Delhi is contrasted by the 'expanse of drabness.' Chaudhuri's description of Delhi throws light as much about the life at Delhi as about the social and political behaviour of Indians.

He then turns his attention from Delhi to the social life in India. His observations again show his insight into human nature, his wide reading and his awareness of social psychology of Indians. "The Hindu society," according to him, "is basically genetic in its outlook and looks upon social life only as an extension of the family, clan or tribe. It is very difficult for us to get out of this mould of social life, which is really tribalism and to acquire genuinely social behaviour." (41) None who is acquainted with the Indian society can deny the truth of Chaudhuri's observation. He illustrates it by pointing out how the Indians in the streets address one another as bhai, or bahen or baba.

Marriages, illnesses and death anniversaries are very important occasions of the Indian social life. Far from being the celebrations of the events concerned, these occasions are turned by Indians, rather farcically, into those of pomp and show and prestige and what not. Chaudhuri therefore, does not generally attend the wedding of his friends or relatives. "Rather than go through that experience I prefer to be a Diogenes." (44) Wedding ceremonies in India are occasions for showing off one's wealth and stature. Therefore wedding invitations are sent even to strangers who happen to be big officers. Sometimes weddings serve as occasions for intimidating bride's or the bridegroom's side. Nowadays this habit has been "extended into a general attempt at intimidating neighbours, relations, and clients into a proper respect or fear of the host's wealth and position." (46) Some of the wedding invitations contain special sentences like "some central Ministers are expected to attend," and the host's bureaucratic servility to his superiors and his arrogance towards his inferiors are comic and irritating simultaneously. Like marriages death-anniversaries also are turned into occasions of pomp and show. Far from making people unhappy, deaths in some families act as good riddance and add to the happiness of the surviving members like sons and daughters-in-law. Sometimes the surviving relatives are very insensitive to the death of a person. Chaudhuri offers an instance of how the people behave comically and practically even at the funeral ceremony at the burning ghats at Delhi. Again, deaths have a serious impact on the sexual life of the surviving members who are likely to indulge in sex in order to forget their sorrow of having lost somebody. Likewise illnesses are important events in Indian life in that whenever a person in a family is taken ill, it becomes mandatory on the part of the relatives and friends to go and see, console and enhearten him and the members of his family. But even this is turned by Indians into a farce: "It is the traditional Indian habit of making illness, and more especially a serious illness as frivolous a social gathering as a cocktail party in New Delhi." (52) The visitors who flock to the house of illness are quite likely to forget the sick man and indulge in their gossip and noise. This is how Chaudhuri shows the farcicality of the main events of Indian social life which testifies to his keen observation and sharp thinking. He is able to support his general observations of life with examples of his personal experience.

Chaudhuri switches his attention to the social behaviour of Indians. The first feature of the Indian behaviour is the ridiculous acceptance of his inferiority, which paradoxically enough, masquerades as superiority complex. Chaudhuri is never tired of repeating the fact that the Indian is notorious for his lack of perception which is the result of the lack of social education. "The Hindu society never learned to value man as man, as an individual, as a personality, without reference to his worldly status." (59) It is basically because of this exaggerated importance attached to the economic status of man, that the Hindus cannot understand the total behaviour of man. Even their description of a man's character is so simple and elementary. Their poverty of perception could be seen in their description of a man's character in a word or two.

"What I cannot explain about my people is their extraordinary insensitiveness to points of character. 'He is a good or a bad man' is the final summing up of a man's character with us, and I have hardly been able to get any idea of another man's personality from the talk I hear at secondhand about him." (59)

The economic poverty or wealth of the Indians plays a very significant role in deciding their behaviour. Whereas poverty makes them cherish the ideas of class-hatred, wealth instigates them to show it off on all the possible occasions such as large parties. This leads Chaudhuri to comment upon their behaviour. According to him, the Indians are not properly educated in the social behaviour. They can be very sociable in streets and bazaars but not in close gatherings as they lack the capacity for intelligent conversation. In India, there are, roughly speaking, two approaches to talking. According to one, they believe in the notion that the stature of man consists in his being a taciturn. It may even be said that taciturnity is proportionate to his dignity. "To withhold *Kathamrta* or nectar of speech, is recognized as a means of asserting one's importance." (63) By contrast, talking incessantly is the mark of the undignified people. The Indian attitude towards talking may be said to be quite utilitarian, in that it is employed either for out and out pornographic purpose or for the profitarian purpose or for that of self-aggrandizement. The Indians are generally very fond of talking smut which provides a compensation for their sex-starvation. "In them, perhaps the most innocent and friendly thing is the lading out of smut, which becomes more salacious among the 'England-returned' ones, who have been able to shed either their 'ingenuous shame' or Hindu prudery through their stay abroad." (63) Another typicality of the Indian indulgence in smut is that more often than not it is directed against the absent ones and is therefore eloquent of the talker's malice. Otherwise talking is employed only for utilitarian purposes like money-making, matchmaking, disputations among pandits, homilies from holymen and altercations between doctrinaires or competitions. All these habits go to prove Chaudhuri's conclusion that the Indian social behaviour is marked by gregariousness rather than by genuine sociability.

Chaudhuri, then, jumps from the wider entity i.e., society to the one of the most important components of that entity i.e. woman.

He has chosen to comment upon woman as she happens to form one half of the totality of life as much in India as anywhere else. But woman has been an object of special interest and concern in India because of the ambivalent approach of men towards her which is again caused by the rigid puritanical background. In spite of the modern introduction of democracy into the Indian society, Chaudhuri is forced to say that "there is hardly any intercommunication between the sexes." (69) He is right when he points out the reverse method of improvement of relation between men and women in India. As it is, there is no social mingling between the two sexes, and the Indian authorities have wrongly taken a decision to solve the problem by putting the cart before the horse i.e., by introducing co-education before paving the way for social mingling. This observation obviously holds a mirror to Chaudhuri's sociological imagination. There is indeed, no doubt that the Indians suffer from "an acute sex-consciousness" (70) which is easily attributable to their puritanical upbringing and atmosphere. That is why there is bound to be a perpetual tension between their natural instincts and their puritanical code of behaviour. Chaudhuri, therefore, remarks, "As things stand, any kind of natural and friendly intercourse between men and women has been made very difficult, if not impossible. The accepted code of conduct is to keep mum about women in public and talk smut in private." (71) Obviously talking smut in privacy is the natural result of the public restriction and disapproval of the exchange of views and feelings between men and women.

It is because of the unusual social restriction about sex, that the Indians become sex-obsessed and therefore begin to read Kama Sutra repeatedly. Chaudhuri's historical sense enables him to clarify the fact that Kama Sutra was originally meant for the courtesans of India, but it is wrongly read by one and all in the modern days. In spite of the sexual taboos in India, paradoxically enough, sexual promiscuity could be seen on a large scale there. Chaudhuri offers one of his own experiences in Delhi office where a pretty-girl-steno-typist was the object of rivalry between his male colleagues. The popularity of the concepts like 'boyfriend,' 'girlfriend,' 'call girl' and 'dating' is the sign of the promiscuity, concealed or otherwise. Chaudhuri's keen observation cannot be rejected by anyone who has an awareness of the Indian society. He points out the shift of promiscuity from one area to the other. 'What has really happened is that the area of the irregularity shifted. Thus, instead of being confined to family relationship, it has spilled out into social relationships, so that the liaisons are now with the friend's wife, instead of being with the sister-in-law. In other words, it is a change in the veneer." (77) The puritanical restriction which is responsible for the secret solutions sought for by men and women, should, according to Chaudhuri, be relaxed a little so that social mingling might be made possible. "We have driven the only alternative to arranged marriages of the traditional type, which is love-making, into the streets and parks, and made lovers literally street walkers. I would have unrestricted meeting between men and women for this purpose even at the risk of having some adultery." (78)

Chaudhuri's observation about the Indian women is quite in keeping with his observation about the Indian life in general. Women's beauty, according to him, is not generally attended by the proportionate mental or spiritual beauty. There can, of course, be exceptions to this, but the general rule is quite unmistakable. The appearance of a woman in India can be quite deceptive and may be quite contrary to her inner nature. Chaudhuri offers a personal example. Once he saw an elegant woman clad in sepia and gold saree walking in a garden of Delhi and naturally thought her to be quite graceful and aesthetic minded as she carried a bunch of flowers with her. But as he went ahead for a while, he saw her stealing the flowers from a tree in the roadside compound. He was rather puzzled to see her chased by the shaggy mongrel and running away giggling. Chaudhuri has obviously shown the contradiction in that lady between her sweet appearance and ugly behaviour. It is this dichotomy in character that is described by him as 'dimorphism.'

Chaudhuri's discussion of the joint-family system of India is full of subtle observation and incisive remarks. "At its best the joint family is co-operative society based on the blood tie and a smaller and more closely knit replica of the village community." (100) The joint family system produces a particular type of behaviour, in fact, it is a miniworld in itself. Family quarrels caused by women folk are quite common in it. The women who take the initiative in the querulous adventures seek the help of their husband-dogs. Most often, it is the pent-up emotion caused by the cumulative quarrels that eventually creates divisions in the family. One of the aberrations of the Hindu society is the peculiar relation between the mother-in-law and the daughter-in-law. In fact, a wild kind of a law of inductiveness is always operative in the Indian family where the daughter-in-law is ill-treated by the mother-in-law in the first half of their life and the mother-in-law is ill-treated by the daughter-in-law in the latter part of their life. Thus both of them have to undergo the two stages of serving and reigning in the reverse order. Chaudhuri's sociological imagination helps him to remark that the joint family has a tendency to erode and undermine the spirit of adventure and self-help in its members. The relationship between the different members of the joint family is governed by factors like sex, status and age. For example, a son in the family will be more communicative with his wife and mother than with his brother's wife or his father or with the children. Chaudhuri's subtle observation shows that there is generally more intercommunication between women than between men. The mothers discuss anything and everything in the presence of their daughters but the fathers do not do so in the presence of their sons. One more peculiarity of the Indian joint family is that the grand-children are generally closer with the grandparents than to the parents.

Chaudhuri then discusses the problems and conditions of the working women in India. These women are rather forced by the circumstances to earn their livelihood and keep themselves and the members of their family away from the wolf. Sometimes their salary helps them to save some amount cumulatively until it grows big enough to be an attractive dowry for the highly-stationed grooms. Thus employment of woman seems to be a stop-gap arrangement. Chaudhuri describes the condition of the working girl and the change of the locale very convincingly. "In my young days, when a girl was withdrawn from school or college in anticipation of marriage, we used to say that she was in the waiting room. At present a far larger number of girls are to be seen in the same waiting room, but it is now an office, and not the home. A bigger difference is that for many the train does not arrive at all; formerly, at the worst, it was unpunctual." (138) Thus the feminine resort to a job is ultimately connected with the problem of marriage. India which is undergoing a transition from traditional to modern way of life, the educated woman who is neither purely traditional nor purely emancipated will have to lead a life of forced spinsterhood or to seek surreptitious satisfaction without losing her dignity in the society. Most of the time she will be waiting for something great to happen in her path of husband-hunting. Thus, late marriage of girls is invariably encouraged by the matrimonial Micawberism. Another reason for the girls' attraction for jobs is the economic independence which they enjoy and the consequent love and obligation of the members of her family who depend upon her earning. "In a living society even the relatives of a girl do not feel embarrassed to be under financial obligation to her lover." (150) The married working women are more independent and arrogant than the jobless housewives. Chaudhuri shows how it is a Western imitation. "The Indian phenomenon is really derivative. Its practical emergence is due substantially to the impact of Western influences, and its apologia is wholly imported. To cut the matter short, as in political ideas, economic organization, literature and art, or fashion, here too we are faced with a case of imitation, the working woman being only the economic counterpart of the woman in jeans." (146) Again, the kinds of jobs preferred by the modern women are only desk-jobs and not the heavy ones like agricultural or industrial or military ones. Chaudhuri points out the three main interests of the married working woman in a priority order: "In the emotional life of our womenfolk three loves—for husband, for child, for saris—constitute a harmonic triad, in which the last love is the treble, the second middle register, and the first the bass note." (153) Whereas love of money is the characteristic quality of the working girl, love of clothes happens to be the dominant feature of the married working woman.

Marriage in Hindu society is attended by certain peculiar characteristics. It has typical antecedents and consequences in Hindu society. Whereas in ancient India marriage was basically meant for the procreation of children, in the modern India it has come to mean a "means of enjoying the pleasure of sexual intercourse without the attendant risk of conception." (158) Chaudhuri has obviously shown how procreation, the primary goal of ancient marriage, has become the secondary one in modern matrimonial world. This phenomenon shows the extra importance given to the sexual aspect of marriage. Chaudhuri says that the very origin of matrimonial attraction is sexual in nature. He uses his typical aesthetic vocabulary to describe this process. Love, which eventually paves the way for marriage, has 'geometrical basis.' (159) Since, more often than not, love begins on the visual level, the sight of the feminine body, plays a very important role in the amorous process. "The geometry of linear curves and of spheroids is, in a manner of speaking, interwoven with love," Since falling in love is caused and intensified by the curvilinearity of the pattern of the feminine body, the inward beauty or grace or sublimity transcending the physical attractiveness are not at all cared for in India. Thus love is rooted in the visualness of beauty and physicalness of attraction. It is this superficial attraction that sets a number of young men to daydreaming. Thus physical or sexual attraction plays a very important role in love from the boys's or girls's point of view. But when the same has to be referred to the family for sanction the economic consideration also creeps in. Chaudhuri rightly remarks, "the marriages are sordid scrambles for money." (170) In the matrimonial bargain, the bride's father pays an undue attention to the economic status of the groom's family and never cares for the groom's mental or moral achievements. Chaudhuri, therefore, says that "In my young days some fathers and mothers talked about the character or talents of the young men, nowadays nobody pays any attention to these things." (171)

Having discussed the antecedents of marriage, Chaudhuri goes to analyse the consequences of marriage as seen in the routine life of a couple. Since most of the marriages are made possible only on account of mutual physical attraction, they are sure to crumble as the foundation of physical attraction wears into nothingness. Marriage at this stage remains only as a technical one which is marked by the absence of true vitality. The husband and the wife cease to be so and begin to take a neighbourly interest in each other. Chaudhuri's presentation of this phenomenon is so clear that it needs no addition. "After the physical attraction has worn off most husbands and wives feel only a neighbourly interest in each other and sometimes also neighbourly animosity and hatred. . . .

As married life advances, it ceases not only to be a marriage of true minds, but even of bodies. In many families the physical revulsion of old husbands and wives from one another shows itself painfully." (72)

Another important feature of Indian society is the secretiveness of lust. The only difference is that whereas some people begin with it, some others end with it. The sex-starved young men and women and the sexually dissatisfied married couple will be always trying to have underground means of satisfaction without tarnishing their image in society. Chaudhuri rightly remarks: "In Hindu society so long as appearances are saved nothing is wrong." (177) In some aristocratic or snobbish families, the couple will be practising prostitution with mutual connivance or understanding. That is why the slogan like "Bourgeois marriage is legalized prostitution" written by the youngmen on the walls of a women's college are more a dream than a satire.

Chaudhuri's views, again, on the Indian unitary family are very insightful. He says that the dominant note of Indian family is staticity which discourages all kinds of liveliness. "Most Indian homes are stagnant, stuffy, or even stifling in their psychological staticity and for this reason if a member of the family happens to possess a lively spirit he is driven out from the home to show it in places which cannot be civilized in its expression. The wet blanket is thrown about so relentlessly at home that few persons treat it as anything but a lair to sleep or an eating house which supplies such bad food that good living has become identified with wish frequenting meretricious restaurants where cuisine is never looked upon as the first attraction." (185) The absence of interest and boredom are two important features of the Indian family. Sometimes the interests of the young men and women are curbed by the parents: "I have always been dismayed by the indifference to hobbies shown by my countrymen. Actually, many parents consider them to be moral delinquency in their children, and never allow them to have them when the children are obedient." (186) This kind of suppression of the interests of the youngmen and women is responsible for the cumulative frustration which asserts itself at the earliest opportunity. "The revolt of the youth in India begins with the suppression of their interest in early childhood." (187) The things of the mind like literature, art, music, drama etc. are not generally encouraged by the parents who think that everything except an earning of livelihood is redundant and even a waste. Many times, Indian family life involves soulless living together, without a renewal of love and faith in the members. Thus a sensitive man is likely to be terribly lonely in spite of being surrounded by his kith and kin. Chaudhuri offers a conjugal instance to illustrate the problem of maintenance of the family. "To send off a wife to her father's house, as it is customary to do in Hindu society, may be like sending a car for periodic overhaul to a garage, but to live with her calls for a different kind of attention, which, to continue the analogy of the car, is like providing cooling and lubrication all the time engine is running. Try to run it without these and it will not be long before it disintegrates." (192) Indians have a remarkable talent for being unhappy and making others unhappy. Chaudhuri suggests that it is better to have a divorce than to endure constant nagging and bickering. He therefore says, "I would rather die of family cholera, which is divorce, than have its dyspeptic, which is bickering." (193)

The essay *To Live or Not to Live* is discursive, analytical, explicatory and elaborate in its style; it helps the reader to understand the man-woman relationship from a liberal point of view. The clarity of views expressed in this essay is remarkable and speaks of Chaudhuri's sharp intelligence and stunning scholarship behind it.

NOTE

1. Nirad C. Chaudhuri, *To Live or Not to Live* (Delhi: Hind Pocket Books, 1970).

Chaudhuri's Sartorial Vision in *Culture in the Vanity Bag*

BASAVARAJ S. NAIKAR

Perhaps no Indian writer has thought so seriously about the Indian clothes and the philosophy underlying them as Nirad Chaudhuri has. He is such a keen observer of life around him and such a minute scholar that he is amply qualified to relate his observation to his wide and historical scholarship and evolve a very interesting sartorial philosophy about Indians. One might easily say that *Culture in the Vanity Bag*[1] is an Indian parallel to Carlyle's *Sartor Resartus*. Whereas Chaudhuri's book is historical in perspective and analytical in method and realistic in style, Carlyle's is romantic and synthetical in its overall approach to the problem. Chaudhuri's analysis is, as usual, tinged with satire and intellectual humour. The sophistry that he brings in the analysis and perspectivisation of the whole problem is indeed very admirable. The highlights of his arguments may be seen in the following paragraphs.

Chaudhuri, who has observed the Indian life very keenly, is able to show the connection between the Indian clothing and the Indian history. Clothes are, obviously, the external manifestations of the innermost cultural habits of men adapting themselves to the peculiar geographical, social, religious and even political phenomena around them. That is the reason why Chaudhuri says that "the evolution of clothing in India has been only a part of the historical evolution of the peoples of India, possessing similar features, following similar lines, and producing similar results." (xi) Although the present India is a 'museum or warehouse of cultures' exhibiting a motley of clothing, having a group or individual autonomy, their origin and development could be traced to the historical movements which swept India from the earliest times to the present.

Chaudhuri offers a taxonomical break-up of the evolutionary history of clothing in India. The first category of these, according to him, is the Mongoloid clothing which consists of two pieces of 'loom-woven clothes' "one of which is thrown around the shoulders and the other, the main piece, wrapped round the waist." (14) This type of clothing is used mainly by the Mongoloid peoples in the Himalayan regions.

The second category, according to Chaudhuri, is the aboriginal one which consists of one piece of cotton cloth, "anything between eight to fifteen feet in length and thirty to forty-five inches in width. With a slight difference in the design of the borders, it is worn by both men and women. Men wrap its middle section round the waist, pass the left-half section between the legs and tuck it behind, while the right-hand portion is sometimes tied round the waist and sometimes folded and hung in front." (15) The women wear the same with a slight variation. This is the simplest and most basic costume worn by all the aboriginal peoples of the Central Indian plateau and the Deccan.

The Aryan costume, which forms the third category, is an elaborate form of the aboriginal costume. It consists of a long piece of cloth worn as the main garment by both men and women. It is known as dhoti when worn by men and as saree when used by women. "The dhoti is worn roughly in the same fashion as the cloth of the aboriginal man, but it is longer and wider, and is worn with so many folds, gathers, and tucks that it gives the impression of much fuller draping. More especially, the gathers and folds in front are heavier and hang lower." (16) Similarly, the saree is an elaboration of the aboriginal woman's cloth. "A section of about four feet of its length is gathered in front and tucked in at the middle point of the front waist line, and thus constitutes the main feature of the Hindu manner of wearing the saree. All over northern India women wrap it over the lower limbs like a shirt but in South India Brahmin women tuck the left end at the back like their men folk, though modern women are giving it up." (16)

Sometimes an add combination of the aboriginal and the Aryan costume is formed and worn by the labouring population. It is called 'decency-clout' and is used by these people due to poverty and for convenience of work.

The nomadic costume forms the fourth category of clothes. It is "the first and earlier of any sewn costumes worn by a particular ethnic group permanently settled in India." (18) Further, it is "a harmonious whole from head to foot" (18) which is made up of a full shirt with deep and ample gathers; a closely fitted bodice; a waistcoat. "The ensemble has a linear unity and rhythm of surprising beauty and dynamism" (18) and because of the addition of bright colours and bold designs, gives an impression of a very strong individuality. This costume is worn mainly by the people of Rajputana from Kathiawar to the West of Delhi to the east.

The Muslim clothing of the fifth category consists of sherwani or achkan and kurta or kamiz for men and salwar-kamiz-dupatta ensemble for women. These costumes are worn by the Muslims of India, the Hindus of Punjab, the Sikhs and also the Islamised Hindus of Hindustan.

The European clothing, which forms the sixth category, consists of the standard garments of men and women like suit (pants, shirt, coat, hat and tie) and skirt respectively. These clothes are adapted by a large number of Indians who, once used to it, never go back to the Indian costumes.

After offering a taxonomical picture of Indian costumes in general, Chaudhuri enumerates the chief component of the typical Hindu costumes. He rightly says that "the correct Hindu dress must be unsewn. Next, it must have two essential *garments*. A Hindu must be, whether male or female, a person of *two* garments. These are the dhoti or sari for the lower limbs, and a scarf for the upper part of the body. In Sanskrit the two pieces are called *Vastra* and *Uttariya* respectively." (22) Chaudhuri also discusses the mode of wearing the *vastra*. He says that "being *dvivastra*, a man of *two* garments, a Hindu must also be *trikachcha*, a man of three tucks, and the places at which these are to be put are the back on the alignment of the spine, navel and the left side of the waist." (23) After showing the relation between the Hindu garments and the sacred prescriptions, Chaudhuri makes certain observations about the purpose of the Hindu's wearing of certain types of garments in certain styles which testify to his sharpness of perception, boldness of judgement and freedom from inhibition. He, for example, takes up the traditional Hindu prescription that a man should take off the back-tuck while urinating. But Chaudhuri asks a simple, straightforward and uninhibited question as to why a Hindu should take off the back-tuck when he can perform his nature-call without taking it off and that too when the back-tuck is the most unnecessary to take off. Then Chaudhuri explains in his typical fashion that this habit or rather prescription is founded upon the usual Hindu habit of non-thinking.

The dropping of the back-tuck by the Aryans is attributed by Chaudhuri to the aboriginals of India. The back-tuck, for example, is not used by the unmarried Brahmins and non-Brahmins. This habit of wearing the dhoti without the back-tuck perhaps suggests the defective status of unmarried Brahmins and all Hindus of non-Brahmin castes.

After offering a taxonomical picture of the basic Indian costumes, Chaudhuri examines the philosophy of clothing in India in general. Clothing in India, especially among Hindus, had not only utilitarian role but an aesthetic role also to play. Clothing is used not merely to cover the body from the climate, but as a means of self-assertion and self-protection. It is used in India to show off one's superiority over the enemies. "There is no doubt that in the true and honest Hindu tradition of display, women's clothing is aposematic." (32) That explains the Hindu woman's habit of over-dressing without feeling the slightest sense of embarrassment. In this respect, clothing has an asexual rather than inter-sexual significance. Even in matrimonial bonds, for example, clothing plays a role subordinate to that of physical attraction. Chaudhuri, therefore, points out that "in wedlock the access to the body is so untrammelled that artificial attractions are wholly superfluous." (32)

The urban and the so-called civilized (or cultured) people of India attached a lot of importance to the aesthetic role of clothing. The extra attention shown by women to clothes is more often than not motivated by the sexual desire to attract the male attention. Sophisticated habits of clothing are, therefore, associated with courtesans and brothels among Hindus. But the Muslim did not bother much about the 'sublimation of the brothel,' as he "could have any blend of sensuality and refinement in the harem itself." (34) The extraordinary sexual importance attached by the urban Hindu to clothing sometimes leads him to draw wrong judgement about woman's character. Chaudhuri, as usual, supports his observations with illustrations from his personal experience. Once in Delhi Chaudhuri saw "two gorgeously dressed Punjabi young women" who were described by a bypasser as 'Randi hogi'—'Must be whores.' (35) On another occasion, one of Chaudhuri's senior servants asked the sweeper woman to change into cleaner dresses, the husband of the latter is said to have remarked that only the whores among sweepers put on finery. Sometimes, the sexual significance attached to clothes in India is intensified by the accompaniment of feminine coquetry. Thus gorgeous or sophisticated dressing earns the label of a *demi-mondaine* for a lady whether she wants it or not.

Chaudhuri rightly points out the close connection between jewellery and clothes. He is also quite correct when he attributes the Hindu sartorial surplus to their numbness of sensibility caused by the Indian hot climate. "For one thing, the Hindu sense organs are so enfeebled by too much glare, heat and noise that they cannot take in at best more than half of the sense phenomena presented to them, and so there must always be, if there is to be any effect at all, an overdose." (36) He further points out how ostentation was not considered by the Hindu *monde* as morally wrong. That is the reason why there is a good deal of sartorial magnificence even in their routine life. "At cocktail parties in New Delhi, for instance, I often observe Western women looking at the magnificent Indian ladies with a puzzled expression, as if they were wondering whether they were not seeing a mirage of the ranks of duchesses, marchionesses, and countesses at a coronation ceremony in Westminster Abbey." (36-37)

The element of Hindu excess could be seen both in jewellery and in clothes. Chaudhuri exhibits his capacity for minute observation and intelligent connection of things and features of life when he says that gold is the most important metal used for ornaments by the Hindus. Gold is preferred by Hindus because of a variety of reasons. First, the Hindu ornament was based on the gold standards i.e. economic status of the metal. Second, it had a sacred status.

Third, it offered the best security for the people at the time of crisis in their life. It is because of the sacrosanctity of gold that it was meant only for the upper parts of the body and was forbidden for the lower parts which deserved only silver ones. Because of its economic status, it offered them an unfailing security. "So their ornaments were often their only resource, a sort of marriage settlement, and never knowing what the next turn of the wheel of fortune might bring, they clung to their gold as if it was their lifebelt." (38) It was also because of its intrinsic worth that gold could be the cause for creation of contradictory responses in the Hindu women. It "always raised the women to a higher level of mental life." (39) That is why these women "would give the gold to a husband, son, or even relative in trouble, to be sold or mortgaged, and never say a word or take credit." (39) On the other hand, they could be so possessive of gold that they could be totally callous to their near and dear ones. "The love of gold would drive out the love of husband and child from their heart, make the mere idea of a lover a dirty smear, and turn them into chrysel enhantine statues with a demoniac soul." (39)

Chaudhuri rightly equates the Hindu woman's attachment for gold to her madness for saris. "The motive of self-assertion and acquiring worldly importance explains the extraordinary craze our women now have for saris. They go on buying them regularly even when they cannot and do not wear a fraction of their stock. They are the hoarders of clothes, corresponding to the male hoarders of money." (42) It is on account of this madness for sari that the Hindu women make it a point of reference and comparison in their familial and social life. They also make it a means of endearment between friends and relatives; a test of husband's preferential love and also a means of social estrangement and matrimonial derangement. Thus jewellery and clothes, as aptly described by Chaudhuri, provide the best chance of expression for the Hindu feminine moods which blow hot and cold alternately if not simultaneously.

It is very difficult to have an affirmative answer to the question whether we have an Indian dress in India. Chaudhuri, therefore, says in this typically categorical fashion that "just as there is no *Indian nation*, there is no Indian dress." (49) He further states that India "became a museum of diverse cultures fairly early in its history." (49) Since India had been conquered by foreign races, there was bound to be a battle between the Hindu and the non-Hindu clothes as also other things of culture. The first battle was naturally to be between the Hindu clothes and the Muslim ones. Whereas the Hindus believed in non-sewn garments, the Muslims believed in sewn garments. Because of the exclusiveness of the Hindu culture, it never encourages either the proselytisation of Hindu clothes or the adaptation of Muslim clothes. But the Muslim culture, because of its at least one-way traffic of proselytisation, encouraged the adaptation of its clothes by the Hindus. As a religious policy the Hindus did not like the use of Muslim clothes at all except by way of self-denigration or contamination. Chaudhuri is perceptive enough to show the evolution of the sartorial battle between the Hindu and the Muslim culture. He shows how in spite of the initial Hindu hatred for the Muslim clothes, the Hindus—some of them at least—adopted it for the purposes of pleasing the Muslim leaders and authorities in social life. Chaudhuri rightly relates this habit of the Hindus to their national character when he says that "Hinduism forgives every transgression of Hindu standards out of opportunism, but no adherence to any non-Hindu value from conviction. So if a Hindu showed signs, either through his opinion or his behaviour, that he was acquiring new loyalties or even remaining Hindu, widening his personal life by adding non-Hindu qualities, mental or external, he was without any compunction thrown outside the pale, whoever he might be, and no less a Hindu than Raja Rammohun Roy was excommunicated in this manner, though he is rightly looked upon as the creator of the modern Indian mind." (55) The religious conflict between the Hindus and the Muslims was reflected in their sartorial conflict also. The ambivalence in the former is repeated in the latter also.

With the British conquest of India, the sartorial battle between Hindus and the British repeated the pattern of the older battle between Hindus and Muslims, of course, with slight variations. The Hindus, in spite of their religious rigidities, jumped at the opportunity of imitating the British (or Western in a broader sense) clothes for the purposes of fashionableness, snobbery and worldly success, although the British did not like the Hindu imitation of their clothes, as they thought it to be tantamount to the contamination of the superior British culture by the inferior Hindu culture. But the Hindus did not bother about the British superiority-complex at all. Consequently the Hindus went on adapting the British clothes like suit, tie and hat for their social life, if not for their private, religious or sectarian life. The boldest of the Hindus were the Anglicized or 'England-returned' ones who affected the British clothes and maintained costly wardrobes with real style and gusto. Thus imitation of British clothes was a virtue allied to other habits like, for example, speaking and writing English, quoting Shakespeare and Milton; "airing rationalism and contempt for Hindu image worship; eating beef; and drinking until dead drunk." (59) One might easily say that imitation of the British clothes was the strongest aspect of the Westernization of Hindus.

Among the many effects of the British clothes on Hindus was the growing Hindu tendency towards covering the body. "With the coming of British rule, the practice of covering the body became more general; in fact, to remain bare-bodied except when being comfortable in summer in private, became more or less rare. . . . In addition, the women have made the petticoat an integral part of their dress." (61)

In India, there is no strict connection between clothes and morals. "In other words, the moral connection is a secondary relationship, a matter of association of ideas." (72) After categorically showing the absence of moral connexion with clothes, Chaudhuri shows how the pattern of clothes of particular culture, though originally decided by the immediate climatic conditions, are not likely to be changed to the new climatic conditions into which the people concerned are thrown. Thus, for example, the British refused to change over from their suit to anything Indian in spite of the horrid climate of India. Similarly, the Muslims were unwilling to give up the shalwar and kameej in spite of their being inconvenient in the Indian climate Thus, each culture believing in the validity and sanctity of its own clothes, refuses to respect those of the other, except for utilitarian purposes.

He offers a contrastive picture of the Muslim clothes and the Hindu clothes. The Muslim clothes had a "combination of magnificence, purity, and strength" at least until the time of Aurangzeb's sons in India. But the Hindu approach to clothes was governed by a dual idea that "personal adornment through clothing ought to be a combination of the highest and the most refined beauty of the nude with that of clothing and ornaments. It fused what are regarded as incompatibles and it did so with glorious success." (81) The dual aesthetics of the Hindu clothing, according to Chaudhuri, suffers from two handicaps: one, its effect depends "as much on the body of the wearer as on the quality of raiment, and not all men and women could boast of perfect figures" (81); two, it lends itself to misjudgements on moral counts, although at the other extreme it attains an unearthly purity.

The battle of clothes in India, says Chaudhuri, has not any dignity or elevation about it, though it has been fought perpetually all through the Indian history. It has, therefore, become a mere squabble. Chaudhuri puts forth his views very frankly, "the battle of clothing in its current phase is of a low quality. Just as the governance of the country by the present Indian ruling order, which I call Brown Colonialism, is a caricature of British imperialism, the conflict of clothes is also nothing better than degenerate aping, without any ideal or principle behind it." (87)

The Hindus had been also slavish in their imitation of the European clothes that they easily tolerated the public conveniences including interminable railway compartments being earmarked for 'Europeans only.' Chaudhuri points out the height of paradox when he says that the government-owned Ashoka Hotel of Delhi would not be able to admit the Buddha himself if he were to come now in his usual garments as represented in Gandharva art. That the Hindu piece of cloth i.e. dhoti should be forbidden in the hotel owned by the Hindu government is indeed beyond all sense and logic. Too much dependence by the Hindus upon the white mythology is obviously satirized severely by Chaudhuri when he says: "That above every fluttering national flag in India today I see its 'idea' in the Platonic sense—a transcendental Union Jack." (91)

Then Chaudhuri shows how even the great Indians like Rajendra Prasad, Jawaharlal Nehru and Indira Gandhi had taken to the Muslim and European garments respectively. Jawaharlal Nehru, who was brought up in the Islamic garments, changed over to the European clothes when he was at Harrow and Cambridge for his education; took to dhoti for the utilitarian purpose of participating in the Indian independence movement and switched over to pajama and shirt which are still popular as 'Nehru pajama' and 'Nehru shirt.' Likewise, Mrs. Indira Gandhi had taken to frock and hat when in England for her education; then she changed over to sari in India although she kept her head bare; but after her assumption of the status of Prime-Ministership of India, she began to cover her head with the end of her sari in the true Hindu fashion.

Like everything else in India, clothing has also been reduced to the ugly minimum. Chaudhuri never tires of stating and illustrating this very Indian truth. He shows that the Gandhi-cap and the Jawahar waist-coat are no better than their old counterparts. The adoption of Gandhi-cap by the 'miserly Congress Party' is an evidence of the extra-ordinary poverty of aesthetics exhibited by the Congresswallas. Similarly the adoption of Jawahar-coat which is an adaptation of a Muslim garment makes it very difficult for the Westerners to distinguish between Indian diplomats and butlers. These instances are a proof of the lack of any sound aesthetic basis for the sartorial habits of Indians. Even in their imitation of the Western clothes, the Hindus are so poor that they easily make a farce of it. They neither use the standard material for their garments nor stick to the original shape of the Western pattern, nor are able to maintain them properly. In spite of the Indian compromise with sartorial predicament, they continue to indulge in their arrogance and snobbery.

The beauty of clothes has, of course, got to be supported by the beauty of the human body. Chaudhuri shows how the Hindus have failed to achieve the necessary concordance between the body and the clothing. The linear beauty of woman when seen from a lateral angle, depends a lot upon the poetic cascade of long hair, but as Chaudhuri deplores, the Hindu woman, nowadays has begun to spoil it by cutting her hair, thus playing the sedulous ape to the Western woman. He also shows the folly of the Hindu woman who instead of achieving a 'glossy finish' for her hair by oiling it, turns it into 'horse hair' thereby spoiling the crinal beauty. Similarly, the Hindu woman's habit of powdering her face takes away the ivory look from her and turns her skin into a 'suede leather.' The habit of painting the lips with red does not always produce the happy effect. The contrast between the red colour on the lips and the dark face of the Hindu lady is so sharp that it creates a meretricious look. The growing habit of 'mammary and even mamillary ostentation' and 'the exhibition of the posterior' by the Hindu lady is deplorably ridiculous, sensual, ugly, provocative and shameless. Obviously, all these recent habits of the Indian-Hindu woman are shown by Chaudhuri to be anachronistic and incongruous in the Indian context and produce a look of cheapness and vulgarity.

Sometimes the sartorial fashions become so unhealthy from the Indian point of view that they become matters necessitating police control. Chaudhuri says: "The fashions have even become a police matter, because they are being connected with a scandal which is growing in all the big 'Indian cities." (133) The dowdyism, eve-teasing and molestation of girls and women, which have been growing in the streets and on the University campuses in India are all directly or indirectly caused by the 'provocative' and 'glamorous' methods of feminine dressing or clothing, which have a touch of sensuality. Chaudhuri is very correct when he shows the connection between the cheapening of clothes and the vulgarity of the Indian film world. "Our cinema has reached a level whose degradation is not approached even by the lowest films from Hollywood." (139) Then Chaudhuri shows how the Indian politician also has a large share in contributing to the sartorial ugliness of the people.

Culture in the Vanity Bag shows Chaudhuri's serious approach to the sartorial habits of Indians. He analyzes the philosophy of clothing in a very sophisticated manner armed with the historical sense. He has shown how the Hindus are casual and mindless in their imitation of the Muslim or British clothes and how they are not bothered about contradictions in their sartorial habits. The book is historical, analytical and satirical at the same time and holds a mirror to Chaudhuri's microscopic intelligence and incisive analysis.

NOTE

1. Nirad C. Chaudhuri, *Culture in the Vanity Bag* (Bombay: Jaico, 1976).

Thy Hand, Great Anarch: Autobiography as History

BASAVARAJ S. NAIKAR

Whereas *Autobiography of an Unknown Indian* depicts the first fifty years of his life, *Thy Hand, Great Anarch!* may be said to be an extension and a complementary sequence to it. There is no clear-cut division between the two autobiographical works as far as the time and theme are concerned. *Thy Hand, Great Anarch!* which includes some facts of his early life microscopically picturized in *Unknown Indian*, aims at giving a relatively vaster picture of his later life. If the *Unknown Indian* offers a close-up picture, *Thy Hand* offers a panoramic picture of Nirad C. Chaudhuri's life. Insofar as its width and large rhythms of life depicted in it are concerned, it assumes the dimension of an epic. It happens to be one of the lengthiest autobiographies ever written in the world. The one autobiography that can easily be compared with *Thy Hand* is perhaps Bertrand Russell's. Normally autobiographies are likely to be arbitrary and slipshod, but writers like Nirad Chaudhuri have shown how even autobiograhies could be written seriously, systematically and artistically. As Northrop Frye has pointed out, the writing of autobiographies involves artistic selection and concentration:

> Autobiography is another form which merges with the novel by a series of insensible gradations. Most autobiographies are inspired by a creative, and therefore fictional impulse to select only those events and experiences in the writer's life that go to build up an integrated pattern. This pattern may be something larger than himself with which he has come to identify

himself, or simply the coherence of his character and attitudes.[1]

Although *Thy Hand* can be loosely called an autobiography, its detailed study shows that it is not a pure autobiography; it contains a heavy dose of memoir as well. An autobiographer records his own experiences as a participant in the events of life, whereas a memoir-writer records his experiences as an observer of other people and events happening around him. Thus the heavy element of memoir which is just a little less than half of the whole book may be said to be complementary to the autobiographical element in it. Thus Chaudhuri the participant supports Chaudhuri the spectator in giving a comprehensive picture of not only an extraordinarily sensitive Indian, but of the large spans of historical events and movements.

As far as Chaudhuri's individual experiences are concerned, *Thy Hand* offers a greater number of details than the *Unknown Indian*. For example, he describes his intellectual growth by detailing the reading of important books. His reading of Fallodon's *Recreation*, a collection of lectures delivered at Harvard University disturbed him very deeply. But he immensely enjoyed reading Margot Asquith's *Autobiography* and was deeply influenced by Vallery-Radot's life of Louis Pasteur, journals like *The Nation*, *Times Literary Supplement* etc. These details are not mentioned in *Unknown Indian*. The charismatic influence of his teacher Bibhuti Babu on his intellectual life occupies a good deal of space in *Thy Hand* which does not find a place in *Unknown Indian*. Chaudhuri describes the poverty, personal peculiarities, love affairs, outward callousness and inward tenderness of Bibhuti Babu very realistically and graphically. The reader is easily convinced about how and why Chaudhuri was deeply influenced and inspired by Bibhuti Babu. He acknowledges the help and encouragement he received from Bibhuti Babu to write and publish his articles in the British owned magazines like *The Statesman*.

Chaudhuri describes his mania for buying books even when he was unemployed and his chronic poverty. His inability to pay the rent of his room (while trying to do his M.A.) and the dues to the booksellers and his humiliation by the landlord are narrated in a very touching manner. His poverty is closely associated with the unemployment. His temporary appointments with magazines like *Sanibarer Chhitti* and *Prabhasi* do not solve his financial problems. But his appointment as Secretary to Sarat Chandra Bose not only lessens his financial anxiety, but enriches his experience of life in general and of political life of India in particular. Again he works for *The Modern Review*, *The Free Press Journal* (renamed as *Free India*) and many other journals including the Bengali ones. Because of his incurable poverty, he was compelled even to resort to ghost-writing, though it was not approved by his wife. Later he was appointed as a literary assistant to a very wealthy Bengali Ph.D. holder, namely Satya Churn Law for five years from 1937 to 1942. Since Dr. Law was an ornithologist and maintained many aviaries, Chaudhuri's close proximity with him helped him to gain a scientific knowledge of Indian birds. But that did not solve his financial problem. A little later, Nalini Kanta Sarkar took pity on Chaudhuri and helped him to get a job in All India Radio of Delhi with a high salary which was almost triple of what he used to get earlier. Thus Chaudhuri's long drawn poverty fortunately came to an end. His wife never complained or quarreled with him about his poverty—which is an evidence of greatness rarely found in modern Indian wives.

In *Thy Hand,* Chaudhuri offers a detailed picture of his professional life which is not given in *Unknown Indian*. He mentions the details of his strenuous life. As he worked with two masters i.e. Sarat Chandra Bose and Dr. Law, he had to shuttle between them almost all through the day. Consequently the strain of work told upon his health adversely. Though Chaudhuri was only forty years, he looked like a men of seventy years. But the one great advantage of working with Sarat Chandra Bose was that it helped him enrich his experience of life and he could observe the Indian political life from very close quarters. He describes Sarat Chandra Bose's discipline, liberality, generosity, efficiency and anti-British views very minutely. The diverse kinds of people including young and old, normal and peculiar who used to visit Sarat Chandra Bose, extended Chaudhuri's knowledge of human nature.

Chaudhuri's appointment in the All India Radio at Delhi at the age of fortyfive brought a remarkable change in his life as far as his financial security was concerned. He records his impressions about Delhi very honestly. He, for example, suffered a lot in the summer heat of Delhi and even had a heat stroke. But he was quite successful in his career as a military commentator and earned the admiration of British officers for his intelligence, good English (both spoken and written). Thus he had some temporary professional satisfaction in the All India Radio of Delhi. But this sense of satisfaction did not last long. At the time of retirement Chaudhuri's publication of his *Autobiography of an Unknown Indian* caused a great deal of jealousy among his colleagues who tried to harm him materially. His service papers were not properly recommended or attended to, in spite of his serious attempts and appeals. Consequently, he was retired on the due date, but his gratuity was not sanctioned to him on technical grounds. Thus his professional career ended on a note of disappointment. Finally after retirement he was offered the job of an editor of an English bulletin on a meagre but fixed salary. *Thy Hand, Great Anarch!*, thus, offers a panoramic picture of his professional life from his youth upto his old age with all the oscillation of his financial status. The reader cannot help pitying the financial insecurity of Chaudhuri in spite of the latter's being a brilliant scholar of international reputation. Chaudhuri has, obviously shown how a sensitive soul is compelled to suffer in the callous bureaucratic set-up of India.

Chaudhuri's literary or scholarly growth is closely linked with his professional life. *Unknown Indian* has already described his scholarly quest microscopically, but *Thy Hand* offers some more details of his scholarly life which are complementary to those of *Unknown Indian*. His scholarly attitude and obsession could be seen in his habit of voracious reading of encyclopaedic range. Eager to find a direction for his life in the form of a vocation, he went on reading several classics including Margot Asquith's *Autobiography*, Vallery-Radot's life of Louis Pasteur and journals like *The Nation* and *The Times Literary Supplement*. He mentions how his bibliomania in spite of his chronic poverty was disapproved by his relatives. One can easily perceive how in his life, reading, reflection and journalistic publication went almost hand in hand, thereby helping him consolidate his vision of life gradually and microscopically. Though he was initially interested in Bengali literature, he could not approve of the crude treatment of sexual life in it. He, therefore, grew disillusioned with it so much that he finally gave it up. But he kept his interest in journalistic writing in English alive and was appreciated by many intelligent British officers. Because of his scholarly pursuits, he was in epistolary contact with great scholars of the world. Being a student of history, he was in touch with the great historian Arnold Toynbee and used to get replies from him for his queries.

Thy Hand assumes the meta-autobiographical dimension in its description of the genesis, composition and publication of the earlier one i.e. *Autobiography of an Unknown Indian* which may be compared to a box within a box. *Thy Hand, Great Anarch!* thus achieves a sort of self-reflexivity and reveals several interesting details. Chaudhuri mentions how in 1947 he thought he might die within two or three years and how he decided to write his autobiography as he could not write a history of India for lack of facilities required for it. He is typically frank and honest in confessing that his insomnia and distress egged him on to write his autobiography. He mentions how he took nine months to write the first draft of it. He wanted to publish it abroad, but did not know any publisher. But luckily his colleague in AIR, Melville de Mellow, took the manuscript to England and arranged for its publication by the Macmillan publishers of London in 1951. Chaudhuri was naturally very grateful to Melville de Mellow. The book was reviewed very favourably in the western press especially in England and America which gave Chaudhuri a sense of fulfilment. It also gave him some sort of material success. It widened the vista of his social life including the circle of friends. Consequently he was invited by the BBC to go to England for five weeks in 1955.

But there was also a negative side to the publication of the autobiography. The Indian reviewers condemned the book totally. Krishna Menon, the High Commissioner to London was said to be very angry with it. Chaudhuri's success created great jealousy among his close Bengali friends who tried to harm him materially. A close friend of his wrote an anonymous letter to the Government Department to proscribe the book. Though the green-eyed monster played havoc with Chaudhuri's life, he could not harm him totally. On the contrary, it inspired Chaudhuri to write more and more so that he could scale greater heights of literary success.

The family life depicted by Chaudhuri in *Thy Hand, Great Anarch!* is more elaborate than the one briefly mentioned in *Autobiography of an Unknown Indian*. The emotional ups and downs experienced by him are graphically described here and touch the chords of our heart. Like any autobiography written honestly and realistically, it offers a wealth of material for psycho-analytical critics. The first major event in his emotional life happens to be the death of his mother when he was only twenty six. As he mentions, this event had a very deep influence upon his mind and made him very sad and pessimistic in life. Under the pessimistic influence of his mother's death, he wrote a story about funeral ceremonies.

Although Chaudhuri had the juvenile habit of dreaming about a girl of seventeen years, he was not lucky enough to go in for a love marriage. Though he postponed his marriage by about ten years, he was compelled by the contingencies of his life to get married finally to an educated girl in 1932. But after marriage, he never repented it as his wife happened to be not only educated but very understanding and cooperative. Chaudhuri honestly confesses that his marriage gave him an emotional stability and a direction to his life. That is the reason why he says, "Had I not married my life would certainly have been lost like a river in a desert. Marriage made the river cut through rock and push through shoals to reach the sea."[2] He also mentions how he was lucky in the sense that although he was physically unimpressive, he was given the daughter by his parents-in-law considering his 'education.' Chaudhuri, thus, settled down to the regular matrimonial life. Later he narrates the expansion of his family gradually. He got a male child who was pet-named as 'snubby' and christened as Kirti-Narayana. Again joy and sorrow went on alternating in his life. Chaudhuri, for example, lost his father when he was thirty six years old. A little later he lost his mother-in-law also who was about fifty years old and who was worried about her son-in-law's financial insecurity.

Chronic poverty seemed to be a very close companion of Nirad Chaudhuri. His life was not a bed of roses but one bestrewn with thorns all along. He was so impecunious that he could not pay the bill for the daily milk required for his children. Chaudhuri is very honest in acknowledging the humanitarian help of the milkman who went on supplying milk to his family although he was not sure of the payment of his bill. Similarly he records with gratitude a boy-servants's loyalty to him and his family. He acknowledges the greatness of his wife who never complained about his poverty or quarrelled with him. This is, indeed, a very rare quality in a normal Hindu wife.

Chaudhuri's honesty of expression and purity of character are at once revealed in his reference to an incident that happened in Delhi. When he was passing through a lane of Delhi, some pimp tried in vain to ask him if he wanted 'a pretty little wench from Bombay.' But the second pimp told the first that the gentleman i.e. Chaudhuri never went to prostitutes. Chaudhuri rightly mentions that "that was the most resounding and prized certificate of character I ever got in my life." (713)

Chaudhuri's sense of humour can be seen in his description of himself as 'Kuttawallah Bengali Babu,' a nickname given by the people of Delhi who used to observe him going every evening with an Alsatian dog.

Chaudhuri happens to be a very keen observer of life around him and has a novelist's capacity to describe the scene in a very graphic manner. He, thus, brings the richness of fictive narration to the autobiography which could have been a bald reportage in the hands of a lesser writer. His microscopic observation and almost photographic capture of the details of Nature and its beauty are remarkable. In *Thy Hand, Great Anarch!*, he has a few passages describing the beauty of Nature of different parts of India. For example, while he deplores the Bengali insensibility to Nature, he mentions his own sudden discovery of the beauty of Bengali Nature by saying that there is a close connection between water and Bengali life. Similarly he refers to river Meghna and compares it with the other lakes and oceans of the world. He describes the autumn season in Bengal in 1935 including the dust in the street very minutely.

Likewise, Chaudhuri's description of the narrow lanes of Benaras and the serene sculpture of Sarnath is very graphic and almost photographic. It is because of his fascination for Nature that he studied the Himalayan hydrography and tried to learn some moral and political lessons from it. Similarly, his description of the Temple of Jagannath at Puri and the ocean is very elaborate and picturesque.

After getting a regular job at AIR, Chaudhuri migrated to Delhi where the contrast between Calcutta and Delhi enabled him to observe the latter city very meticulously. He was really struck by the unimpressive look of the city of Delhi and suffered a heat stroke in summer. He honestly records the dust, dust-storms and locusts of Delhi. His observations of Delhi and its life are very sharp. He refers to seven Delhis and calls New Delhi the eighth one. He observes the habit of the people of Delhi urinating at a wall or a post. He points out the dominance of commercial life in Delhi including wholesale business and import of foreign goods. He observes how the population of Delhi consists of Muslims and Hindus. He shows his scholarly admiration for the architectural beauty and grandeur of Red Fort and Qutab Minar, the melacnholic grandeur of Tughlaqabad. He exhibits the perceptiveness of an art-critic and art-historian in his admiration for Islamic architecture, painting and civilization. He rightly opines that one can study the evolution of Muslim architecture from 12th century to the 18th century of Delhi, although not all the greater monuments are there.

Chaudhuri's close association with Sarat Chandra Bose gave him a rich experience and knowledge of human nature in particular. This aspect of experience was not offered in *Unknown Indian* but it occupies a major portion in *Thy Hand.* Nirad Chaudhuri brings in the richness of fiction and its narration to his autobiography by offering a very graphic picture of his daily experience at Sarat Chandra Bose's house. His description of Bose's palatial house with all its paraphernalia like the furniture, garden, servants, maids, eastern and western type of cooking is very minute, elaborate and vivid. One easily gets the impression that Chaudhuri has written a chapter of a novel. Similarly he captures the characteristic features of Sarat Chandra Bose's personality like his discipline, liberality, generosity, efficiency and anti-British views. Chaudhuri's close proximity to the great man teaches him one moral lesson of how to face the obstacles or crises of life immediately. Chaudhuri also came to know all the major cross sections of Indian society—rich and poor; normal and abnormal; rational and irrational; educated and illiterate—which converted him from a taciturn into a relatively sociable man by rubbing off his rough edges.

Chaudhuri's autobiographical *Thy Hand* has a big biographical chunk devoted to the life and career of Rabindranath Tagore. But he is very critical of both Tagore and Bengalis. The biographical-critical account of Tagore reveals as much about Tagore as about Chaudhuri's approach. Personally he had great respect for Tagore the poet, although he deplores the Bengalis's inability to understand or rate him in spite of their provincial vanity. He reveals some very interesting facts about Tagore's personal life and temperament. He mentions how Tagore was a product of interaction between European and Hindu life. He also points out Tagore's contempt for English novels (and even the Russian novel *Anna Karenina*) and even greater contempt for English criticism especially that of Dowden. He shows the paradox of Tagore's life by remarking how Tagore had to depend upon Europe for literary recognition and appreciation in spite of his dislike for British people. Similarly he points out Tagore's alienation from the Bengali society and readership and contempt for their cliches borrowed from English literature. His mention of Tagore's further alienation from Bengali society after receiving the Nobel Prize for his *Gitanjali* in 1913 and his inability to get a D.Litt. degree from Oxford University and many other facts are very interesting revelations not easily available in Tagore criticism elsewhere.

One of the striking features of *Thy Hand, Great Anarch!* is that far from being a bald impersonal account, it projects a typically Chaudhurian point of view which is critical and idiosyncratic at the same time. Being a highly original thinker and a widely read scholar, Nirad Chaudhuri never accepts any fact or interpretation blindly. He analyzes everything from his own rationalistic viewpoint and shocks the people including his readers by rejecting popular, fanatic and convenient views. It is not justifiable to brand his rationalistic views as only Anglomaniac. He uses almost Bertrand Russellian type of chopping logic to deconstruct the meaning of people, things, events, and movements. Among many things that Chaudhuri says about Gandhi, a few can be noted here. His opinion that Gandhi's upbringing in the Vaishnava atmosphere was responsible for his quietistic views held later and that he did not have a higher Brahmanic Hinduism is sophisticated as well as acceptable. Chaudhuri's attribution of the western—especially Christian—admiration for Gandhi to the Christian pacifism is very insightful.

Chaudhuri also offers a very subtle and contrastive picture of Nehru and Subhas Chandra Bose and admires their convictions and qualities. They were two towering personalities who could never meet each other ideologically. Chaudhuri's interpretation of the collaboration between Nehru and Gandhi is interesting and realistic as he calls such a collaboration opportunistic and calculated. In spite of his admiration for Nehru, Chaudhuri comments on his British leanings.

Similarly Chaudhuri is very critical of the Hindu-Muslim as well as Indian-British relationship. He points out how the Hindus and Muslims distrusted and hated each other privately although they pretended to the contrary. Likewise he shows that the Indians and the British hated each other on political grounds, although they had cordial relationships in private emotional aspects. Chaudhuri does not spare the Indians either. He points out the paradoxical nature of Indians who hated the British and yet tried to imitate them. He laughs at the Hindus's oscillation between xenolatry and xenophobia; between chauvinism and mindless imitation. Thus Nirad Chaudhuri's observation of the contradictions of people living in India is an evidence of his perceptiveness and clear-cut thinking backed up by his deep knowledge of Indian history.

That Chaudhuri is an extraordinary intellectual is evident in everything that he writes. That he is one of the great modern thinkers of India is incontrovertible. But his thinking is not an abstract one like that of philosophers but concrete one that is typical of historians, sociologists, ethnologists and political thinkers. Since Chaudhuri himself is a very perceptive student of history, his thinking is naturally backed up by a sharp historical sense and contemporary observation. From the childhood itself, he had a fascination for an intellectual life. He says: "I never lost my capacity to think even under the worst of conditions. In fact, it was during this period that I arrived at the ideas about our life, history and civilization which have remained the basis of my interpretation of these things." (392) He had thus a great respect and capacity for 'mental creation,' but he did not like to be trapped in grooved thinking.

He did not have any respect for a closed system of thought which is normally enjoyed by a large number of traditional scholars of India. On the contrary, he has great love and respect for liberal thinking which is based upon past experience and revised by fresh one. His intellectual sharpness, meticulousness, industry, precision and abundance of information are more than evident in *Thy Hand, Great Anarch!* There is ample evidence in it to show how his intellectuality is supported by his bibliomania, journalistic career and intellectual interaction with great scholars of the world. The external evidence for his intellectuality can be seen in many of his brain-teasing books like *The Continent of Circe*, *To Live or Not to Live*, *Hinduism* and so on. His comments on Indo-British relationship, the Indian National Congress and the International situation of the two world wars are pregnant with vast historical and contemporary knowledge.

It is but natural for an extraordinary intellectual like Nirad Chaudhuri to codify the philosophy of his life at least in the evening of his life. Whereas the *Autobiography of an Unknown Indian* was written during the meridian stage of his life, *Thy Hand, Great Anarch!* is written at the dusk of his life. There is, therefore, no attempt at the codification of his world view in the *Unknown Indian*, but *Thy Hand, Great Anarch!* has a place for such codification as it helps him to look back at his past life—doubts, beliefs, dilemmas, frustrations and joys—and generalize the essence of his existence. Hence his generalization or codification tends to be philosophical and formulaic. The crystallization of his world view is marked by his transparent honesty and scintillating ideation. He relegates the codification to the Epilogue of his epical autobiography and names it as *Credo ut Intelligam*, a typically pedantic label. The straightforward observations made in this section are very significant in that they help the reader unlock the mystery of Chaudhuri's life, worldview and interpretation.

Some of the remarks made by him are very interesting and comparable to those of many philosophical thinkers. His frankness as well as honesty could be seen in the confession of his loss of faith in Hinduism as well as all other established religions at the early age of eighteen. Yet he developed some faith as a rational man though he did not care for intuition or supra-rational truths.

He was more inclined towards the matter of fact or cautious interpretations than to imaginative ones of history. But the paradox of his life is that he prematurely realized that there is much sorrow in much knowledge. He honestly confesses that he suffered more from his rational outlook than from his crushing poverty.

Chaudhuri, in spite of being an agnostic, has developed a kind of faith. He says, "I have found peace in a new form of monism. I have been able to realize that the universe and I are one, and not at odds with each other. This is the very basis of my new faith." (945) He has achieved some kind of unity with the world. This union happens to be more an intellectual one than an emotional one. He also knows how he has to undergo the dark night of the soul before achieving the enlightenment of faith. "I would say that intellectual discipline is the purgatory through which a man must pass in order to reach the paradise of faith, and the passage can be, in fact, it often is, torture." (945) Chaudhuri has, obviously, passed through the purgatory to reach the final faith of his life which, he says, is based upon his belief in biology and physics. One should specially note that his faith is not based on religion and mythology. Thus he believes in a scientific or materialistic vision of life. He offers eight points of his belief which can be stated briefly: (1) The cosmos is not material in the ordinary sense; (2) phenomena or matter are subjective sensory perceptions; (3) the distinctions between matter and spirit are fictitious; (4) the universe is a flow or continuum; (5) there is no conflict in the cosmos as a process; (6) body and soul are not distinct; (7) there is neither personal God nor are there many gods and (8) intellectual knowledge is partial knowledge and therefore it is only *credo ut intelligam*.

Many of Chaudhuri's philosophical observations are very deep and interesting and invite comparison with those of other serious thinkers of the world. According to him, man's body procreates, but his mind creates cosmos in a new dimension. Showing the difference between man and animal, he says: "The animal is an automatic creator, but man, besides being that, is also a creator by volition." (952) He confesses: "I myself have arrived at a non-religious view of the universe as a creative process on the strength of the theory of evolution." (955) Though his faith is based on science, he knows that it is nearest to Hindu monism. He confesses that he believes in biological evil and not in theological or ethical evil.

Thus the philosophical strands of his worldview are made explicit at the end of his autobiography. The existential abundance of experience is followed by a process of essentialization. This kind of codification of his faith or vision of life naturally gives a wholeness to the autobiography which shows the transformation of the protagonist's experience into knowledge.

The most conspicuous aspect of *Thy Hand, Great Anarch!* is that only less than half of it can be called autobiography in the strict sense, whereas more than half of it has the quality of a memoir. In other words, Chaudhuri the spectator happens to be more dominant than Chaudhuri the participant. But what one appreciates in it is that the memoir element is organically linked to the autobiographical element. But what disappoints the reader is that the memoir element grows far too unwieldy to balance the autobiographical one. In this respect *Thy Hand, Great Anarch!* invites comparison with Nehru's *Autobiography* in which Nehru the spectator appears to be stronger than Nehru the participant. A large part of the memoir element in *Thy Hand, Great Anarch!* is devoted to the depiction of political picture of India, especially the pre-Independence one. He offers an elaborate picture of the Hindu-Muslim hatred; the dynamic role played by Mahatma Gandhi, Jawaharlal Nehru and Subhas Chandra Bose; the Congress Party, the Hindu-British hatred; governmental and civic politics in Bengal; India's struggle for freedom with exact dates, facts and documentary evidence. The large part of the book, which has the quality of a memoir about it, tries to relate Chaudhuri's individual life to the larger rhythm of national life. Yet one is compelled to say that this section is more enjoyable for political scientists and historians than for students of literature. The memoir element is so dominant that Chaudhuri's strictly autobiographical life appears to be rather insignificant comparatively. This is not to deny the extraordinary importance of the historico-political picture of India offered by Chaudhuri as a contemporary record of life. What is disconcerting to a literary critic is the disproportionate combination of the elements of autobiography and memoir.

Nirad Chaudhuri has given an artistic beauty to his autobiography by the use of his imagistic style. He exhibits his great scholarship in the employment of images borrowed from a wide range of fields of knowledge. The width of his field of references is almost Shakespearean. Geographical images are quite common not only in this autobiography, but also in his other works. For example, referring to his late marriage, Chaudhuri offers a metaphor of river. He says, "Marriage made the river cut through rock and push through shoals to reach the sea." (343) Describing his experience of poverty and insecurity, he says, "It was like being on a raft after being picked up by a ship." (364) He describes the conquest of Bengal through a geographical simile. "The recovery and conquest of Bengal by Clive in 1757 was like the breaking out of a river through the highest section of a mountain range near its source, whereas in the period with which I am dealing in this book the river of the British Empire in India split itself into narrow and sluggish channels in a flat delta to be silted up wholly or to grope its way out in mangrove swamps." (394)

Being an ardent student of history, Nirad Chaudhuri is naturally inclined to use many historical images to highlight his point of view. Referring to the unromantic ugliness of New Delhi, Chaudhuri says that it could not be depicted in a very romantic style. He employs a historical image to convey his sense of irony. "Cleopatras did not lie on the beds of New Delhi bungalows and so there could be no question of raising the ghost of a rose in any of them." (730)

Nirad Chaudhuri employs many socio-political images to convey his ideas powerfully. He describes the shameless opportunism of Indian politicians who showed their true colours after the transfer of power from the British to the Indians, through a very frank socio-political image. "All the nationalist beggars who filed into the enormous buildings bequeathed to them by the fleeing British, realized what treasures were to be looted by them, and they must have thought their sacrifices were at last rewarded." (383) Chaudhuri's comparison and contrast between Mahatma Gandhi and Stalin is expressed through a political simile, "In nothing else have Western writers gone more wrong about Gandhi than in overlooking his insatiable love of power and implacability in its pursuit. In this he was in no way different from Stalin. Only, he did not have to kill because he could eliminate his opponents equally well by means of his non-violent Vaishnava method." (528)

Chaudhuri offers a very interesting animal image to describe Mahatma Gandhi, "On the animal plane Gandhi suggested the primitive tarrier to me." (437) Such an image can speak of Nirad Chaudhuri's uninhibitedness and liberal imagination.

Likewise he is quite fond of using medical imagery whenever it is required. Pointing out the sympathetic relation between Bengalis and the Japanese, he says, "The truth was that the Bengalis who had become nationalist drug addicts were bringing down the Japanese to their level." (650) At some other place, Chaudhuri describes the Indian officers through a clinical image, "They were overwhelmed by the patriotism and self-sacrifice of Subhas Chandra Bose. He was the man who wiped some of the filth from the body of these dirty military prostitutes." (787)

Many matrimonial images are also employed by Nirad Chaudhuri at appropriate places. Describing the relationship between Subhas Chandra Bose and Mahatma Gandhi, Chaudhuri points out the period of waiting and anxiety for the two brothers through a matrimonial image, "For Subhas Bose and his brother Sarat Bose these months were a period of fervid pre-material honeymoon." (500) When in 1939. Paderewski sent a telegram to Gandhi for sympathy towards Poland longing for freedom, Gandhi sent a very sympathetic reply. But he also knew that "to ask the Indian people to have any sympathy for the Polish people at that time was like asking a wife to have sympathy for the cast-off mistress of her husband." (552) Nirad Chaudhuri's use of the matrimorial image to describe the political situation is an evidence of his liberal thinking and imagination.

Because of his wide range of scholarship and voracious reading, Nirad Chaudhuri employs a variety of literary images in *Thy Hand, Great Anarch!* as also in his other works. The international range of his literary scholarship could easily be sensed in his imagery. When Nalini Kanta Sarkar took pity on Chaudhuri and helped him to finally get a job in All India Radio in Delhi, Chaudhuri was very grateful to him. He describes his own dire need through a literary image: "I accepted the offer at once. For me it turned out to be like the camel's thrusting of its nose into the Bedouin's tent." (405) Referring to the Bengali envy, Chaudhuri says that all the great Bengal produced in the 19th century was "a group of Dantean figures, in death sleeping far away from their ungrateful country." (665) Chaudhuri describes his own rational growth in a literary-cum-eschatalogical image, "I would say that intellectual discipline is the purgatory through which a man must pass in order to reach the paradise of faith." (945)

Nirad Chaudhuri is very fond of using Biblical imagery (which is part of literary imagery) to describe various situations of life. It shows his subtle understanding of the Biblical lore and his imaginative capacity to use it appropriately. Nirad Chaudhuri employs a Biblical image to describe Mahatma Gandhi's relationship with the Working Committee to Congress, "Mahatma Gandhi was never a member of the Working Committee. But he hovered above it like the Holy Spirit, and sometimes even descended in the form of the dove of peace." (444) Referring to the corruption of the Congress members, Chaudhuri says, "It was as if the Congress organization as Adam had been coaxed by the practical leaders as a Congress Eve formed out of the ribs of Gandhi, to eat the forbidden fruit." (445) Chaudhuri opines that Indian politicians like Subhas Chandra Bose would be happier in prison than being pestered by visitors. He, therefore, says: "Forced imprisonment was for them what self-imposed retreats were for devout Christians." (478) Nirad Chaudhuri makes very harsh comments on Nehru's pro-British policies, "Joan of Arc was inspired in her patriotism by the vision of the Virgin, but Nehru was both inspired and sustained in his by the apparition of Britain as the Evil One." (543) All these Biblical metaphors testify to Nirad Chaudhuri's sound knowledge of Christian theology as well as very perceptive observation of Indian things, beings and situations.

Since Nirad Chaudhuri knew the private as well as the public face of the Gandhian Congress, he describes it through a theatre-image, "or varying the metaphor, I would say that I saw something of the greenroom behind the lighted stage and the actors without the make-up as well as with its application." (434) One can easily understand how the metaphor is resonant of many things connected with drama-acting.

Sometimes Nirad Chaudhuri uses architectural imagery to drive home his point. That is ascribable to his sound knowledge of art-history and theory. He describes the ICS officers and clerks through an architectural image. "When Llyod George described the Indian Civil Service as the steel frame of the Government of India he forgot to mention that the Bengali clerk was its concrete foundation." (729) Referring to Gandhi's encouragement of bogus membership of the Congress by rich people, Chaudhuri says, "While this was happening on the ground floor of political life, on the upper floors there was vicious competition for office and other profits." (456)

Thy Hand, Great Anarch! is, thus an important autobiography which gives a very honest picture of Nirad C. Chaudhuri's life of continuous struggle and of the major historical events of Indian life in general. Although one may not like the disproportionate elements of autobiography and memoir in it, one feels that both the student of literature and the student of modern history can benefit from it by turns.

NOTES

1. Northrop Frye, *Anatomy of Criticism* (New York: Atheneum Press, 1970), p. 307.
2. Chaudhuri C. Chaudhuri, *Thy Hand, Great Anarch!* (London: Chatto and Windus, 1987), p. 343.

Atmaghati Bangali: A Dis/Passionate Critique

RAMA KUNDU

Calcutta being the original stronghold of the British in India, Bengal had to come in early and direct contact with the colonial 'culture' and 'anarchy' alike and naturally the response of the English-educated Bengali elite of the first generation was ambivalent towards the British as evidenced by writers like Dinabandhu Mitra, Bankimchandra, *et al* around the mid-nineteenth century. They registered their fascination for the European culture, its 'sweetness and light' as well as their rejection of the 'barbarism and philistinism' as manifested in the practice of the colonists. Rabindranath Tagore subsequently came to represent the maturest response to this new wave; he assimilated and transcended both the Western influence and the Indian heritage to offer a new approach of living exchange on equal levels. Nirad C. Chaudhuri, born towards the end of the nineteenth century, after twenty-six years of Tagore, exhibits an interesting outlook. He seems to have overcome the contradictions that characterized the early Bengali elite, but not in the Tagorean way. His preference for the British—as people, culture, society—is unambiguous; he shows no oscillations like many writers of his earlier generation between their commitment to the indigenous tradition and their longing for the new ways shipped over from England.

Personally, too, he has chosen a life of self-exilement in Oxford since 1970. Even before that, since 1942, he has been outside Bengal. But this should not necessarily mean that he has forgotten Bengal altogether. *Atmaghati Bangali*, published in 1988, on his ninety-first year, bears evidence to the writer's nostalgia for the place where he was born and lived for fifty-five years. However, even nostalgia may not mellow the critic within a man like him. The present volume bears ample proof to the complex response of Niradbabu to his motherland. Chaudhuri's English books are widely read. But his few Bengali books are understandably not so well-known or publicized. This book gives intimate glimpses of the Bengalee/'Bangal' (his own term) hiding within the 'continent'al Saheb.

Atmaghati Bangali is planned to cover the span of the entire nineteenth-century Bengal as also occasional references to the twentieth century. But the focus has been laid on a very limited area/section of the Bengalee society and culture; it is the highly educated section of Bengal who were never too many.

This second Bengali book by Nirad C. Chaudhuri (the first one was also about the Bengalee life, i.e., *Bangali Jibane Ramani* 1968) projects a thesis: the Bengalee life had once touched the acme in various fields under the impact of English language and literature; but since the turn of the century, and especially since 1935, Bengal has started on a declining course; symptoms of decadence are appearing everywhere. This saddens the writer. So, in order to remind the Bengalee of his lost glory, and of the forgotten history of his Renaissance that Nirad C. writes this book with the fond hope that this remembrance may bring them back from their present 'suicidal' (*atmaghati*) course and turn towards another Renaissance.

Chaudhuri's book is, as it were, Gibbon in miniature in the Bengalee context. It is about the rise, decline and fall of Bengalee life during a certain period of recent history. In this volume the writer assumes the role of a social historian—quite entertaining though—as he sums up within the brief span of 200 pages the social-intellectual life of the Bengalee over a phase of more than hundred years. It was a phase which, according to Chaudhuri, marked the 'blossoming' of a new consciousness in the social and individual lives of the Bengalee under the impact of Western education. The writer lovingly describes this 'blossoming'; but his ulterior aim is to expose the subsequent tragedy of Bengal compared to its earlier promises and excellence.

The material is arranged into ten chapters. The first chapter, "Rebirth of the Bengalee," traces the change in the 'Bengalee life'

(Chaudhuri's 'Bengalee life' applies to a very limited section) to the inauguration of the Hindu College in Calcutta in 1817. With the introduction of English as the medium for education, and with the establishment of the University of Calcutta in 1857, this process of change was further strengthened and the new Bengalee consciousness began to take a mature shape and expression. The writer defines this development as a 'mental revolution' or 'Renaissance' of Bengal. In this connection, he also alludes to the other Renaissance of Bengal which had been ushered in the sixteenth century by Chaitanyadeb with his new cult of love. Chaitanya too had appeared against a similar backdrop—a society stagnated by unquestioning surrender to irrational/inhuman rites and rituals. The writer also shows that the cleansing effects of Chaitanya's cult of humanism based on devotion and love had already disappeared from the pre-British Bengal, and its place was usurped by coarse vulgarity. Around mid-nineteenth century, the educated Bengalee's acquaintance with English literature brought an over-all change to the scene. "The new generation of Bengalis saw in the intellectual life of Europe a force to extend their mental horizon." (19) Chaudhuri's perceptive mind recaptures the fascination and enthusiasm of the new generation of Bengalees around the time and their joyous response to the surge of new ideas. As the educated Bengalee found his own heritage inadequate, he naturally turned toward the vista of Western thoughts and life freshly opened up before him. The new way was so indisputably attractive that there was no difference of response in this respect between the liberal and conservative elites of Bengal as represented by Bankimchandra and Vivekananda. The real difference rose between the Sanskrit-educated pundits and the English-educated elites who did not understand each other's language. The writer reiterates Vivekananda's view that as Europe had once "drawn from the fountains of the Greeks" Young Bengal drew from the fountain of European thought through English language.

Chapter Two, "On the Eve of the Renaissance," explodes the myth that the Bengalees were the direct inheritors of ancient Hindu civilization and the heritage continued unimpaired till the British advent in our socio-cultural life, and as a result there was the glorious synthesis that determined and coloured the new Bengalee life of the nineteenth century. The writer holds that everybody in those days would have spoken in terms of the merging and synthesis of East and West. Even Tagore too had propounded this message of synthesis and exchange in his 'Bharattirtha.' All the Bengalees, including the writer himself, had accepted this message with respect and trust. But later, around 1925, the turn of thing in Bengal had set him wondering if there was really any clash or synthesis here between Eastern and Western civilization. He argues that actually people were paying lip-service to the programme of upholding some so-called 'Indian tradition,' while blindly following the Western way at the same time. Niradbabu seems to find an explanation in the social situation of Bengal on the eve of the British onslaught. He maintains that the Bengalee daily life during this period had no connection with the pre-Muslim Hindu civilization and its ancient scholarship and culture. As a result, our life had assumed the easy simple rural way which is defined by the writer as 'folk civilization.' One mature culture had disintegrated and its place was not yet taken by an appropriate substitute. (The British influence had been so eagerly absorbed here because it was expected to fill in this void.) Chaudhuri takes care to remind the reader that two mature trends were still present in the eighteenth century Bengal: the Islamic civilization and the Hindu pundit's study of the 'shastras.' But neither of these formed the main current of Bengalee or Indian culture. The Islamic civilization was mainly confined within the cities and among the rulers, and did not spread among the common Hindu or the poor rural Muslim. The pundit's pursuit of knowledge was also confined within a special and necessarily small circle. The greater mass lived in a primitive, juvenile state. Even the memory of a past and the feeling of a continuity and wholeness that is present in all mature societies was lacking here. The *Ramayana* and the *Mahabharata* operated during this period as the only collective memory of the multifaceted achievements of an ancient Indian civilization. The author suggests that the process of this racial oblivion had probably started with the establishment of the Muslim rule. The Hindu ruler and the aristocratic Hindu society which provided a frame for a rich Hindu culture had been either destroyed or too enfeebled to sustain the ancient trends of a rich civilization. But, the author points out that there was also a positive sequel to this development. This was the period when countless folk religions, folk rites, folk literatures and folk songs sprouted. This rural culture was our only treasure on the eve of the British advent. The author thinks that is the reason why after the re-discovery of the glory of the ancient Hindu civilization in the nineteenth century the educated Bengalees (as also other Indians) became indifferent to their immediate past and became fantasized by their remote past which was often distorted by wishful thinking and too coloured by imagination to emerge as a real strong basis for a healthy cultural exchange on an equal level.

The second chapter is a quite perceptive study of the scene, and an appropriate sequel to the first chapter. But the promise created thus is withdrawn in the subsequent chapters which seem to be often too bookish and marred by casual/one-sided and sometimes absurd observations. Chapter Three, "The Spread and Use of the English Language," starts by rejecting the very common notion that the British had introduced English education to have clerks and employees at low cost as "pure and shameless lie unparalleled in history." The author shows how actually, when English was adopted as medium of education in 1835, all high-ranking British officials residing in India were against the measure.

In this chapter Chaudhuri also casts light on a comparatively unexplored area of our social history: how the knowledge of English literature had come to influence the domestic life of an average educated Bengalee. There was an extraordinary harvest of Bengali translations of European classics and Bengali essays on the European literature, arts, history, philosophy, and both women and men of educated families avidly read them. An interesting feature of this period which Niradbabu rightly points out was that the Bengalee gathered knowledge through English but the newly shaped Bengalee mind found complete and powerful expression of this assimilated knowledge in Bengali literature. The writer contends that the influence of this English-oriented Bengali literature on young minds ran to any extent. He assumes that young men and women tried to shape their lives according to what these writers wrote. Again, the Bengalee writer of the day gathered his material from this new Bengalee life too. Thus the writer and the reader—literature and life—mutually influenced and involved each other. He also points out that English education also enlisted social prestige and was indispensable for a professional career—an observation which is still applicable to Bengal in the 1990s.

Chapter Four, "Result of English Education," refers to the initial excesses caused by the new education. Thus immediately after the opening of the Hindu College, Westernization came to include not only Shakespeare study but also taking wine and beef. Such excesses were ridiculed by eminent Bengalees like Dinabandhu Mitra, Madhusudan Dutta, among others. Bankimchandra, however, had made an objective evaluation of this imitation, conceding the possibility that a conscious imitation of the positive things might also lead to self-improvement.

By means of a few select examples, the author tries to show how pervasive the imitation was. In his characteristic entertaining style (and also a bit nostalgically), Niradbabu recounts the introduction of Western-modelled furniture in rich and upper middle-class houses including hanging lantern, table lamp, mirrors, pictures of landscape as well as pictures/sculptures of naked/draped beautiful women; the extra set of perfect European dress for formal occasions in addition to the indigenous dress for normal occasions; more radical changes took place in the women's dress including use of chemise and shoes. The writer claims that even daily speech used in domestic transactions underwent a change from strong slang to soft sophistication. He also recalls how women of rich families, instead of wasting the entire time in the kitchen, started sewing, knitting, carpet-designing, and, of course novel reading. Sewing was considered a necessary qualification for marriageable girls. Chaudhuri alludes to Tagore's *Gora* as illustration of this new generation of women, and also of the charm they exercised on the young men of the time.

Chapter Five, "Marriage, Conjugal Life and Love," shifts focus from external details to the internal life, the deeper subtleties of man-woman relationship. The basis of the argument here is that the impact of English education was apparent in all the aspects of mental activity in Bengal at the time including man-woman relationship. True, the ritualistic details of marriage remained the same (and these are still continuing more or less unchanged). But at the imaginative level, there was a shift from ancient eroticism or medieval vulgarity to a romanticized emotion. This observation, though interesting, appears at best naive over-simplification if one only looks up the documentary records regarding the woman's lot in Bengal. Romantic/Platonic love could be the subject of literature, or was to be found in the life of very few individuals; but never the general experience. At least where the woman was concerned, it was and has been more or less the same situation of cynical sexploitation through centuries. Thus when the writer contends· "But there cannot be any doubt that due to the new education under the British regime the conjugal life of the Bengalee got completely transformed," (67) it seems too naive an assessment. No less naive is his claim that in those days loyalty to one's wife was a norm of the English society, and the English-educated Bengalee also tried to cast himself into that mould; one would like to ask—'was it so?' and 'how many?'

Again, the writer mentions the occasional conflicts of conscience that arose in the mind of the young Bengalee of the nineteenth century regarding the question of priority between religiosity and love. He explains this moralistic tendency as something anachronistic to the Bengalee tradition and defines it as imported puritanism from England to which was added the old mother cult of Bengal; and the two together made love appear fascinating as well as an embarrassing emotion.

Chapter Six, "Love," continues the attempt to establish that the new concept of love as a romanticized Platonic ideal rather than sex-oriented eroticism was accommodated in the Bengalee life in both marital and extra-marital situations. In this context, the writer makes the fantastic claim that due to the influence of *Romeo and Juliet*, the age of marriage (for girls) in Bengali novels was raised from eleven to sixteen; also teenaged girls (in the novels of Saratchandra for example) emerged with the unrestrained vigour and expression of their romantic love. A new respect for the body of the loved one was seen which was completely absent in the Pre-British tradition-bound Hindu society. Also the careful cultivation of post-marital love stabilised and strengthened the bond between the couple.

Chapter Seven, "In Search of the Woman," describes the enlightened Bengalee's (male) search for the ideal woman in his life;

it was in a way a search for personal fulfilment through the female partner. This reflected a new respect for and appreciation of the woman as an individual which was non-existent in the tradition of Bengal. Again, the woman was considered a kind of succour (that is also a role) for the inevitable sorrows in the man's life which usually came from two main sources: the injustice, contempt, oppression perpetrated by rich/powerful fellow countrymen; secondly from the subordination to the British and the resultant feeling of humiliation. According to the author, the Bengalee male had only one means of salvaging his self-esteem; it was through the love and kindness of the female partner. That the woman was not just a bedtime partner of the husband and a full-time maid servant for the husband's family was (and is) of course a new and reassuring perception; but one wonders how far this perception worked (and works) beyond the pages of imaginative fiction.

Chapter Eight, "Strength of Character and Love of God," brings out how "During this age the Bengalee had shown extraordinary talent as well as strength of character," thanks to the Western puritanic teachings of new morality, manners and austerity. The author mentions Vidyasagar as a supreme example of this phenomenon, for whose likes, principle was an inward or personal view of right conduct.

This perfectly valid observation is followed by an absurd thesis about the Bengali's newly acquired idea of God who came to be looked up to as the saviour in his personal love-life. Here Chaudhuri seems to speak without any basis but his personal feelings and family memories. Hence his argument—though the educated Bengalee Hindu observed all traditional rites, at heart they were conditioned by the Brahma concept of God as propounded by Rammohun—might appear rather surprising to scholars in the area. Though the monotheism of the Brahmas has been traced back by Rammohun himself to the *Upanisads*, according to Niradbabu, the God of the Brahmas was the Christian's God: "There was no doubt about it." (171) However, he finely brings out the common Brahma's conscious attempt at the time to distance himself from the Hindu heritage and environment, which brought him closer to the Christian in thought and life-style. In an atmosphere often marked by unconcealed mutual contempt between the two sects, i.e., the

Hindus and the Brahmas, the latter tilted—rather heavily—towards the West. In his characteristic charming way, Chaudhuri describes the Brahmas of this period who never admitted that they were Hindus by origin and heritage; they used to read the Bible and the European theological texts rather than the ancient Indian literature and scriptures; the idea of community prayer was also taken from the Christians.

In this context the author makes the arbitrary claim that the God of the Protestants had not only conditioned the Bengalee attitude to God but also indirectly influenced his attitude to marriage; earlier it was considered the safe way to have carnal pleasure and children; now an extra dimension was added to it under the Protestants' influence who were against celibacy and held that marriage was ordained by God. Thus marital love came to be considered God's blessing and ordained by God.

In the same chapter, however, Chaudhuri points out a significant historical truth when he says—it was the time when one remarkable and admirable habit of the Bengalee elite was to weigh and assess his own faith and conduct continuously, whether the issue was love of God or pursuit of mortal love. Whatever opinion they arrived at in either public or private matters, whichever course they took or way they behaved, they tried to weigh and consider the arguments on both sides; they did not do anything without this painstaking self-probing—a practice sadly missing in today's Bengal.

Chapter Nine underscores the gulf between today's Bengali life and that of the nineteenth century. The two are, according to the author, so different that today's reader in Bengal may find it difficult to visualize the previous century, and may even find his descripton unbelievable. Chaudhuri also admits here: "in fact the life about which I have written was not the folk-life of that age either; . . . it had far transcended the mundane family life or community life." (183) But the problem, as he rightly perceives, was that even this 'higher' life could not get completely separated from the 'low' or average, and the consequence of the contact was rarely happy. Throughout the nineteenth century, the main feature of the history of Bengal was the clash between the prevailing traditions and the new trends. Here the reader gets an anticipation of the oncoming depression of the last chapter as Chaudhuri points out—with his characteristic boldness and clarity—the negative sides of the situation. He says, where the new trend won in this clash there was happiness, and where it was defeated there was disaster. Here the writer contradicts his earlier enthusiasm to admit that although in the national field the new emerged victorious on the whole, it was not so in the personal sphere. Not only in novels and stories but also in real life, there were such characters who had been shattered due to this clash.

However, a glorious aspect of the time, as the writer recalls, was that a large number of people were motivated towards non-materialistic efforts. If one did nothing else, then at least he would have devoted himself to study. Some became writers, some religious missionaries. Since 1905, when the freedom movement started in right earnest, many became either Congressmen or terrorists. How to earn money or run the family were not questions that bothered them; they were serious idealists who left their mark in various fields of contemporary history; the writer affectionately calls them 'Apanbhola' (unselfconscious) whose number has strikingly fallen in today's Bengal; with his enjoyable self-confidence Niradbabu also includes himself in the list of these 'Apanbholas' among whom have appeared all the excellent Bengalees of modern times.

The tenth and the last chapter, "The Fall of the Bengalee," is more contemplative than descriptive. The writer is saddened at the unrestrained decline of the Bengalee life which turns him a fatalist: "Like the individual," he says, "the life of a community is also conditioned by fate." (197) Here the focus shifts from the past to the present, and the writer makes certain generalizations about the Bengali character, alluding to some of its extraordinary qualities and some serious defects. He holds that in the nineteenth century, the Bengalee had tried to rise and had risen in various fields of public as also private life by dint of his own effort. Even then he could not overcome the innate faults and weaknesses of his character. Anyway, those were kept restrained at the time by his urge to create a new way of life. But since 1917-18, the Bengalee spirit had again started flagging and the defects again swelled up to cover the virtues like weeds in a garden. Here Chaudhuri makes a volley of attacks on the various weaknesses of the Bengalee character with particular emphasis on his lack of firmness. Thus when he served and sacrificed for his country that was an unconscious instinctive act, and the same instinct now drives him along the route of suicidal self-destruction. The book concludes on a note of deep sadness: "I had been in Delhi from 1942 to 1970, and in England since then. But it is less easy to forget one's own race as it is to forget some persons. Yet this remembrance brings nothing but sorrow." (200)

II

Regarding the significance of the Western influence on nineteenth century Bengal, and its tremendous impact on the socio-cultural situation here there is no dispute among critics and no dearth of scholarly research. Niradbabu does not add much in the way of scholarship or explorative analysis in this field. But the book derives its special flavour from the author's personal involvement; he passionately tries to understand the reason of the transience of Bengal's brief Renaissance because he is as emotionally moved by its sad termination as he is nostalgically stirred by its happy memory; an intimate personal touch in every page makes the book what it is.

Neither does the author claim to have made a theoretical discourse or a made-to-order thesis. He clearly points out the difference between his portraiture and that of the present-day Bengali writers with their "loud smatterings of all the fashionable Western cliche." He declares: "I am not prepared to impose geometrical 'cubes' on a natural scene." (183) However, one has got to admit that Niradbabu's honest personal impressions/responses—though never dull—are sometimes no less puzzling than those made-to-order 'cubes.'

Again, there are too many small and not so small holes in the texture of the argument. Also, the unqualified appreciation of the British on almost all the scores may not seem too savoury to a people who had been so long under the British rule. Many of his observations—especially those on the woman's situation—are based purely on his own limited personal experience and on contemporary Bengali novels, and consequently show a serious lack of proportion. Moreover, the rambling style of relaxed recollection frequently hinders rather than helps in projecting an argument pointedly. The argumentation is also not always consistent; it is sometimes brilliantly perceptive, and persuasive, sometimes wildly fantastic, and surprisingly absurd on occasions. The narration is in the tenor of personal recollection, and does not carry the impression of a painstaking researcher's exploration; rather it is frequently weighed down under the pressure of oversimplifications, generalizations, too many diversions.

These are the obvious blemishes of *Atmaghati Bangali*; but the book is much more than these. Nirad C. Chaudhuri can never be accused of one folly, i.e. parochialism. But his apparently sharp criticism of the Bengalee, his grievance against and pain for them only further underscore his love and nostalgia for the place which he has left for ever. This book, written in Bengali, on the Bengalee, in the writer's ninety-first year, bears evidence to this love expressed in the language of passionate criticism. The book combines a touching nostalgia with scathing chastisement; this is also self-criticism, because even when he criticizes, Chaudhuri does not forget that he himself is also a Bengalee. And that accounts for the unique effect of his exhortations.

Sometimes the very boldness of Nirad C.'s comments seems fascinating. For example, his critique of the so-called Bengalee Marxists of today: "The new logicians of Bengal boast: we are Marxists. If they had the least insight into their own character, they would know that they were but repeating Bankimchandra: "The Bengalee is controlled by circumstances, circumstances are never controlled by the Bengalee. Marx had said the same thing about mankind. Such utter lie has never been voiced by any eminent man of talent; because man can control his environment he has risen above animality." (189) The cause of the writer's sorrow is that the Bengalee as a race has failed in this test. Similarly 'outrageous' are his observations on Saratchandra and the weaknesses of the Bengalee character. Nirad C. cannot forgive Saratchandra, in spite of his excellence as a novelist, for his attempt to justify the cowardly, selfish, good-for-nothing characters whose wrongs are typical of the race, and cannot be excused by any means. He also severely castigated what he finds to be the major defects of the Bengalee elite—his contempt for the non-Bengalee, his fondness for pandering his little knowledge, and the inability to see his own past, present and future unbiasedly with reason and intelligence. He thinks that it is this ineptitude that has rendered the Bengalee so vulnerable today.

Indeed, the book as a whole may be considered one long bold exhortation by an "old man with an eagle eye" who has perceived from afar the decadence that has set in here. There can be no dispute among honest, conscient joys Bengalees that West Bengal today is going through a steadily declining path of decadence and slow suicide. *Atmaghati Bangali* is meant to be an appeal-cum-warning to the 'decadent Bengalee of our times who has been cut off from his own indigenous springs of creativity; at the same time, caught up in the throes of ape-like imitation he has forgotten his glorious nineteenth century history of learning and assimilation. That is why Chaudhuri's volume on Bengal remains highly relevant for us today who are undergoing the direct experience of the agony of 'waste' Bengal.

One last query: why did Nirad C. write this book in Bengali? Was it meant to be a very special and exclusive message for the Bengalees alone?

The Self-Destructive Tagore: A Critical Reading

MOHIT K. RAY

Atmaghati Rabindranath or *The Self-Destructive Tagore*[1] constitutes the second volume of Nirad C. Chaudhuri's second Bengali book, *Atmaghati Bengali* or *The Self Destructive Bengalees* (1992), his first Bengali book being *Bengali Jibane Ramani* or *Women in Bengali Life* published in 1968. *The Self-Destructive Tagore*, again is supposed to be in two volumes, the first volume dealing with the period from Tagore's birth (1861) to 1913, the year he received the Nobel Prize for Literature. The second volume which according to Chaudhuri, is to cover the period from 1913 to Tagore's death (1941) has not come out so far. It is doubtful whether it will ever be published. So, here, we are concerned only with the first volume of *The Self-Destructive Tagore*. This book is divided into two parts and each part has a separate introduction. The first part is entitled "Prabhat" or "Dawn" and the second part is entitled "Madhyanha" or "Noon." Chaudhuri uses these diurnal terms possibly bearing in mind that the word "Rabi" in "Rabindranath" means "sun" and the career of Rabindranath can be likened to the diurnal movement of the sun—from sunrise to sunset. Chaudhuri obviously uses these terms metaphorically. As the sun is hottest and strongest in the meridian, similarly Tagore was at the zenith of his glory in 1913 when he received an overwhelming reception in the West and also the Nobel Prize for Literature. Moreover, the first part is intended to give an idea of the real Tagore and the second part is purported to show how the conflict between the real Tagore and the contemporary Bengali society gave birth to a 'false' Tagore who virtually committed suicide.

Tagore scholarship, over the years, has become a heavy industry, and serious scholars devoted to Tagore studies all over the world, have made, and are still making significant contribution to it. Then, why did Chaudhuri, not certainly an acknowledged Tagore expert, decide to write a whole book—ostensibly in two volumes—on Tagore? Furthermore, though a great writer of great accomplishment, Chaudhuri with his idiosyncratic theories has already stimulated a lot of controversy. In this connection, Verghese observes: "Chaudhuri is an Indian who is anti-Indian, an Anglicized Hindu who is critical of other Anglicized Hindus, an Indian writer in English who sees no virtue in Indian novels in English, a historian who believes in objectivity, but leans heavily on subjective dogmas, a radical non-conformist who supports the caste system and cow worship, a rationalist who is not above prejudices and hatreds, a believer in social equality who hates the 'plebeians,' a cynical individualist who cares very much for social relations and human happiness."[2] The grand old man is not particularly noted for his modesty or humility. However, on the occasion he has apparently been modest, because in this case his subject is Tagore whose stature is so high, the activities are so diverse, the achievements are so immense that it is well-nigh impossible for anybody not to feel dwarfed by contrast. Anyway, interestingly and intriguingly, Tagore is the only Bengali poet Chaudhuri thinks worth considering or worth writing a book about. His writings show that he has genuine admiration for Tagore's achievements but this admiration is fraught with tones of lamentation, almost elegiac, for the path Tagore had taken to counter the scurrilities and vilifications of the countrymen. And since it is against his grain to mince matters, and whatever he writes as much by sincerity of feeling as by courage of conviction, Chaudhuri deserves serious attention.

In the Introduction to the first part of the book, Chaudhuri says that Tagore has never been properly estimated: either he has been completely deified or aboutely rejected. In other words, either he has been heavily over-estimated or unduly under-estimated. Chaudhuri claims to attempt the first objective assessment of the total Tagore—Tagore, the artist and Tagore, the man. Chaudhuri states his thesis very succinctly:

> I think, possibly, at last, I have been able to grasp the essential Tagore that I have been looking for throughout my life. But, to my mind, the image that I get is not really one but two. It is the image of a divided self. On the one hand, we have the image of a Tagore who is completely absorbed in himself, and on the other, it is the image of a Tagore committing suicide. Inseparability of these two images is the hallmark of his life. He could easily ignore the envy and attack of his countrymen by his remarkable talent for self-absorption. But without doing that he chose a path that brought him untold misery, and so, is more a case of suicide than self-immolation. (3-4)

Chaudhuri begins his first section by referring to Tagore's famous story "Kshudita Pashan" or "Hungry Stone" and compares the Bengali ethos as a quagmire on account of the mud-slinging nature of most Bengalees. Many talents are destroyed by it, many promises are blighted before they can be realized. Tagore in his life-time was also a target of attacks and vilification but, thanks to his extraordinary personality and rare genius, he did not succumb to it. The quagmire could not devour him up nor could it spoil his literary expressions but it filled his life with sorrows and sufferings. Chaudhuri concludes this short section with the statement, "First of all we must find out the cause of this sorrow." (5)

This opening gambit of Chaudhuri presupposes certain things: (1) The Bengali society is a quagmire. (2) It is inimical to the development of a talent. (3) Tagore overcame this opposition by his mighty personality. (4) The struggle made his life painful. It is debatable whether all the presuppositions are valid, but on the assumption that they are *donnèes* Chaudhuri raises the question: If Tagore had overcome the opposition why was he filled with sorrow? The book attempts to search for an answer to this question and then questions the answer when it is 'found.'

The very title of the next section, "Dependendence on Unworthy Countrymen," spells out the cause of Tagore's life-long sorrow. Chaudhuri says that Tagore knew the character of the Bengali people very well—he had known it through his personal experience—but strangely all his life he pined for the love and admiration of the Bengalees. He tried to get some consolation from the admiration of the west, but failed to get over his longing for the love and affection of his own people. The statement is again debatable. It is really true (1) that Tagore looked westward *because* he had not received the due recognition from his own countrymen and (2) that he failed to get over his longing for the love and affection of his people?

The first chapter "Saisab o Balyakal" or "Childhood and Boyhood" is concerned with the childhood and boyhood of Tagore. Chaudhuri here focusses on the rigours and austerity with which he was brought up by his ever-vigilant father. The hallmark of Tagore's character even at this stage as evidenced from his various actions, is love for freedom. Chaudhuri characterizes Tagore in the words Charlotte Bronte used for Emily Brönte: "Liberty was the very breath of Emily's nostrils: without it she perished." (14)

The second chapter, "Balya haite yauubane" or "From Boyhood to Youth," tries to trace through a fine psychoanalytic study, Tagore's awakening to love. In this context, Chaudhuri draws parallels between Tagore's attainment of youth and Chateaubriand's. He refers to two incidents—one from Chateaubriand's life and another from Tagore's—to bring home the point that a young man is first awakened to love through incidental physical contact with a girl. Such an experience which is often overwhelming opens up strange new worlds to a man. It is, however, very doubtful whether the incident (26) that Chaudhuri refers to is really the first experience of love for Tagore. I have a feeling that Chaudhuri is reading too much into the incident.

In the third chapter, "Pablo and Francesca," Chaudhuri explores the nature of the relationship between Tagore and Kadambari Debi (wife of Tagore's elder brother, Jyotirindranath Tagore). Tagore and Kadambari Debi were of the same age-group and the relation between the two was very sweet and friendly. But four months after the marriage of Tagore, Kadambari committed suicide. Speculations are still rife about the mysterious circumstances leading to the suicide. Chaudhuri has marshalled a lot of facts and carefully analyzed some significant omissions and commissions in the writings of Tagore to suggest that there was a romantic affair between the two. The suicide of Kadambari has put a permanent stigma on the character of Tagore who never cared either to confirm or to contradict the scandal. Whatever may be the fact it must be admitted that the way Chaudhuri has made out a case is a testimony to his fine perception of the nature of romantic love and his keen insight into human character.

The fourth chapter, "Nirjharer Svapnabhanga" or "The Awakening of a Spring," continues the same theme of romantic love and reinforces it. The experience of first love is like the sudden gushing out of a spring from a dark cave under the earth, into the open, sunlit world. Metaphorically it also stands for the sudden spurt of creativity, an expression of intense joy, celebration of the pleasure of life and love.

The fifth chapter, "Mrtyusok" or "Bereavement," treats the same theme of love from a different angle. Chaudhuri brings under sharp focus the particular chapter of the same title "Bereavement" in Tagore's *Jibansmrti* or *Reminiscences* and pounces upon one sentence: "Meanwhile there were a number of deaths in the family." A close reading of the relevant chapter of Tagore's *Reminiscences*, according to Chaudhuri, clearly indicates that although Tagore talks about many deaths, he is actually concerned with one death—the death of Kadambari. Experience of death, however, did not cripple Tagore; on the contrary it gave a new dimension to his view of the world. He realized that death provides the distance necessary for a full and impartial appreciation of the world in all its glory. Tagore was a deeply pious person and it is on account of his strong religious feeling, an absolute trust in God and after-life that he could easily defy death and look upon it as a portal to eternity. As separation sharpens the feelings of love, so death, a permanent separation, Chaudhuri contends, gives permanence to the feelings of love.

The sixth chapter, "Kadi o Komal" or "Sharps and Flats" is also an excellent psychoanalytical study made on the basis of the poems published in Tagore's *Sharps and Flats* of Tagore's conflicts at the crossroads of life. Chaudhuri writes:

> At this time Tagore was at a crucial juncture of his psychological existence, he was moving from one kind of life to another. One was tied to the past, the other looked forward to

> the future. Death, bereavement, bondage were the drawbacks of the past; the future promised birth, joy and freedom. (52)

Chaudhuri perceptively suggests that the book *Sharps and Flats* is full of rich materials necessary for writing the biography of the poet's mind. Chaudhuri then proceeds to examine the nature of the conflict and the source of it. By drawing parallels from the poetry of Vigny, Chaudhuri contends that Tagore wanted to break out of the destiny-dominated routine life of the East and enter the western world of free will. This is his transition from the old to the new. Chaudhuri believes that such a radical shift cannot be effected only through intellection; it requires a strong emotional drive. And such an emotional upsurge is generally occasioned by the impact of some incident or experience. We may not have any quarrel with Chaudhuri for these views, because they appear quite sensible and therefore acceptable. But when Chaudhuri confidently locates this experience in Tagore's love for his wife, one cannot so readily accept the thesis. It needs a more thorough research and detailed psychoanalysis of various other factors to arrive at such a conclusion. However, what Chaudhuri has suggested has certainly the status of probable hypothesis.

The seventh chapter, "Bangali Rabindarnath" or "Tagore—a Bengali," is the concluding chapter of the first part of the book. The chapter shows how the wanderings of Tagore in different parts of Bengal in connection with his estate managements gave him an excellent opportunity to enjoy the sights and sounds, the flora and fauna, the landscape and the river scape of Bengal. The whole immensity of Bengal with her trees and foliage, rivers and meadows, her mornings and evenings made a deep and lasting impression on Tagore. He had developed an emotional bond with the natural beauty of Bengal; it had practically entered his soul and made him a Bengali poet. Chaudhuri believes that Tagore's exposure to the natural beauties of Bengali during a formative period of nearly a decade made him out and out a Bengali. Chaudhuri concludes this chapter by referring again to the role of love, particularly the marital love, in shaping his life.

There is no doubt that Tagore loved Bengal and had harmonious relationship with all the aspects of Bengal. There is also no doubt about the fact that Tagore was a Bengali to the core of his heart, but to suggest that he was just a Bengali to the point of being clannish is to ignore the broadness of Tagore. He was a man who considered the entire world his home and was an internationalist in the true sense of the term.

II

Part II of the book also begins with an Introduction in which Chaudhuri says he would cover the period from 1901 to 1913, which he describes as the meridian of Tagore's life. He also contends that it was till 1913, that the scurrilous criticism of his countrymen notwithstanding Tagore was able to preserve his self-absorbed composure. Then he gave in. The little happiness that he got after this as a man was like the splendour of the setting sun.

In the first chapter entitled "Sahityik Krititva o Pratistha" or "Literary Achievements and Recognition," Chaudhuri says that whatever Tagore wrote during the first forty years of his life is comparable to the achievements of Wordsworth, Byron, Shelley, Keats, Tennyson and Browning. While Shelley, Keats and Byron died before they could reach forty, the other three lived long, but they did not produce better work after their fortieth year than what they did before. Only Tagore and Hugo continued to write consistently better as they advanced in age. Chaudhuri, of course, admires the versatility of Tagore's genius but ignores the fact that all the Romantic and Victorian poets rolled together cannot match Tagore in range and profundity of subjects, variety of form, sincerity of feeling, depth of passion, felicity of expression, and in the all-embracing sweep and magnificence of synthesis. The only poets comparable to Tagore in terms of greatness are, actually Shakespeare and Goethe. In protean plasticity and creative fecundity he is easily comparable with Shakespeare. And he is comparable to Goethe in more ways than one. Both had long life crammed with crowded activities. Both had varied experience and both lived life intensely at all levels. In both, noble physical presence was combined with prophetic vision, and both had remarkable command over their age.

Anyway, by citing many examples from the writings of Tagore,

Chaudhuri tries to establish that Tagore's creativity to rise higher even at this time. This is, in fact, labouring the obvious. It is common knowledge that like Picasso's, Tagore's creativity moved from one form to another. Attaining perfection in one form he passed on to another. So much so that when Tagore died at the ripe old age of 80, Buddhadev Bose, an eminent Bengali poet, deplored that Tagore had a premature death. The point is that at 70 Tagore had taken to painting and gave the world some 2000 pieces which are now considered of great artistic value. They are treasures of Art. Similarly, in poetry, in the last decade of his life he was experimenting with new form; he was trying new themes and techniques.

The second chapter "Bhasa, racanariti o bhaber aitihasik dik" or "Language, Style and the Historical Side of Thought," is on Tagore's language. It was, as Chaudhuri rightly claims, the mature form of the Bengali language that was evolved in the nineteenth century. But, he says, it is not written anymore, and he is not certain whether it is still understandable either. But the example of Tagore's prose that he cites to substantiate his views does not bear out his contention, and the 'modern' Bengali version of the sentence that he gives is no Bengali at all.[3] Although he says about the modernized version that "a Bengalee will have no difficulty in understanding it," I, for one, just cannot understand it. Chaudhuri says that unless one has a working knowledge of Sanskrit it is not possible to understand Tagore's prose or poetry, let alone relish it.

Here Chaudhuri shows, unfortunately, very poor understanding of the nature of language. There are diachronic and synchronic aspects of language. A living language is never frozen in time. It constantly changes, it is always in a flux. The language of one decade is never the same as the language of its previous decade. It is as true of Bengali as it is true of English. When we read an author we have to bear in mind the historical period in which that writer was born and brought up, and the corresponding state of language at that time. Nobody would quarrel with Chaucer or Shakespeare for writing in a language that is no longer spoken in the contemporary English speaking world. Bankim, the great predecessor of Tagore wrote in a highly Sanskritized Bengali. Most common readers today have to frequently consult a dictionary in order to understand it. But Bankim's contemporaries had no difficulty in understanding him. And Bankim is not only a great writer but also like most great writers—like Dante, for example—helped develop the vernacular language. We can really appreciate the contribution of Tagore to the development of the Bengali language if we just compare the state of Bengali before and after him. Moreover, it is also not true that Tagore always used Sanskritized Bengali. In fact, Tagore was always very conscious, particularly in writing poetry, of the aesthetics of sound and always tried to effect a perfect correspondence between the sonic and the semantic.[4]

In this chapter Chaudhuri also analyzes Tagore's fascination with the image of the ancient as reflected in his famous long poem, "Bharattirtha" or "The Sacred India." Chaudhuri discovers in Tagore's mythicizing of the past an obvious influence of European Romanticism. To my mind, however, Tagore's recreation of the ancient Hindu and Buddhist myths and legends has more affinity with Renaissance Humanism than with the European Romantic Movement. In this connection it is worth recalling what Asit Bandyopadhyay, the great historian of Bengali literature, writes about the nineteenth century Bengali sensibility. He writes:

> The religion of man, generally known as Humanism made an impact on the nineteenth century Bengali sensibility. In place of Candi, Mansa and other goddesses man became the centre of interest. . . . It does not mean, however, that the old divinities left the scene for ever. . . . They reappeared in mythological writings. . . . But they were humanized. In other words, gods reappeared like ordinary human beings and fellow compatriots with whom we can enter into an emotional bond.[5]

The third chapter, "Sok o Nirbed" or "Bereavement and Despondency," is about the series of bereavements in Tagore's life that started with his wife's death in 1902. Tagore was then 41. Failing to find any satisfactory explanation for this suffering, Chaudhuri falls back upon fatalism. The poet's first memory of death was recorded much later, after 26 years of the event. But immediately after his wife's death, he had written a bunch of poems. Chaudhuri says: "I have never read such touching poems on the death of the dear one." (95) She is imagined as one who had just been a guest in this world, now that she has left only another guest is to be waited for. Obviously this second guest is death.

An even more terrible thing happened to the poet before the end of the year—the death of Rani, the second daughter, at the age of 13. Rani was not a common girl, she was rather indifferent to material comforts or glamour and preferred to be left alone with her books. Why did not Tagore allow this quiet girl to carry on her studies and instead married her off in great haste, at the age of 11 to a most ordinary middle-class youth? Even his youngest daughter Mira thought that this indicated a lack of practical approach which made him a great poet but not a practical father. Rani fell ill before long and soon died of tuberculosis. The poet had stayed by her bedside during her last days and used to read out passages from the Upanishad to help her through her imminent journey into the other world.

Soon after Rani's death he lost his youngest son Shamindra who died of cholera in Munger in 1907. The poem that Tagore wrote in reaction to this death registers the terror and confusion of a perturbed mind which is thrashed down by disaster. But the same poem, an extraordinary in Tagore, for the spiritual chaos it records, ends on a positive note: he inspires himself: "Cast away your fear, rise from idle cowardice/ Stir up the strength of your mind in joy." (99) Chaudhuri interprets this as resulting from a growing conviction in the poet's mind that death was the eternal counterpart of life, which moved him to make an effort to come to terms with death.

In 1918 Tagore had to face death again in the form of the demise of his eldest daughter, Bela. But by that time he seems to have developed a kind of detachment which started in 1902 with his wife's death. Chaudhuri uses a beautiful analogy to bring out the state of the poet's mind: "the bare forest of autumn" (100)—the poet's own phrase for this phase.

He also takes care to point out the difference between Keats's autumn and Tagore's. Unlike Keats, Tagore had his God by his side, so he could transform his bare forest into a temple of worship. The sorrow that came to his life in the course of unavoidable circumstance and which could not be prevented by any earthly means, found an aesthetic expression in his poems, especially in the poems of *Kheya*, *Gitanjali* and the songs of *Gitali*. In these poems and songs, characterized by a mellowed detactment, Chaudhuri notes not just music, but "worship of God in tune." (100) This deeply felt response actually echoes the feelings of many ardent admirers of Tagore's song.

The fourth chapter, "Svadesikata o Hindutva" or "Patriotism and Hinduism" is about Tagore's patriotism and Hinduism. Chaudhuri claims that in Tagore's mind patriotism and Hinduism were intimately related. He makes it clear that there was no narrowness in Tagore's patriotism or Hinduism. Tagore's 'nationalism' could be seen as his lifelong effort to be a patriot—not just confined to the exciting programmes of struggle for independence. Chaudhuri relates this to his family tradition; this explains his attitude of humorous indulgence towards the ineffectively but sincere 'Swadeshi' activities by some of his contemporaries. Tagore himself had joined the national political movement in 1905. According to Chaudhuri it was more due to his love for the geographical entity than for his identification with fellow countrymen. As evidence he cites one famous patriotic song of 24 lines, of which only the last line could send a faint political suggestion. During this period, Tagore had written a number of justifiably popular poems and songs, but these do not carry the strain of topical politics. Chaudhuri claims that Tagore's patriotism was not oriented in anti-Britishism; he was also in favour of striking against the stagnation and shackles of orthodox Hindu society.

The fact of the matter is that a visionary as he was, Tagore could clearly see the meaninglessness of the empty rituals of the so-called 'Swadeshi' movement. He could clearly see through the blatant hypocrisy and empty rhetoric of many leaders. His perception of the Swadeshi has been elaborately verbalized in *Char Adhyay* or *Four Chapters* and *Ghare Baire* or *The Home and the World*. Tagore could never support any insane infatuation in the name of patriotism. However, in this context, Chaudhuri discusses the similarity between Tagore's vision of the country as mother-goddess and Bankimchandra's identification of the country with the image of 'Durga' in *Anandamath*, and the ancient Hindu tradition of worshipping a mother-goddess as the source of all inspiration and energy. He quotes at length from *Chandi* to establish his point. He also thinks that the Hindu ideal of feminine loyalty had all along fascinated him.

However, Chaudhuri's claim that Tagore's establishment of the 'Brahmacharyasram' in Santiniketan in 1901 is a further proof of Hindu heritage, may stir controversy. Anyway, as he acknowledges, Tagore's Hindu heritage was not an item of religious faith, but a heritage of nationalist culture. In *Gora,* he rejects orthodox Hinduism in favour of new liberal embracing humanism. He also never believed in the institutional hostility or gregariousness of religion. His preference was certainly for the modern concept of universal brotherhood instead of the sectarianism of religious groups. Religious faith or devotion to God was a completely personal matter with him. In fact, even if Brahma religion is taken as the Protestant form of the Hindu religion, it is evident from the poems, essays and diaries of Tagore that for all practical purposes Hinduism in its ideal form, was, for Tagore, only another name for Humanism.

The fifth chapter "Rabindranather dharma o isvarbhakti" or "Tagore's Religion and Devotion to God" tries to establish that Tagore used the terms "religion" and "god" in his original way. Unless one is sufficiently sensitized to these feelings and expressions, one may be easily misled and Tagore's observations may appear puzzling. Tagore questioned the basis of so-called official religious differentiations, and understood the essential inner religion of every individual. Again, his concept of the finite and the infinite informed his religious thought too. Religion helped to grasp the infinite within the finite.

Chaudhuri reiterates his favourite idea (since 1941) that Tagore was no mystic, though his religion was a deep consciousness, a new sensitivity. Here he cites Abbe Bremond's *Priere et Poesie* at length in support of his argument that a poet cannot be a mystic. He also cites St. Augustine's *Confessions*, *Rigveda* and *Upanishads* to explain mysticism. He contends that Tagore's religious life was only apparently based on the Upanishad but not actually. Both the after-world and this world found accommodation in his religious life. In spite of his sufferings, bereavements and troubles, he believed that in after life all this will find fulfilment. Yet he also loved this world with all his poetic emotion and attachment. He had never given up this life like St. Augustine or St. Teresa of Plotinus.

Chaudhuri fails to realize that Tagore's mysticism is very much different from the esoteric mysticism we are so familiar with. That is why he is regarded as a devotional poet and not a mystic poet, though devotion is also a part of mysticism. But a study of his writings clearly reveals that he is a mystic of the first order. He is love-and-beauty mystic. Mysticism holds a belief that the Ultimate Reality exists and it is knowable only through some non-rational or supra-rational faculty. Tagore's faith in the Ultimate Reality was simply unshakable. On the subjective side, he considered himself as a tiny creature overwhelmed by a sense of his own insignificance in contrast to the vastness of that Ultimate Reality. On the objective side, this experience relates to the mysterious Reality which is both terrible and beautiful at the same time. We can never comprehend it, we can only apprehend it at the most, and that too, not through reason but through intuition, because intuition is the only faculty adequate to this knowledge. And Tagore's intuition is motivated by love. He says time and again in the essays in *Santiniketan* that man's freedom and fulfilment is in love, which is another name for perfect comprehension. By this power of comprehension, this permeation of being, he is united with the all pervading spirit who is the breath of his soul. W.B. Yeats wrote in his Introduction to Tagore's English version of *Gitanjali* that Tagore "has been content to discover the soul and surrender himself to its spontaneity." Indeed, the Reality which haunts the poet through all his experience is a kind of universal self-consciousness. Beauty is the lover-poet's gift to Nature. We can never know the real character of sense objects unless we look at them through the lover's eyes. The world then assumes a new significance in its totality as the tabernacle of the living God. Then one sees in the plenitude of nature, in its multifarious forms, sights, sounds and smells what Hopkins calls 'God's grandeur.' Everything then is realized as the true objectifiction of the Ideal which is the most real among reals breaking into the ever-changing and ever-new forms of beauty through the mediations of the recipient poet. Everything, then, is seen as the outflow of divine love which pulsates, throbs and thrills the universe. We must hasten to add, however, that

Tagore was fully aware of the dual aspects of Nature—the terrible and the beautiful. Yet he saw Nature, as he saw Life, as a reconciliation of opposites. He therefore accepts all the beauty and the ugliness, and this profound acceptance forms the spiritual substance of his mysticism.

In this chapter Chaudhuri also comments on Tagore's devotion. Tagore often had spoken of his feeling that within him operated the joy of expression of an inner God. Chaudhuri relates this feeling to the God of Debendranath and then proceeds to suggest that Tagore's God is neither Upanishadic nor Christian. Tagore's devotion to God includes, like Wordsworth's skylark, "the kindred points of heaven and earth" and Tagore's God is androgynous—both male and female—like the Greek Hermaphrodite or the "ardhanarisvara" of the Hindus. I do not understand what relevance this section has to the central thesis of the book.

The last two chapters—the sixth chapter, "Vilayatyatra 1912" or "Journey to England: 1912" and the seventh chapter "Vilayte Ananda" or "Joy in England" can be taken together as they are concerned with Tagore's visits abroad and his delight in these foreign tours. In 1878 and 1890, Tagore had gone to Europe under pressure and had not liked it much. But in June 1912, he decided to go abroad after 22 years. It was a changed attitude. He felt an urge within to come out. Chaudhuri quotes from the writings of Tagore of this period to show how delighted he was on being able to set out for the world at last. The foreign tour was, for him, a kind of pilgrimage. He wanted to learn the secret of the success of the Europeans, the spirit behind their attainments.

Tagore also carried with him the manuscript of *Gitanjali* on the tour, which was to bring him world recognition soon. Chaudhuri describes in detail how Tagore met the literary luminaries of the time—Yeats, Rothenstein, Wells et al, and the well-known circumstances leading to the publication of *Gitanjali*. Chaudhuri elaborately describes these months when the poet, according to Chaudhuri, had been deeply and fully enjoying his tour, *because* there he got a recognition which was denied to him at home. According to Chaudhuri, after his return to India in 1913 till his death in 1941, Tagore had never found happiness and peace; he became the target of venom and hostility. Tagore, the man, was eclipsed by his mighty public images.

Chaudhuri concludes his discussion with a surprising analogy: "As an injured tiger beats retreat into its den to have some peace, Tagore, too, had to take some hidden shelter panting and limping, during this last, long, lonely spell of life." (153)

III

Chaudhuri's central thesis that Tagore, in spite of his recognition in the West in 1913, continued to hanker after the admiration of his countrymen, particularly the Bengalee community, did not get it and, therefore, felt miserable till his death, and died like a wounded animal nursing its wound in the privacy of a cave, is just not tenable.

It is true that the western response to Tagore was simply overwhelming and Tagore naturally felt very happy about it. It may be true that he expected the admiration of his people which he so eminently served. It is also true that Tagore underwent immense sufferings in his personal life. But it is not true that like a wounded animal Tagore had to take some hidden shelter, during his "last, long, lonely spell of life," from 1913 to 1941.

A close look at the last poems of Tagore would at once give lie to Chaudhuri's thesis. As Browning's protagonist says "Shall we receive good at the hand of God/And evil not receive?" So Tagore also accepts joys and sorrows meted out to him, with matchless equanimity. What Eliot said about Baudelaire is partly true about Tagore: "He had great strength . . . to suffer." Tagore, in fact, arrived at a conviction that without sorrow there is no real happiness. One must pass through the purgatorial fire to attain the bliss of paradise. During eighty long years Tagore saw life and saw it whole, and his vision crystallized most clearly in the last period of his life. In this connection, Ayub writes:

> In spite of all these hesitation-conflict-obstacles-impediments the earnest pursuit of Rabindranath in the last phase was to realize in his own heart that 'merciless' God who is the greatest seer, the greatest spectator who witnesses through his delightful contemplative eyes, the creation and destruction of

> endless nebulae, the rise and fall of human civilization—as if a great drama full of conflicts, and sharp pleasure and pain is being enacted just for his pleasure.

And again:

> During the last period of his life Tagore's physical and mental pain was as excruciating as misery and sin at the international level were unbearable. Even then, unlike his western counterparts he did not lose the balance of his mind. The contemplation of Nataraj gave him a kind of profound, almost ascetic serenity. On the other hand his faith in the indomitable power and infinite possibility of man saved him from the clutches of bitter pessimism till his death.[6]

It is therefore not unnatural that in the fortieth poem of *Ses Saptak* (1935) or *The Last Septet* we find him after a tired and troublesome journey through life, after "the searing sighs of an aggrieved heart/ blew dry leaves over the horizon" standing before the Immortal Primal. And in the fortyfifth poem, he says: "Much have I suffered/ Yet I have liked it,/ Have loved it."[7]

In the tenth poem of *Patraput* (1936) or *Foliage*, Tagore reaffirms his faith in man: "At the fading center of your halo man has witnessed his glorious form from time to time . . . and has declared. 'We know that we are children of the Immortal. We have seen the appearance of the Supreme Being, brighter than thousand suns, across darkness.'" In the title poem of *Nabajatak* (1938) or *The Newborn*, we again hear him saying, "The child of man brings the message of hope again and again. The new dawn will possibly bring the light of emancipation." And in the poem "Janmadine" or "On the Birthday" in *Nabajatak*, Tagore refers to the failures, insults, ignominies and bitterness that he had experienced but claims not to have been overpowered by them. As the caves and cracks and crevices cannot mock the totality of a mountain, similarly all these trials and tribulations could not shake his faith in man. In other words, the greatness of the total cannot be annihilated by the deformities of the parts. Six months before his death, Tagore wrote. "Honeyed the heavens, honeyed the dust of the earth: this is the great fulfilling chant of life I have received and treasured in my heart." And just a week before his death, he dictated his last verse: "He who has found his way into an unruffled acceptance of the deception receives at thy hand the gift of an inalienable peace." (Sen's translation)

Towards the end of his life, Tagore arrived at the final reconciliation of the joy and pain. He absorbed all kinds of pain and pleasure and transcended them by reconciling all opposities, all the disparate elements, all the separate parts into a magnificent, harmonious whole where all dichotomy is resolved. To compare Tagore to a wounded animal is to do great dishonour to him.

A man of Chaudhuri's scholarship and intellectual capabilities could do much better justice to Tagore had he chosen to. Instead, he tries to cut Tagore to size, to his own size possibly, and gives us a very partial, narrow, parochial and distorted view of Tagore. He claims to have found, at last, the key to Tagore's character, in supercilious disregard of the unique and phenomenal quality of Tagore's genius which can never be summed up in a simple mathematical formula.

Chaudhuri's efforts remind me of what Tagore said in the twenty fifth poem of *Rogsayyay* or "From My Sick-Bed": "It requires little skill to belittle the great by trivial, contrary evidences."

NOTES

1. The original Bengali title of the book is *Ātmaghātī Rabīndranāth* (Calcutta: Mitra and Ghosh, 1992) which can also be translated as "Tagore committed suicide." I have chosen to write on this book, because the book is not accessible to the large community of Chaudhuri's readers who do not know Bengali, and the book is yet to be translated into English. Furthermore, the book is about Tagore about whom everybody knows, and with whose writings everybody is more or less familiar.
2. C. Paul Verghese, *Nirad C. Chaudhuri* (New Delhi: Arnold Heinemann India, 1973), p. 116.
3. I do not quite understand why Chaudhuri tries to ridicule the prose of Tagore as well as the modern Bengali prose. This reminds me

of the notorious scandal of the Matriculation Examination of Calcutta University of 1914 when, reportedly, Sir Asutosh Mukherjee, the then Vice-Chancellor of Calcutta University got a Bengali question paper set by Dinesh Chandra Sen, in which candidates were asked to rewrite "in chaste and elegant Bengali" a given passage from Tagore.

4. Take, for example, the following two iines occuring in close proximity in the poem, "*Prithvi*" (The Earth): (i) "*meghaloke ūdhāo prithvī*" and (ii) "*nilāmburāsir atandra tarange kalamandramukharā prithvi.*" The first line describes the beauty of the earth as seen in a floating cloud. The line, accordingly, is ligh., smooth-flowing and free from consonantal clusters.

   Compare with this the other line. It is highly Sanskritized, full of consonantal clusters and long compound words, so much so that one can hear the rumbling ocean in the line itself.

5. *History of Modern Bengali Literature* (Calcutta: Modern Book Agency, 1986), pp. 7-8.
6. Abu Sayeed Ayub, *Rabindranath o Ādhunikatā* (*Tagore and Modernity*) (Calcutta: Dey's Publishing, 1968), pp. 116 and 123, my translation.
7. Taraknath Sen, *A Literary Miscellany* (Calcutta: Rupa, 1972).

Three Horsemen of the New Apocalypse: A Dispassionate Meditation on a Decadent Civilization

TAPAN K. GHOSH

It is a phenomenon, unique in literary history, that a writer remains creative with his coruscating intellect, photographic memory and relentless spirit of enquiry in the hundredth year of his life. Nirad C. Chaudhuri, noted scholar, critic and thinker, celebrated his hundredth birthday on 23rd November, 1997. At such an age, most people, having passed through the inevitable process of physical and mental decline, wait in a feeble and uncreative state for death. But Nirad Chaudhuri has ignored the burden of age and decided to write a treatise on the decline and fall of the contemporary civilization. His latest book, *Three Horsemen of the New Apocalypse*, published by Oxford University Press in the centenary year of his birth, unquestionably proves that even in the twilight of life his intellect remains as formidable as before and that he still commands a refined and lively language to express his thoughts. In this respect, he is really nonpareil.

A man of rare intellectual courage and a fiercely honest and unsparing critic of men, morals and manners in our time, Nirad Chaudhuri has always shown an uncanny fascination for decadence and decay. Indeed, decadence has become an obsession of this eminent writer and he has returned to the subject in untiring repetition even at the risk of being unpopular. From *The Autobiography of an Unknown Indian* (1951) to *The East is East and The West is West* (1966), one of his major pre-occupations has been the decline of Indian and Western civilizations. In between, he has contributed numerous articles to British and Indian Press denouncing the barbarism which is threatening the life and culture in these two societies. In *Three Horsemen of the New Apocalypse*, he brings to bear the accumulated wisdom of a life spent in dispassionate pursuit of knowledge, on his central concern: the worldwide disintegration of civilized life. The book reveals his phenomenal erudition, profound historical sense and highly individualistic world-view.

Briefly defined, the subject of *Three Horsemen of the New Apocalypse* is 'decline and fall of Western civilization.' It may remind the readers of Spengler's celebrated work, *Decline of the West*. But Chaudhuri categorically states that his latest tour-de-force is not a 'refurbished version'[1] of Spengler's book. The term 'west' has a different connotation in his work. As he explains:

> Western civilization today is no longer exclusively Western. It has expanded all over the world, but in doing so it has not remained a whole one: it has two clearly marked divisions. There is the inner circle which is fully lighted and is occupied by peoples of European origins; around it is a very much larger circle, which is the penumbra of the central sun and is occupied by diverse non-European peoples. (10)

It is with the decline of the 'inner circle' and its penumbral regions (in Asia and Africa) that the author is concerned.

The book, divided into three parts, explores the reasons and the historical perspectives of this decline. In part one, Chaudhuri informs the readers, briefly but precisely, of (a) the methods he consciously followed in writing this book; (b) his fundamental assumptions about human life and the universe on which the entire thesis of the book depends; and (c) the present state of his mind in which he views the world. In the second part, he considers the concepts of individualism, nationalism and democracy and their extant debased forms and arrives at the conclusion that these three are mainly responsible for the decadence of contemporary civilization. They are the 'three horseman' of the 'new apocalypse.' In the third part, he presents a graphic but authentic picture of decadence in England, India and America. He also refers, in connection with the elaboration of his arguments, to various autobiographical incidents and personal experiences which is a familiar style of his writing.

Chaudhuri's method of thinking and writing is geometric. His model, in this respect, is Pascal. The geometric method "makes those who want to understand a phenomenon, ignore a whole array of facts which are plainly visible to find some fundamental feature which has to be detected by a priori reasoning." (7) This is a recognized method in science of understanding a phenomenon in the material order. But Chaudhuri extends it to the human order to explain human activities and affairs: "When I have been confronted with a problem in human affairs I have always tried to reduce it to its simplest." (7) But the application of this method, however convenient it may be to the practitioner, entails some risks. For example, an aspect of a complicated problem which one views as its essential elementary feature, may not appear to be fundamental in the perception of another, but equally discerning, person. It may also lead to over-simplification. But Chaudhuri prefers his practical good sense to the spirit of finesse favoured by problem-mongers who "revel in multiplying complexity." (8)

He next sets out his fundamental assumptions about the universe and human life, his belief in reasoned faith and in what he calls the psychological evolution of the human species, frankly drawing on European thinkers like Pascal and Alexis de Tocqueville. According to the scientists, who devote themselves to cosmology, the universe is not a material body; it is a process and flow of energy in different directions. It has a beginning and an end. With the help of Thermodynamics, they have mathematically proved their hypothesis that the total energy of the universe will one day be dissipated and the universe will cease to exist. While Chaudhuri accepts the scientists' theory of the nature of the universe, he rejects their hypothesis about its duration, because he regards it as "an expression of scientific nihilism." (13) It deprives all human achievement of its permanence and renders meaningless every creative effort of man. He has deep-seated faith, which is not necessarily connected with any religion, in human endeavour and in the permanence of human achievement. He believes that the flow of energy in the universe has a direction and that there is a definite purpose in evolution which makes it meaningful. The purpose is two-fold: on the one hand, there is the attempt of the species at better adaptation to circumstances; on the other, there is the creation of new form of animal existence. It will be absurd to think that the evolution of species from amoeba to man is totally fortuitous. In that case, human rationality and perception of values would become self-deception. As he writes in the second part of his autobiography, *Thy Hand, Great Anarch!*:

> I believe that in its flow the universe is purposive, and the purpose has been partly achieved, but for the greater part it remains to be fulfilled, and in this purpose are included all that the mind of man, yearning after perfection, has regarded as the highest values, e.g., beauty, goodness, righteousness, or holiness. (1987: 955)

He further asserts that man's unity as a species has been achieved zoologically, because as a species of animal, man is the sole survivor in a zoological family called 'Hominidae' and in a zoological genus called 'homo.' Since no new animal has appeared on earth after the emergence of man, it can be assumed that in the animal world the zoological evolution has come to an end. Chaudhuri thinks that the next stage of the evolution will be psychological through which new psychological species of man will appear. It is not unimaginable, he says, that "in some five hundred or thousand years a particular psychological species of man will find that he is not quite like other human psychological species, although he will also admit that there are common features." (17) This theory of psychological evolution is, however, nothing new. Bernard Shaw, and long before him Nietzsche, had written about the evolution of man into superman. Chaudhuri presents it as a 'teleological corollary' to his cosmological assumption.

His third assumption is that the life-cycles of individuals and nations are analogous. Just as an individual is born, grows to manhood, arrives at the acme of his achievement, and then begins to lose vitality and gradually passes through old age to death, so does a nation. Sometimes, a nation, after passing through the process of decline, totally vanishes from history; but sometimes it continues in a devitalized and uncreative state. When a society continues to exist in an etiolated condition, it is called a decadent society.

The last of his fundamental assumptions is about the value of public opinion. He believes that public opinion does not shape the course of history: it simply follows historical trends.

Everything written in this book was kept in the author's mind long before he set it down on paper. But the death of his wife in 1994 brought about a sea-change in his attitude to life. The event 'shed a wholly different light' (23) on what he wrote subsequently:

> For me the Night of Time has descended on the lighted universe. That has made a radical change in my life. In my vocation as a writer I had always been an engage, totally immersed and involved in the affairs of the world. But suddenly, I lost all interest in that world. (24)

He now views the world and its affairs from a distance, as one views a familiar landscape from a hill-top. He sees it "very brilliantly" but also "softly, with a new chiaroscuro." (24) Indeed, anyone reading the book will notice the difference. The zeal of an 'engage,' the familiar pungency in his style, the brilliant irony and devastating satire that marked his earlier writings are absent here. Like a wise man, mellowed by bereavement and sorrow, he now looks at the world dispassionately, softly but as a whole.

In the second part, he traces the careers of the three horsemen, namely individualism, nationalism and democracy. Beginning with the lexical meanings of these three words, he traces their history and shows how these concepts have assumed debased forms in the twentieth century and substantially contributed to the decadence of civilization. Individualism, which literally means "belief in the individual's supreme worth and importance, as well as in his right to act as he pleases," (27) is a nineteenth century concept. In fact, the first citation of the word in *The Oxford English Dictionary* dates from the first half of the nineteenth century. But in course of time the term came to signify an extreme assertion of individual freedom and a revolt against authoritarianism. This kind of individualism came from America where the term is used to mean that "an individual has the right to pursue self-interest in the form of acquisition of money and fulfilment of all desires, good or bad, also amenities of life, without external constraints." (29) The principle is embodied in the American Declaration of Independence. The domination of authoritarian doctrines and absolutist regimes in Europe, in France, Germany and Russia in particular, from the middle of the nineteenth century is responsible for making individualism a driving force of the process of decadence in Western civilization. Individualism, as it is understood today, is "just unrestrained self-indulgence, more especially in regard to money and sexual relations." (44) Though primarily an American concept, it has spread inexorably to all countries of the world and has proved to be a formidable agent of disintegration.

Nationalism, too, has acquired a degenerate form in the present century. Nationalism, as it is understood now, is totally different from historic nationalism. In the past, the main inspiration of nationalism came from the desire to free a subject nation from foreign domination. At present there is no direct foreign rule in any country of the world. Moreover, imperialism as an assertive and expansive form of nationalism[2] has also disappeared. No country today, however powerful and aggressive it may be, can think of occupying another country and imposing its rule on it. Even if any such attempt is made, it will be foiled by other free nations. [The recent gulf war over the Iraqi aggression against Kuwait is an example.] An altogether different form of nationalism has appeared in the place of historic nationalism. Nirad Chaudhuri calls it 'new Nationalism.' It is "a self-sufficient and disinterested passion" (59) and it receives its strongest urge from national pride. The new nationalism has generated a strong sense of national identity for each nation which results in xenophobia. The neo-nationalism at its typical is now found among those peoples who have been emancipated from European imperialism. The colonial experience and "the extensive transformation of the societies of nationalistic peoples" (60) have added a new colour to their sense of national pride. It has become "nationalistic inferiority complex." (60) These peoples constantly suffer from a feeling of being confronted by inimical forces and nurture unending grievances. This, in turn, breeds an "impotent hatred" (60) in them. This depraved form of nationalism is the main source of wars and conflicts, expansive military preparations and terrorism in the present-day world. "The mental life of the mankind of our times," remarks Chaudhuri, "has one overriding emotion: hatred generated by conflicts of every kind, personal and social." (61) And this ubiquitous hatred has accelerated the decline of human civilization.

Next comes democracy, the third horseman of the new apocalypse. Democracy, which literally means the rule of the people, is, in the opinion of Chaudhuri, "the domination (for some the tyranny) of the majority" (62) over the whole society. Modern democracy, as it is practised all over the world, is, in fact, the American form of democracy and its fundamental doctrine ('government of the people, by the people, and for the people') was asserted by Abraham Lincoln in 1863. Political democracy, with its parliamentary and representative government, came to be accepted universally as the only form of democracy after the end of World War II. A new democratic ideology, which is at once assertive and aggressive, has appeared in recent times. Chaudhuri calls it "total democracy." It seeks to assert its power not only over the political realm but over all aspects of life—economic, social, cultural and educational. The supporters of total democracy want to give all these aspects of life the form desired by the majority of the people. They totally disregard quality and prize only quantity. Democracy has, thus, become the same as egalitarianism. Chaudhuri points out a 'glaring inconsistency' (67) in the present form of egalitarianism which reveals its true character and which is immensely harmful for the civilization. The egalitarians accept "inequality in the physical powers and skills of men." (67) But the same champions of equal rights fiercely assert that all men are equal in mental powers. In the name of equality, the supporters of total democracy, with their animus against mental capacity, have reduced the human mind "to its lowest common denominator" (67) and made all kinds of cultural development and excogitation impossible. Egalitarianism (Chaudhuri describes it as "the assertion of the rancour of the futureless") is, thus, a major agent of decadence. Western civilization, which is now in decline, lacks the strength to resist its malevolence.

The decline and fall of civilizations is a historical phenomenon and it had occurred repeatedly in human history. Decadence, as *Webster International Dictionary* defines the term, "presupposes previous maturing and usually a high degree of excellence; it implies that the falling takes place after a thing (such as a people, a literature or other form of art, a branch of knowledge) has reached the peak of its development." (72) In Chaudhuri's consideration of decadence, the term is totally divested of its moral connotations. He thinks that the decadence of a nation is as natural as the physical and mental decline of a man. A nation becomes decadent "when it has lost its political and economic power as well as its cultural creativeness." (72) It is in this sense that the geographical space called Europe and its penumbra, i.e. the countries which were once under European colonialism, are decadent.

In the last twenty-seven years, after he had settled permanently in England in 1970, Nirad Chaudhuri has unremittingly written about the degeneration of the English people and their culture. He wrote his first jeremiad against British decadence in 1979 in an article published in *The Times Literary Supplement.* He remarked in that article that the idea of a world-wide decadence of civilized life had always haunted him: "My preoccupation with decadence has nothing to do with my age. . . . It has grown out of my whole life and has been treading at my heels like the Foul Fiend even to the shores of the Pacific at Vancouver." In another article, entitled "Why I Mourn for England," published in *The Daily Telegraph* (February 20, 1988), he regretted the passing away of the old English spirit and denounced the country's moral and mental decay illustrated most strikingly by the dwindling literacy he found around him. In this book, referring to various personal experiences and newspaper reports in his somewhat detailed account of British decadence, Chaudhuri informs his readers why his despair about the present-day English society is so deep-rooted. The decadence of the English people is all-embracing: "There is not a single aspect of English life to which decadence is not spreading and deepening its invasion—national personality, politics, social and economic life, education and culture." (76) Love of money "in the extreme form of addiction" (83) and licentiousness—the two passions which are typical of decadence—are manifest in the British character. The most decisive impact of decadence on the social existence of the British people is seen in the disintegration of the basic unit of the society, i.e. family, and the absolutism of the State which is evident in its attempt to bring all individuals directly under its control. The destruction of family has dispensed with "the protective barrier which absorbs the shocks of political changes or revolutions among the people." (89) It results in individual's helplessness and growing sense of alienation on the one hand, and increasing interference of the State in every aspect of society on the other. Chaudhuri regards the Welfare State as a decadent state because he believes that "mere welfare of the mass of people of a state can never restore the greatness of a people." (94) It only fosters decadence, "especially in the expression of national life in its culture." (94) In every aspect of national life in Britain—language, education, culture, morality and religion, national character, political leadership, dress and food-habit, individual and familial relationship—he finds a steady degeneration. And he is convinced that civilization in Britain is a glorious monument in ruins.

The picture in India is not different. India has not escaped the contagion of Western decadence. According to Chaudhuri, there had been in India two previous periods of decadence: "the first for about two hundred years before the Muslim conquest at the end of the twelfth century; the second, in the eighteenth century, after the death of the last great Mogul emperor Aurangzeb. The first decadence brought about the extinction of the ancient Hindu civilization; the second, of the Indo-Islamic." (109) He first diagonsed the present decadence in India in the nineteen twenties and wrote in *The Autobiography of an Unknown Indian* (1951): "everything about us was decaying, literally everything ranging from our spiritual and moral ideals to our material culture, and nothing really live or organic arose to take their place."[4] The second part of his autobiography, *Thy Hand, Great Anarch!* (1987), describes the whole process of this unadulterated decay. The only relieving feature in Indian decay is that "it does not exhibit the malignity which is seen in England. It is only a comatose senility." (111) Chaudhuri thinks that the emancipation of the country from British rule could not release sufficient energy and idealism to bring about a rejuvenation of our national life. In an article, published in *The Statesman* Festival Number, 1994, under the title 'British Rule is Dead, Long Live British Rule,'[5] he wrote that although the British had left India in 1947, the system of government created by them remained in all its features and in its spirit. The government of India after Independence was thus an ersatz British regime which pursued the political concepts of the foreign rulers and shamelessly aped their arrogance and airs. The most striking aspect of the government was its absolute falsity: "Nothing was authentic, nothing sincere, nothing disinterested in it." (113) The political feebleness of the national leaders to face any challenge, the lack in them of the spirit of political enterprise, the dynastic rule initiated by Nehru, the emergence of a dominant order of hucksters in all walks of life and the staticity of the bureaucratic system—"a solid, egocentric and rootless order, which by its very nature, is not only uncreative, but even unproductive"[6]—contributed to the political decadence in post-Independence India. The recent governments are in no way better than the earlier ones. The decadence in political life has its counterpart in social and cultural life. The most obvious manifestation of socio-cultural decadence is "the popular and lowest expression of Amricanism" (119) and three important aspects of this decadence are (a) "single-minded, sordid and dishonest" (120) pursuit of money, (b) licentiousness and (c) falsity of mores. The decadence in India is as pervasive as it is in Europe. But there is a difference between its manifestations in the two continents. As Chaudhuri remarks: "As a cultural satellite of the War, India was bound to share its decadence. But there is a difference between the two manifestations. The Western rouses a civilized man to anger; the Indian benumbs him into despair." (124)

The author finds no ray of hope in America either. In fact, he thinks, the latest decadence in human history "has its centre of diffusion in the United States." (133) The 'impressive' and 'revolutionary' achievements of the Americans in the field of technology, which have immensely improved the standard of living, have failed to make them immune to decadence and infuse a vitality into their national life.

Decadence is a world-wide phenomenon, although it is now manifested in an absolutely new form. The novelty of decadence lies in the fact that it is appearing in an age when the economic basis of civilization has changed from agriculture to industry. The stupendous achievements of technology have brought about an economic revolution in the West. This revolution is now being fostered in Asia and Africa by the Western countries. The peoples of these continents have inevitably caught the virus of Western decadence. "The absolutely new power of making things established in the West and spreading rapidly and irresistibly all over the world," says Chaudhuri, "is not making any difference to the expansion of Western decadence everywhere." (135) Although in some Asian and African countries religious fundamentalists are making futile attempts to resist modernization and Western decadence, the people of the West have accepted it as a normal condition of life. Decadence is, therefore, no longer militant, it is triumphant. Like the mythical Greek goddess Circe, it has succeeded in captivating human mind. Chaudhuri sees no hope of regeneration in near future and the book ends on a note of despair: "Everything beyond is uncertain, and the foreground is vide et meant, empty with nothingness in it. I wish I could see man's great age coming anew—it may; but I cannot see how it will." (137)

In its ultimate admission of the inevitability of decline and of the impossibility of any renewal of the present civilization, the book is disconcerting. But in many respects, *Three Horsemen of the New Apocalypse* is a valuable contribution to contemporary history. Here Chaudhuri records his mature wisdom on a subject of universal concern in closely-knit arguments and in measured prose. His age has left no mark on his writing; nor has he allowed his predilections and dislikes influence the presentation of his subject. He has tried to remain objective throughout the book. In the Preface, Chaudhuri admits that he has taken Machiavelli, Thomas Hobbes and Alexis de Tocqueville as his models in choosing the form of the book. Like these great European thinkers, Chaudhuri is not given to "looseness of thinking" or "imprecision in writing." The absence of looseness does not result in rigidity or dryness. On the contrary, it makes the book a highly readable and disinterested meditation on the twentieth century as it is nearing its end. It is true that some of his observations, however astute these may be, and fundamental assumptions may appear unacceptable to many. One may not agree to his assumption that there is a purpose behind the flow of energy in the universe or to his postulate about the psychological evolution of the human species. Again, his strong dislike of democracy, because of its baneful impact on mental life, may appear to be elitist. Moreover, the elite of a society are more responsible for the debasement of democracy than the general mass of people. The steady erosion of political values, the degeneration of the democratic institutions, and the prevalence of financial and political scandals in India of today, for example, are largely the contributions of the ruling elite. Again, he has marked individualism as an agent of the decline and fall of Western civilization but ignored its contribution to the development of modernism. There is no gainsaying the role of this concept behind the most distinctive cultural achievement in the modern age. His views about American decadence and technology and his judgments on the two dominant passions of British and Indian peoples, namely money-making and promiscuity, and on American decadence and technology are as challenging as they are thought-provoking. Like all his previous writings, this book will also spark off controversy. But it is the sign of a live and creative mind in an author that it can provoke readers and stimulate their thoughts even at the age of hundred. At once absorbing and disturbing, *Three Horsemen of the New Apocalypse* will remain a remarkable landmark in apocalyptic literature and an enduring testament of this celebrated scholar, humanistic thinker, and dispassionate critic of East and West.

NOTES

1. *Three Horsemen of the New Apocalypse* (Oxford University Press 1997), p. 10.
2. Chaudhuri thinks that nationalism and imperialism are two aspects of the same political urge: "the first being its defensive aspect and the second its assertive." (56)
3. Quoted by the author himself in an article entitled "A Sterile Intelligentsia," *The Times of India*, May 25, 1980.
4. (Tenth Jaico Impression, 1994), pp. 424-25.
5. It was subsequently included in his collection of essays, *The East is East and The West is West*, ed. Dhruba N. Chaudhuri (Calcutta: Mitra and Ghosh, 1996).
6. "British Rule is Dead, Long Live British Rule!" Qtd. by the author in *Three Horsemen of the New Apocalypse*, p. 117.

"England Unmade Me": The Anguish of Chaudhuri in *Three Horsemen of the New Apocalypse*

SHYAM S. AGARWALLA

My critique of Chaudhuri's *Three Horsemen of the New Apocalypse* would be circular, rather than linear. It is about death in religious vocabulary. All religions, all faiths, speak of the ultimate journey of the man, that is, death. Chaudhuri quotes four lines from Wordsworth's poem *Ode on the Intimations of Immortality* on page 46. The first line, "Our birth is but a sleep and a forgetting," tells us that birth is just falling asleep, and just like falling asleep, and just as we forget the world in sleep, similarly, at birth we forget what happened to us in our previous existence. A. Hamilton Thompson comments: "Wordsworth in this stanza recalls the platonic doctrine of a former existence in which the Soul contemplates God and those ideal forms which are the archetypes of the forms of death. According to Plato, all learning acquired in the earthly life is reminiscence, in which the soul learns to recognize the reflections of the ideals with which it had been conversant in its earlier home."

Lord Krishna tells Arjuna in *Srimad Bhagavadgita*:

> Vasami jirnani yatha vihaya navani grhnati naroparani
> tatha sarirani vihaya jirnanyanyani samyati navani dehi (Chap. 2, ll. 22-23)
> As a man shedding worn-out garments, takes other new ones, likewise the embodied soul, casting off worn-out bodies, enters into others which are new.

Lord Krishna tells Arjuna not to grieve over death:

> Jatasya hi dhruvo mrtyurdhruvani janma mrtasya ca
> tasmadaparihary e'r the na tvam socitumarhasi (Chap. 2, l. 23)
> For in that case death is certain for the born, and rebirth is inevitable for the dead. You should not, therefore, grieve over the inevitable.

Chaudhuri quotes Tagore, Walter Pater and Pascal to prove the religious concept of death which, often, turn the weak into passivity, docility, social and political sensitivity. He develops the community spirit, lives on his conscience, cultivates societal mind and heart.

To develop Chaudhuri's point further, I, for instance, take up Leo Tolstoy and Chekhov, of the nineteenth century Russia. In *What is Art*, Tolstoy laughed at the absurdity of opera and ballet, and in *Resurrection* he spoke of the Mass as "words and magic" in such a way that the Church considered it blasphemy and excommunicated Tolstoy. He preached "true Christianity" based on the Sermon on the Mount and the fundamentals of Christ's Gospel: "Love thy neighbour" and "Do not resist by violence." These two maxims, according to Tolstoy, were sufficient guides for living in accordance with Divine Will. Marc Slonim beautifully sums up Tolstoy's concept of human approach to divinity:

> He denied the divinity of Christ and the immortality of the soul, and refused to cope with metaphysical problems, confining himself to morality. . . . Simplicity, purity, naturalness, resignation—those, according to the sage of Clear Glades, were the fundamental virtues of man, and their practice could, in his opinion, lead to salvation . . . the kingdom of God was within us, and the renovation of mankind could be accomplished only by the reform of the individual, by the concentrated efforts of millions of separate wills.

For some years Chekhov was attracted by Tolstoy's moral policy of non-resistance to evil by violence, but by 1890, after his voyage to the Island of Sikhalin, a penal colony, he abandoned that doctrine and re-asserted the value of struggle, and a belief in liberalism. "Reason and justice tell me," he wrote in his half-joking manner, "that there is more humanity in electricity and steam than in chastity and vegetarianism." In modern India, Tolstoy was an exemplar for Gandhi and Nehru was an executant of Chekhov's liberalism. In *Gooseberries*, Chekhov challenged Tolstoy's didactic tale of *How Much Land Does a Man Need* by saying, "It is customary to affirm that man needs but seven feet of earth. That, however, will suffice only for a corpse. A human being needs more than seven feet, more than a whole estate—he needs the whole world. "Tolstoy, like Lord Buddha and Lord Mahabir in India, had advocated asceticism, looked askance at religious preachings, but didacticism laid aslant his path. His ascetics looked for an ashen person, shrunken, submissive, stomachless, and stolid. Yama, for Tolstoy, Wordsworth, Tagore, Pascal, and Peter, is like a conning tower, which directs firing on hapless or helpless human beings, clock-wise. Tolstoy does not subscribe to immortality and divinity but, at the same time, his didacticism portrays him as an ascetic, devoid of individualism and liberalism.

Chekhov, on the other hand, advocates individualism and liberalism. In his own words, he believed "in health, intelligence, talent, inspiration, love and absolute freedom, freedom from coercion and falsehood." This sensitive, delicate artist was a convinced positivist and humanist with the ideal of fully developed harmonious individuality. Death does not strike fear in his heart. Death does not make him moralize on mortality and immortality. Death does not give him searing pain nor seclude him from society or company. Sackcloth and ashes are repugnant to him, as deprivation of liberty is *depayse* for an epicurean.

Chaudhuri retextures the origin of man and woman in this world, biologically: "So, religion leaves us in the same uncertainty about man's life in the world and individuality as intellectual inquiry so far seen has done. The religious view of life is anti-biological. Indeed, all religions in their basic stand are a revolt against biology." (47) I have written about the biological evolution of man in my book *Religion and Caste Politics*: "It is an accepted version of the biologists that the superiority of *homo sapiens* is based on two things: (a) complex nervous system, and (b) brain. The earthworm has no specialized nervous system i.e., it is not regulated from one centre or brain. It has absolutely no consciousness. If it is cut into two, both parts would survive without being conscious of the happening. Thus, it is consciousness that differentiates human beings from animals . . . Gifted with these two assets, man has acquired consciousness, or more correctly, what the Germans call, *geist*. . . . A plausible deduction that we can make from these reasonable hypotheses is the relationship between human consciousness and religion. Consciousness makes a human being, first, to understand the things around, and then manipulate, or control the forces of nature. . . . Therefore, the concept of religion is the result of mature human consciousness, i.e, a quality that enables man to perceive a symmetry first, and, then conceive a purpose or meaning of the symmetry."[2] As man was helpless in the primitive age but endowed with consciousness, he attributed all the things to some supernatural power. Sir Alfred C. Lyall calls it "natural religion." So, the religious view of life, arising from "natural religion" to modern religious views, is the product of consciousness, which is a specialized nervous system, an accepted version of biology. So, the religious view of life is not anti-biological, but is a finished product in the factory of biology. After all, consciousness or specialized nervous system is the main cause of either religious or secular concepts. If man considers this world to be an evil place, it is because of his progress from "natural religion" to the religion of God(s), "the invention of God(s) was not a single person's invention, whether an Indian, or an African, or a Polynesian. Out of this invention issued two things—devotion and rituals and ceremonies. . . . People literally believed in the rituals and the ceremonies which they performed, be it the Christian (Catholic) belief in the conversion of the whole substance of Eucharistic bread and wine into the body and blood of Christ . . . man understood the symbolic meaning of these rituals. This was the genesis of metaphysical religion, philosophical speculations . . . the moment human consciousness reached the level of abstraction, religion manifested itself in a new form."[3] The question of evil in human nature is an abstraction, which man developed as he progressed from lower consciousness to higher consciousness.

Erich Fromm, a great German/US social psychologist, throws

light on this aspect of religion and human nature by narrating the biblical myth of man's expulsion from paradise: "Man and woman live in the Garden of Eden in complete harmony with each other and with nature. There is peace and no necessity to work; there is no choice, no freedom, no thinking either. Man is forbidden to eat from the tree of knowledge of good and evil. He acts against God's command, he breaks through the state of harmony with nature of which he is a part without transcending it. From the standpoint of the Church which represented authority, this is essentially sin. From the standpoint of man, however, this is the beginning of human freedom."[4] He reasons us with the birth of the concept of individualism, contradistinguishing it with God's command and bondage to authority. Proceeding on the same wavelength of reasoning, he proclaims:

> Acting against God's orders means freeing himself from coercion, emerging from the unconscious existence of pre-human life to the level of man. Acting against the command of authority, committing, a sin, is in its positive human aspect the first act of freedom, that is, the first human act. In the myth the sin in its formal aspect is the eating of the tree of knowledge. The act of disobedience as an act of freedom is the beginning of reason. The myth speaks of other consequences of the first act of freedom. The original harmony between man and nature is broken. God proclaims war between man and woman, and war between nature and man. Man has become separate from nature, he has taken the first step toward becoming human by becoming an "individual."[5]

The angry eyes of God in Christianity compel man "to fall into evil ways unless protected by God's gift of grace." (47) But this is the beginning of individualism, a blessing in disguise. Once again, biology intervenes between man and God, endows man with reason, wards off fears of divine evil and makes him a free man, lovable and loving, free and sinless, encumbered by guilt of sin, repentance, and coercion. Religion is one aspect of human consciousness. Biology, therefore, deserves pitas from religion. Man is a biological species, nonspecific with God, who is also a product of higher consciousness of man. The questions of evil, human suffering, "the lust of the flesh, and the lust of the eyes, and the pride of life," (47) may not have answers in holy scriptures of religions, but Ockam taught that man's nature has not been really corrupted by sin; to him, sin is only a single act which does not change the substance of man. The Tridentinum very clearly states that the free will co-operates with God's grace but that it can also refrain from this co-operation."[6]

As to the question raised by Chaudhuri: "Why does God send man into this world, to have an intermezzo who has no real, eternal life" (47), the answer lies in Calvin's God who, in spite of all attempts to preserve the idea of god's justice and love, has all the features of a tyrant without any quality of love or even justice. In blatant contradiction to the New Testament, which Chaudhuri quotes profusely, Calvin denies the supreme role of love and says: "For what the schoolmen advance concerning the priority of chastity to faith and hope, is a mere reverie of a distempered imagination."[7]

Chaudhuri writes about decadence of Western civilization, of the English people, and of India and the United States. He finds the meaning of decadence in the Webster International more satisfying than the OED. Decadence 'presupposes a previous maturing and usually a high degree of excellence; it implies that the falling takes place after a thing (such as a people, a literature or other form of art, a branch of knowledge) has reached the peak of its development.' Chaudhuri rues the ruderal growth of contemporary English civilization on the rubbish of decadence. He prefers his solidarity with the Victorian morality to softly approach the decadence. I will take into consideration two signs of decadence in the English people, viz., love for jewellery by English women and passion for money by the English people.

Every age creates its own likes and dislikes, pride and prejudice, and habits and social mores. Chaudhuri criticizes Englishwomen, "especially the young, [who] seem these days to have fallen for the Oriental habit of overloading themselves with jewellery in their workaday appearance. . . . Both of these are unoriental, for the pearls are synthetic and the gold fake. To speak of the gold only, a respectable Oriental woman would have only 22 carat." (81) Chaudhuri writhes at the thought of his 'dear' Englishwomen imitating the Oriental habit of adornment. He has been away from India for more than two decades, when he had written his last book. Indian workaday women no longer wear 22 carat jewellery. And they cannot afford to. Even the elite women in India use 22 carat jewllery in family functions or festivals only. They use jewellery, made of synthetic and the fake gold, to adore themselves in their workaday appearance. The violent England is as much unsafe for the real gold jewellery in the neck of a workaday woman as violent India is for her womenfolk. It is not the sign of decadence, as bolting of a house is not the sign of decadence.

Nirad C. Chaudhuri's disdain for money-grubber and spendthrift in England is understandable. In *A Passage to England*, Chaudhuri regarded the Englishman as showing a general 'non- attachment' to money. He refuses to discuss the problems and methods of acquisition openly. "Chaudhuri admits that there is a good deal of prudery over this, but he fails to see in the Englishmen's attitude to money the sordidness which he finds among Indians. In their monetary transactions the Englishmen believe in smoothness which is unthinkable in India."[8] The Eighties had broken the illusion of Chaudhuri. Malcolm Bradbury vividly portrays the Eighties in England: "If the Fifties had largely read culture with a moral vocabulary, the Sixties with a sociological one, the Seventies with the language of personal consciousness, the Eighties quickly introduced a new discourse founded on myths of money. It was no longer the radical sociologists and the consciousness-gurus, but the post-Keynesian economists who provided the times with their going rate of exchange. The theory they delivered, "monetarism," came to dominate not only the economic and political but the cultural spirit of the day. The welfare-state consensus of the post-war years was now proving both intellectually and economically overspent. New economic realities—no less fictional than any other interpretative realities—took over; fiscal interpretation was applied to all manner of things, and not least to matters of culture and art. The age of the "free market" (which proved not as free as all that) and the commodification of culture had come, and the climate had changed."[9] Mrs. Margaret Thatcher is the inaugurator of this "inauspicious" age of "monetarism." Chaudhuri writes about it:

> Just to name them, the first is love of money in the extreme form of addiction, and the unceasing pursuit of it. . . . Among a decadent people money at their most innocent are merely like ants or working bees. There is zoological innocence in their activity; but in man's pursuit of money it acquires moral repulsiveness by becoming wholly sordid. (83)

The "Thatcher Revolution" had brought about a well-established liberal consensus to an end. Where the traditional liberal-left view had stressed the modern collectively, the "great society that redistributed wealth to all its members, the new view emphasized individualisms and sought to roll back the frontiers of the state. The bourgeois individual was reconstructed, the moral self (imperfectly) recovered rules of individualism and entrepreneurialism were applied to most aspects of life. Society, said Mrs. Thatcher in a phrase much quoted against her, "did not exist." But her meaning was perfectly clear: society consisted of a "nanny state" organizing all in the presumed best interests of each, but was the sum of its individualisms, the achievement of its most energetic selves. The USA, England, and other Western countries rapidly began to adopt the "free market." Asia did not lag behind. South Korea, Malaysia, Thailand, and Singapore opened up their markets to multinationals. India, first under late Rajiv Gandhi, and then under P.V. Narasimha Rao, has adopted the policy of the "free market" and "monetarism."

Martin Amis had written his novel, *Success* (1978), in ironically Thatcherite slogan. And in the following few years no writer of fiction better caught the note of the British Eighties, with its immediate gratifications, its apocalyptic anxieties, its cynicism and its underlying alarm. *Money: A Suicide Note* (1984) was a perfect title for the times. "As Saul Bellow said, it seemed for a while in the Eighties that money was the one thing that didn't stink," Amis wryly explained, "Everything was questionable, but money was a vital substance you knew where you were with." "While making love, we often talk about money," reports the grabby, grubby anti-hero of *Money*, John Self. "I like it. I like that dirty talk."

The Anglophone Chaudhuri mourns for the loss of "non-attachment" of Englishman for money and justifiably, in the light of the transition of the "welfare-state consensus" to "free market" state. Another Anglophone Salman Rushdie's novel, *The Satanic Verses* (1988), has a main theme of fragmentation, violence and disorder of a multi-cultural but incoherent Britain, ruled by a "Mrs. Torture." Malcom Bradbury writes: "Rushdie's *The Satanic Verses* has a surreal London going crazy in a period of extravagant heat-wave. Some critics called this the most improbable feature of the book. So common was the end-of-the-world news, the catastrophic gloom, the disaster vision, that it became a relief to turn to those writers who practised the art of sceptical and critical comedy; Rushdie himself, Anthony Burgess, the admirable William Boyd, Angela Carter, Michael Frayn, David Lodge and Howard Jacobson, who were capable of suggesting that even the age of apocalypse deserved satirical attention, and might even have a comic silver lining."[10]

Chaudhuri is incapable of seeing a comic silver lining in this age of apocalypse. He, like early T.S. Eliot, finds Britain going into the cycle of decadence and waste. If I apply his conclusion on greed for money on all "free market" states, all states in this world, including the communist states, become sites for decadence, which is not wholly true.

Nirad C. Chaudhuri's analysis of nationalism is based on some presuppositions and some propositions. I would deal with his propositions. He writes: "The new nationalism has created a strong sense of national identity for each nation which is different from other national identities. Conscious of being *we* not *they* is strong and ineradicable in the present-day nationalists. This makes them xenophobic. . . . But in contemporary nationalism xenophobia has become aggressive and active. It has created a feeling that all foreigners are potential enemies." (59-60)

Hans Kohn, in his books, *The Idea of Nationalism, The Age of Nationalism*, and *Nationalism, Its Meaning and History*, accepts nationalism as an integral part of the story of liberty. In its essential aspects, therefore, nationalism represents the attempt to actualize in political terms the universal urge for liberty and progress. And yet the evidence was undeniable that it could also give rise to mindless chauvinism and xenophobia and serve as the justification for organized violence and tyranny. "It has been the cause of the most destructive wars ever seen; it has justified the brutality of Nazism and Fascism, it has become the ideology of racial hatred in the colonies and has given birth to some of the most irrational revivalist movements as well as to the most oppressive political regimes in the contemporary world."[11] Nationalism and liberty could often be quite irreconcilably opposed. Dr. Salazar of Portugal, in the name of nationalism, established a "Dictatorship of Reason and Intelligence." He did not like theories of democratic liberty preached in England. His argument was that in the particular circumstances of Portugal, the choice was between anarchy and misery on the one hand and authority and well-being on the other; and that in the political conditions of that nation it is nonsense to pretend, in the name of liberty, "that the administration can be carried out by the mob instead of an *elite* whose duty it is to lead and to sacrifice itself for the rest of the community."[12]

Chaudhuri writes about nationalism in newly-freed-nations, "which has created a type of human personality like the 'freed man' in Roman society, who although free, could never forget that he had once been a slave. . . . All the present-day nationalist people of Asia and Africa have a feeling that they are confronted by hostile peoples, and nurse endless grievances." (60) The feelings of Asians and Africans are not without foundation. Elie Kedourie writes that the very idea of nationalism being a rational and self-conscious attempt by the weak and poor peoples of the world to achieve autonomy and liberty is demonstrably false. Nationalism as an ideology is irrational, narrow, hateful, and destructive. It is not an authentic product of any of the non-European civilizations which, in each particular case, it claims as its classical heritage. It is wholly a European export to the rest of the world. It is not a child of reason and liberty, but of fervent romanticism, of political messianism whose inevitable consequence is the annihilation of freedom. On the other hand, Anthony Smith says that nationalism has often had a great humanizing and civilizing influence. He cites Dvorak and Chopin, or Cesaire, Senghor, Abduh and Tagore. It is misleading to portray nationalist politics merely as secret conspiracy and terrorism or nihilism and totalitarianism.

> Nobody would dispute that these have been features of some nationalisms. . . . But it is only fair to recall the extreme situations in which they operated. . . . Kedourie forgets the uses of nationalism in developing countries, the way in which they can legitimate new regimes desirous of maintaining political stability and keeping a fissiparous population under a single and viable harness. He forgets too the examples of nationalism providing an impetus to constitutional reforms, as in India or Ottoman Turkey, not to mention its uses in legitimizing sweeping social change and modernisation.[13]

As to the charge of Chaudhuri against the peoples of Asia and Africa for "their excessive military preparation," (61) and "unbearable burden of military expenditure," (61) Partha Chatterjee counters: "It is to raise the possibility that it is not just military might or industrial strength, but thought itself, which can dominate and subjugate. It is to approach the field of discourse, historical, philosophical and scientific, as a battleground of political power."[14]

Chaudhuri writes his conception of nationalism and says: "The main and the strongest drive for it (nationalism) comes from national pride." (59) Horace B. Davis gives a similar argument: "Whether to consider nationalism a rationalist, secular, modern movement, or whether to emphasize the more distinctly national elements, many of which are frankly atavistic and irrelevant to modern conditions. . . . Atavistic nationalism cannot be condemned out of hand, when considered as part of a movement for a people to regain its pride and self respect, it has a constructive aspect. . . Nationalism is . . . an implement . . . when used for murder, the hammer is no doubt a weapon, when for building a house, it is a constructive tool. Nationalism considered as the vindication of a particular culture is morally neutral; considered as a movement against national oppression, it has a positive moral content, considered as the vehicle of aggression, it is morally indefensible."[15]

This national pride often leads to wars between Third-World countries, which has led Chaudhuri to say: "nationalism among the peoples of Asia and Africa has led to repeated and continuing armed conflicts." (61) Benedict Anderson, in *Imagined Commu-*

nities, expresses a similar view on Third-world nationalism of twentieth century: "No one imagines, I presume, that the broad masses of the Chinese people give a fig for what happens along the border between Cambodia and Vietnam. Nor is it at all likely that Khmer and Vietnamese peasants wanted wars between their peoples, or were consulted in the matter. In a very real sense were 'chancellery wars' in which popular nationalism was mobilized after the fact and always in a language of self-defence."[16]

Thus, it is all a matter of vanguard intelligentsia coming to state power by "mobilizing" popular nationalism and using the "Machiavellian" instruments of official nationalism. Both Chaudhuri and Anderson strike a pessimistic note.

Chaudhuri's view on democracy is Leavisian. He says:

> Elite is a term which recognizes 'quality' as the supreme criterion in determining the importance of any group of persons in the nation or community.
>
> This standard is rejected by 'total democracy,' which preaches and has popularized the nation that an elite is really an ideological *canaille*, a residual scum. The fanaticism shown by the holders of this view of 'elitism' is terrifying to those who prize quality. The 'total democracy' of today is, in contrast, the champion of quantity. (65)

F.R. Leavis, in his very early publication "Mass Civilization and Minority Culture" (1930), explained the role of the educated minority and their composition: "Upon this minority depends our power of profiting by the finest human experience of the past; they keep alive the subtlest and most perishable parts of tradition. Upon them depend the implicit standards that order the finer living of an age, the sense that this is worth more than that, this rather than that is the direction in which to go, that the centre is here rather than there."[17] From the very beginning Leavis and Chaudhuri place a tremendous burden on the minority, the elites, they alone, in effect, are responsible for, and can change, the health of a modern democratic society.

"Granting that Leavis is concerned with more than a literary minority, his insistence on the crucial importance of the educated minority is in modern democratic society, frequently challenged or resisted. While the importance of the educated public may have been recognized in the nineteenth century of Coleridge and Arnold, in modern society the dominance of egalitarian ideas often leads to a straightforward rejection of the role of minorities. Leavis himself regards the prevalent hostility towards minorities, towards the educated public and thus to standards, as one of the sicknesses of contemporary society."[18] I had written these words in 1995. William Walsh, in his essay on "the literary critic and the Education of an Elite," makes two important observations that seem relevant to any egalitarian critique of minorities. First, Walsh notes that "Civilization, or 'culture' in Coleridge's and Arnold's sense, has always been the direct concern and the immediate product of minorities."[19] The importance of minorities in the past seems a well-settled fact, and there seems little reason to think that the situation had changed in the early twentieth century in the Western world and in the late twentieth century in the Eastern world. Secondly, continuing his defence of minorities, Walsh argues: "Democracy has much to tell us about the quality of moral value of men but very little to say about the equality of intellectual capacity. And capacity, intellectual capacity, is to be the sole measure regulating the composition of the elite."[20]

Chaudhuri commends the elites in his *The Autobiography of an Unknown Indian*:

> They lived in [Calcutta] aristocratic segregation, brought about in the first instance by the orthodoxy of the ordinary Bengali . . . and secondly by their own contempt for those whom they looked upon as the unredeemed rank and file of Bengali society. . . . Most of them had a highly literary culture, well-developed political sense, and awareness of social and political duties. . . . In family life, despite the fact that some affected the ways of the fast and more fell a prey to drink, the general tone was of Victorian respectability, strict discharge of family obligations, steadiness. I use the adjective Victorian in a commendatory sense, as I feel it should be.[21]

He mourns the loss of Victorian qualities in the post-Victorians and calls them decidedly poorer lot than the Victorians. The commination of Chaudhuri against the subalterns is as subtle and ingenious as Dr. Salazar's "Dictatorship of Reason and Intelligence." Dr. Allen's counter-question to Dr. Salazar was as much relevant to him as it is to Chaudhuri. His rhetorical counterblast to Dr. Salazar is convincing:

> Who elects the *elite*, and what is to prevent their title to rule being sheer superiority of cunning or of might? What are the limits of authority? If it is necessary, for the sake of order, to suppress the dissent of the Malignants, what guarantee is there that the reasonable dissent of Benignants will not also be suppressed? What government yet devised by man is really fit to decide in all circumstances, of its own omniscience, what is best for a people? And, above all, how can irresponsible power be prevented from feeding upon itself—how can authority, even if it begins with the most benevolent intentions, be restrained from the vice of all autocracy, which is to regard its own survival as the supreme consideration? All history shows that a monopoly of right is destined, of its very nature, to become a monopoly of wrong.[22]

The examples of Soekarno, Zia, Nkurmah, Idi Amin and Milton Obote, to name a few rulers, send shivers in our minds and hearts.

This has led the visionary historian, Ranjit Gupta, to deviate from this Victorian dogma and say: "The historiography of Indian nationalism has for a long time been dominated by elitism—colonial elitism and bourgeois-nationalist elitism. . . . Both these varieties of elitism share the prejudice that the making of the Indian nation and the development of the consciousness—nationalism—which informed this process were exclusively or predominantly elite achievements."[23] The absence of the subalterns's participation in the colonial period resulted in the failure of the Indian bourgeoisie to speak for the nation.

Nirad C. Chaudhuri sees crisis in Western, English, and Indian civilizations, fearing their decline and fall. The term "crisis" is of Greek derivation, and gains its force from its medical usage as describing the climax of some illness at which the patient will either die or recover. A crisis is thus a matter of life or death, and the only reason the term can be used, over and over again, to describe recurring conditions in modern Europe and America is that they often think of their world as a succession of discontinuities (or "revolutions") rather than in terms of the changing fortunes of one, and continuous, forms of life. For instance, where the Sixties in England had been the age of hippie, the Eighties was the age of the Yuppie. The Russian Revolution in 1917 brought about Communism in Eastern European states. In November 1989 the Berlin Wall came down. It was said the politicians, the New World Order historians announced the "End of History." "What we may be witnessing is not just the end of the Cold War, or the passing of a particular period of post-war history, but the end of history as such: that is, the end point of mankind's ideological evolution and universalization of Western liberal democracy as the final form of human government," wrote Francis Fukuyama in 1989. The ascendancy of Caliban over Prospero, as Chaudhuri laments is not the sign of the decadence of Western civilization or English civilization, but is the End of British Imperialist History and the beginning of Third-World-liberation history. *Three Horsemen of the New Apocalypse* is a prosthesis to prop up the British and the American imperialism, their elitist debunking, and their decedent personality.

Chaudhuri, like W.H. Auden in 1940, is anguished and confused. It is about being unable to be English any more, at, of all times, England's time "of peril":

> The New Year brings an earth unafraid,
> Democracy a ready-made
> And noisy tradesman's slogan, and
> The poor betrayed into the hand
> Of lackeys with ideas, and truth
> Whipped by their elders out of youth,
>
> And culture on all fours to greet
> A butch and criminal *elite*,
> While in the vale of silly sheep
> Rheumatic old patricians weep. (*New Year Letter*)

It was terrible time for Auden to despair in 1940, as it is terrible time for Chaudhuri to despair in 1997. Their epitaph could be "England unmade me."

NOTES

1. Marc Slonim, *An Outline of Russian Literature* (New York: Mentor Book, 1959), p. 117.
2. Shyam S. Agarwalla, *Religion and Caste Politics* (Jaipur: Rawat Publications, 1998), pp. 18-19.
3. *Ibid.*, pp. 23-25.
4. Erich Fromm, *Escape from Freedom* (New York: Holt, Rinehart and Winston, 1941; 1968), pp. 49-50.
5. *Ibid.*, p. 50.
6. *Ibid.*, p. 90.
7. John Calvin's *Institutes of the Christian Religion*, trans. John Allen (Philadelphia: Presbyterian Board of Christian Education, 1928), Book III, Chapter 2, p. 41.
8. C. Paul Verghese, *Nirad C. Chaudhuri* (New Delhi: Arnold-Heinemann India, 1973), p. 56.
9. Malcolm Bradbury, *The Modern British Novel* (London: Secker and Warburg, 1993; 1994), pp. 395-96.
10. *Ibid*, pp. 410-11.
11. Partha Chatterjee, *Nationalist Thought and the Colonial World* (New Delhi: OUP, 1986), p. 2.
12. Quoted in Carleton Kemp Allen's *Democracy and the Individual* (Calcutta: OUP, 1943; 1997), pp. 92-93
13. Anthony Smith, *Theories of Nationalism* (London: Duckworth, 1971), pp. 12-24.
14. Partha Chatterjee, *Nationalist Thought and the Colonial World*, p. 11.
15. Horace B. Davis, *Towards a Marxist Theory of Nationalism* (New York: Monthly Review Press, 1978), pp. 24-31.
16. Benedict Anderson, *Imagined Communities: Reflections on the Origin and Spread of Nationalism* (London: Verse, 1983), p. 146.
17. F.R. Leavis, *For Continuity* (Cambridge: The Minority Press, 1933), p. 15.
18. Shyam S. Agarwalla, *Vikram Seth's A Suitable Boy: Search for an Indian Identity* (New Delhi: Prestige Books, 1995), p. 49.

19. William Walsh, *The Use of Imagination* (Harmondswroth: Penguin, 1966), p. 72.
20. *Ibid.*, p. 76.
21. Nirad C. Chaudhuri, *The Autobiography of an Unknown Indian* (Bombay: Jaico, 1969), pp. 403-4.
22. Carleton Kemp Allen, *Democracy and the Individual*, p. 93.
23. Ranjit Guha, "On Some Aspects of the Historiography of Colonial India," in *Subaltern Studies*, vol. I. p. 1.

A Postcolonial Interpretation of Chaudhuri's Selected Critical Writings

PURABI PANWAR

Like most other English language readers of my generation in India, I have been alternately appalled and fascinated by the writings of Nirad C. Chaudhuri. I have never met him personally, acquaintances of my father's generation who have, recollect his small residence near Mori Gate in Old Delhi where he lived before being invited to tea by the grand old man of letters who is about to turn hundred. At his Delhi residence, tea was invariably served at four with petit four biscuits, among other things. An indication of his love for British traditions which combined with his conservative Bengali roots, give his writings that distinctive character that verges on paradoxicality at times. So, while writing about India and Indians, he is both the insider with his knowledge of history and classics and the outsider who would attack anything he finds irrational, unscientific or simply outdated.

Most of us have read his creative works, *The Autobiography of an Unknown Indian* and *The Continent of Circe* among others, but few are familiar with Niradbabu as a literary critic. I propose to take up two of his literary essays, "Passage to and from India"[1] and "The Finest Story about India—in English"[2] with a purpose to compare the two and assess Niradbabu as an English language critic.

"The Finest Story . . . ," a critique of *Kim* is taken up first though it was written later, to keep the chronology of the subject-novels in order. At the very outset, Chaudhuri remarks, "in *Kim* its author wrote not only the finest novel in English language with an Indian theme, but also one of the greatest of English novels in spite of the theme." (28) Considering that *Kim* was written and published while the British empire was at the zenith of its glory, a few things can be deduced from this.

Though ostensibly on the colonizer's side, Kipling's range of vision about India, socially as well as geographically, is not limited by the Anglo-Indian habit of belittling anything Indian (like referring to the Himalayan mountains as the "hills"). To quote Chaudhuri, *Kim* "is the product of Kipling's vision of a much bigger India, a vision whose profundity we Indians would be hard put to match even in an Indian language, not to speak of English. He had arrived at a true and moving sense of that India which is almost timeless, and had come to love it." (30) A look at Kipling's letters from India[3] and his autobiographical book *Something of Myself and Other Autobiographical Writings* (1990) would have substantiated Chaudhuri's comments but he more or less confines his study to *Kim* in his essay, with a few passing references to *The Jungle Book* and the story "Purun Bhagat."

Niradbabu, with his strong Hindu beliefs, finds the choice of the Lama as a representative of Indian spirituality, somewhat problematic, though not so much as the choice of the Muslim Aziz as the Indian protagonist of *A Passage to India* which will be taken up later. Kipling's choice of the Lama as an exponent of Hindu spirituality is traced to preference based on knowledge. To quote: "His interest in Buddhism was roused by the Gandhara sculptures in the Lahore museum, of which his father was the curator." Recent studies have shown that Kipling had actually met a Lama who was later represented fictionally. In a letter dated May 16, 1902 to Sir Aurel Stein, the great Central Asian explorer and archaeologist, Kipling's father John Lockwood Kipling enquired, "I wonder whether you have seen my son's *Kim*, and recognised an old man whom you saw at the old Museum and at the School." (Hopkirk, 41-42)

Hurree Chander Mookerjee, alias the Babu or R 17 is a key figure in *Kim*. With a razor sharp mind, he can stand up to any one including the whites. Kipling disliked Indian intellectuals who had some English education and tended to question the existence of British empire. Predictably, Hurree Babu is depicted as a comic figure. What surprises the Indian reader is the way Niradbabu plays it down: Kipling's "dislike for Indians who had received a western education was both irresponsible and indiscreet, and in the light of what has followed almost foolish. . . . There was no originality in Kipling's rudeness to us, but only a repetition, in the forthright Kiplingian manner of what was being said in every mess and club." (28) On the one hand Niradbabu takes Kipling's attitude towards educated Indians for granted, on the other he criticizes Forster for not being fair in his portrayal of English officials. How does one reconcile the two attitudes? One is tempted to term Niradbabu's appreciation for Kipling in general and *Kim* in particular, as colonial to an extent.

The saving grace of Niradbabu's essay on *Kim* is his assessment of Kipling as a travel writer, as revealed in the novel. To quote:

> Kipling was equally at home in our plains, hills and mountains, and like all great novelists he remains firmly ecological. There are in *Kim* not only entrancing descriptions of the Himalayas but a picture of the green phase on the great plain that is uncanny in its combination of romance and actuality. We Indians shall never cease to be grateful to Kipling for having shown the many faces of our country in all their beauty, power and truth. (32)

The last sentence, in the passage quoted above, smacks of adulation. The rest of it is a fair assessment. A reference to some of Kipling's travel essays published in *Civil & Military Gazette* and *Pioneer* would have been in order as they preceded *Kim* but also the description in some of these essays is similar to that in *Kim* but more restrained as they were written for newspapers with an official patronage.

A reading of Niradbabu's "Passage to and from India" indicates that there were a number of things in the novel which he did not quite approve of. To quote: "The novel was quite openly a satire on the British official in India. Perhaps in a veiled form it was also a satire on the Indians who were, or aspired to be, the *clients* of the foreign patriciate." (19) So the novel is taken up as "a political essay on Indo-British relations" and in that respect Niradbabu finds it rather inadequate

He views Indo-British relations as largely the conflict between Indian nationalism and British administration which, I feel, is a rather limited perspective, as it ignores the deeper impact of the colonial encounter on the concerned races. In the General Introduction to *The Post-Colonial Studies Reader*,[4] the editors point out the complex developments that rose from this encounter. To quote:

> the eminently prestigious and powerful imperial culture found itself appropriated in projects of counter-colonial resistance which drew upon the many different indigenous local and hybrid processes of self-determination to defy, erode and sometimes supplant the prodigious power of imperial cultural knowledge. Post-colonial literatures are a result of this interaction between imperial culture and the complex of indigenous cultural practices. (1)

It is possible that Niradbabu was himself too close to the colonial set up to be able to assess its far-reaching effects objectively. According to him, Forster's depiction of race relations was limited by the shortness of his visits. "As an Englishman paying a short visit to India he naturally saw far less of Indians in general than of his own countrymen and of the Indians with whom the latter had official business or perfunctory social relations. . . . He could not observe the larger and the more important area without going considerably out of his way and making a special effort." (20) Also, he feels that Forster's "humanitarian consciousness," also termed as a liberal humanistic way of thinking, leads him to sit in judgement against the British official in India.

While one agrees with the second reason, one does not quite agree with the first. There is a depth in Forster's perception of India and his journals and letters bear testimony to the fact that he did go out of his way to meet Indians of all strata of society, from the Maharajas of Chhattarpur and Dewas (where he was political secretary to the Maharaja) to underprivileged persons like servants at the court who find a collective fictional representation in the Punkahwalla in *A Passage to India*. It is the quality of Indian experience rather than the number of days he spent in India on his first and second visits, that should be considered.

Niradbabu's high indignation at the way in which the English officials are portrayed by Forster, is predictable, given his colonial bias. To quote at length:

> Mr. Forster makes the British officials of Chandrapore nervous about the excitement of the Muharram to the extent of making the women and children take shelter in the club. . . . Of this kind of cowardice no British official in India was to my mind ever guilty. . . . As a class, the British officials kept their head. The shortcoming of the British official was not in courage, but in intelligence. (21)

Niradbabu talks of cowardice while to my mind, what Forster tries to convey is a tense situation with political overtones that makes the characters behave in a particular way. The Turtons and Burtons in *A Passage to India* are balanced by characters like Fielding and Mrs. Moore, characters who can relate to India and Indians. Forster had friends in the civil service like Sir Malcolm Darling who, along with his wife Josie, met and made friends with a number of Indians during his tenure in Punjab. The situation in *A Passage to India* is tense because of administrators like Ronny Heaslop, not Malcolm Darling. In that light Niradbabu's comment, "It (the novel) shows a great imperial system at its worst, not as diabolically evil but as drab and asinine; the rulers and the ruled alike are depicted at their smallest, the snobbery and pettiness of the one matching the imbecility and rancour of the other," (22) needs to be modified.

The indignation is intensified when directed towards Forster's Indian characters, generally and specifically. Niradbabu is against the idea of a Muslim character being the protagonist in a novel dealing with Indo-British relations. His reason:

> They [the Muslims] should never have been the second party to the relationship in the novel, because ever since the nationalist movement got into its stride the Muslims were playing a curiously equivocal role, realistic and effective politically, but unsatisfying in every respect. The Muslims hated the British. . . . Yet they found themselves wooed by

> the latter as a counterpoise to the Hindu nationalists, and they did not reject these overtures. (22)

It is difficult that a person of his generation and an erudite scholar at that, fails to take note of the divide-and-rule policy of the English in India, alternately showing favours to the Hindus and Muslims in an effort to (and succeeding) keep the two communities sharply divided. While on the subject of Hindu-Muslim relationship in India, Niradbabu shows his parochialism when he makes a pronouncement against Aziz. To quote: "Aziz would not have been allowed to cross my threshold, not to speak of being taken as an equal. Men of his type are a pest even in free India." (21) Perhaps the critic forgets that Aziz is modelled on Forster's friend Syed Ross Masood who invited him to India and who was known to be as impetuous and volatile as Aziz. One can only conclude that it is Niradbabu's colonial conditioning combined with ethnocentricity that is responsible for his negative attitude towards Aziz.

The same sentiments govern his assesssment of the Hindu characters of *A Passage to India.* According to him Forster "relied mostly on the types found in the Princely States" (21) for his Indian characters and consequently they did not represent modern India. Clearly, he implies that the novel does not focus on English educated, erudite Indians though the locale is British India, a paradoxicality that does not escape the discriminating reader.

However, Niradbabu's opinion of Godbole, "Godbole is not an exponent of Hinduism, he is a clown," (21) is an angry remark rather than a logical one. For a detailed discussion of Godbole, one can look up G.K. Das's article "The Genesis of Professor Godbole."[5] It would be adequate to point out that Godbole's limitations arise not from Forster's intentions to ridicule Hindu spirituality, but his inability to gauge it, and, consequently, represent it credibly or realistically in the intended character.

It is not fair to assess Niradbabu as a critic on the basis of just two articles as I have pointed out at the very beginning of this article. My purpose is to offer the reader a glimpse of a less explored facet of Niradbabu's creativity with the hope that one will explore it further and possibly place him in the English language critical tradition.

NOTES

1. *Encounter*, Vol. II, No. 6, June 1951.
2. John Gross, ed., *Rudyard Kipling the Man, His Work and His World* (1972).
3. *The Letters of Rudyard Kipling*, Vol. I, 1950.
4. Bill Ashcroft, Gareth Griffiths and Helen Tiffin, *The Post-Colonial Studies Reader* (Routledge, 1995).
5. *The Review of English Studies*, Vol. XXVIII, Feburary 1977, pp. 56-60.

Nirad Chaudhuri, UnIndian and UnEnglish

THOMAS AUGUSTINE

Nirad C. Chaudhuri, who died at the age of 101 at Oxford, was the greatest and the most perceptive witness of the twentieth century India. He was an iconoclast, an individualist to the point of egoism, with a love for controversies. His first book *The Autobiography of an Unknown Indian* shot him into fame and since then, the 48 years of his writing life are unprecedented in the history of writing. His incessant cerebral energy enabled him to write a book titled *Three Horsemen of the New Apocalypse* in his centenary year, a testimony of the capacity of his mind to assimilate information and the astonishing faculty of recall that Chaudhuri cultivated. In this connetion, I recall the prodigious intellect of V.I. Lenin. The tale is told of a time when Lenin was straining himself into exhaustion while preparing plans for the electrification programme of the Soviet Union. His wife, worrying for his health, advised him to take time to rest. Lenin paused, picked up a pitcher of cold water and poured it on his head and said, "The machine is now cool."

Most critics have undervalued or criticized Chaudhuri because they ignored his quest. But his quest is clearly set out in his autobiography. Chaudhuri does this by way of a long quotation from Bankim Chandra Chatterjee's novel *Rajani*. In the novel the narrator-hero describes his meeting with Amarnath where the latter does not disclose his business immediately but looks through *The Shakespeare Gallery* which is lying on the table.

A discussion follows of the pictures and of the characters they depict. "From Shakespeare's heroines," Chatterjee continues (in Chaudhuri's translation), "he came to Sakuntala, Sita, Kadamvari,

Vasavdatta, Rukmini and Satyabhama, and he analyzed their characters. The discussion of ancient literature led in its turn to ancient historiography, out of which there emerged some incomparable exposition of the classical historians, Tacitus, Plutarch, Thucydides and others. From the philosophy of history of these writers Amarnath came down to Comte and his *lois des trois etats* which he endorsed. Comte brought in his interpreter Mill and then Huxley. Huxley brought in Owen and Darwin; and Darwin Buchner and Schopenhauer. Amarnath poured the most entrancing scholarship into my ears and I became too engrossed to remember our business."[1] Chaudhuri, like Amarnath Chatterjee, was an erudite scholar and this scholarship became the real business of Chaudhuri's life.

He realized very early in life, during his student days, that the product of scholarship "was not the book but the man." This realization came to him, he says in his autobiography, from a saying by Mark Pattison quoted in one of John Morley's essays. Scholarship and personality are interrelated and "the greater part of his [the scholar's] *metier* is the capacity for experiencing the emotion of scholarship." (199) To know Chaudhuri is to know his scholarship: the man and his learning are irreparable.

With the exception of M.K. Naik, not a single critic or scholar has ever mentioned that his first significant publication is not *The Autobiography of an Unknown Indian* but "Defence of India or Nationalization of Indian Army," a seventy-three page essay, which appeared in 1935. Naik writes: "Chaudhuri begins by emphasizing the demand of the Indian National Congress to transform the whole of the defence service of India from its present (i.e. 1035) to a national footing as one of the indispensable conditions and the natural fulfilment of the ideal of Swaraj, because the right and capacity of defence is an integral part of self-government. Discussing the 'character of the present army,' he argues that the armed forces, as now constituted, are Indian in only one sense—in that their cost is borne by the peoples of India; in everything else they are non-national, though an overwhelming proportion of their personnel is furnished by India."[2]

Chaudhuri goes on to describe armies as the "Condottiere" and the "Burgher" armies, and the latter type was the product of the

French Revolution which saw an amazing liberation of the latent military energies of a whole nation. On the other hand, there was a general decline in the Indian army, because the British deliberately demartialized it by (a) keeping the army as distinct from the general population as possible and (b) depriving the Indian public of the right to carry arms. The USA makes all efforts to train civilians in the art of military training in schools and colleges; in India the people are prohibited to carry arms. The Indian government has followed the British strategy, thus, widening the gulf between civilians and military forces. M.K. Naik interprets Chaudhuri's contention: "The future organizers of a national Indian army will therefore have to restore the military spirit of the people and improve the efficiency of the entire population by halting their physical deterioration, which is the result of a vicious circle of poverty, ignorance and, in some cases, bareful habits of living and unsuitable diet." (102)

The passive resistance and non-violence of Gandhiji, which was followed by Nehru, in post-independence India, not only made Indians lethargic, unhealthy, but have made them solely dependent on the governmental initiatives and encouragements, resulting in the defeat of India at the hands of the Chinese. In 1935, Chaudhuri foresaw what the government in India has not seen even today.

The Passage to England by Chaudhuri has been much criticized and maligned because it was seen to be a tribute to the English, rather than Indians. He writes: "Just as the public in India held the record for futile political demonstrations of all kinds, their Government for its part is pre-eminent among all the Governments of the present-day world for an ineffectual recourse to violence, which in every case reduces the authority of the state instead of restoring it."[3]

Can any right-thinking citizen of India dispute that, by using force and violence, governments at the Centre and States have lost a good deal of physical territory to the ULFA, the PWG, the M.C.C., the Kashmir and Punjab militants? What we have just witnessed in the 1999 Lok Sabha polls is that the writ of the State does not run in many parts of India.

He also compares the English middle-class life with the Indian middle-class life. He says: "The English middle-class life is also simple in its attitude to manual work, which has made the servantless household possible." Compared to England,

> In our society an official of middle-class origins not only does not carry his briefcase, he does not even take a paper to a colleague, he rings for the peon. This peon on his part will carry papers and files but not packages. . . . This same peon will not dust a table, for which another functionary is employed, and the table-duster will not sweep the floor, that being the task of yet another functionary. In our society every rise in status is accompanied by a progressive diminution of physical labour.[4]

Don't we find, in government and semi-government offices, an army of officials and clerks and peons, who shrink from doing any manual labour, because of the consciousness of their position and status? This constructive criticism is neither subjective nor self-righteous. C. Paul Verghese[5] and Chetan Karnani[6] are unduly harsh on Chaudhuri.

Chaudhuri, in his perceptive book titled *The Intellectual in India*, points out: "For the vast masses of Indian peasants and artisans, constituting more than nine-tenths of the population, the intellectual activities meant nothing at all."[7] He rightly says that Hindu society "understood religious greatness, particularly, in its miraculous aspect, it also understood worldly greatness, but had no consciousness of anything in-between, which belonged to the spirit of man." (35) Besides this, poverty is another main cause of intellectual backwardness. Poverty also had encouraged the relation of the extended family which left time neither for leisure nor for introspection.

Even in Indian universities, conditions are not propitious for intellectual effort: "The Indian academic world is laden with a deep somnolence without the justification of deep potations: it is mental vacuum, and not vintage port, which produces the abstracted air on the faces of the professors." (64) Even an outsider like Edward Shils did not fail to notice this tendency everywhere: "The jealousy of an archaic head professor intimidates or obstructs the lively young man with ideas and enthusiasm, dull colleagues deaden the resonance of the atmosphere and contribute towards the slackening of standards."[9]

What Chaudhuri missed to mention was the intellectual colonization of Indians. Joon-Chien says: "Once the process of intellectual colonization for an individual is completed, it acts as a powerful control over him and guides his thoughts, and not infrequently, his actions too. The value and ideals implanted during the process of intellectual colonization become so natural a part of him that, as a mentally subjugated individual, he is not only happy, contented and proud of them but very often becomes their ardent defender and propagator."[10] He further says; "In other words, to get recognition from the Eastern intellectuals, an Asian scholar, as a matter of necessity, has to obtain some sort of recognition from the West first before he can expect any acknowledgement or acclaim from them." (16-17) Tagore, Chaudhuri, Raman, Bose, Ranjit Guha, and Amratya Sen are examples of his contention. It is true, also. Ranjit Guha could not get lecturership in Calcutta, now he is the father of the Subaltern School of Studies.

In *To Live or Not to Live*, Nirad C. Chaudhuri sets out to trace the causes of unhappiness and thereby help others avoid misery in India. The following passage is characteristic:

> That [happiness] comes from realizing some great purpose of working for it to the best of one's duties in life without flinching. . . . A man who is not happy with fellowmen and members of his family may find a compensating happiness in his vocation or in his duty, but he will never be fully happy.[11]

These lines show that Chaudhuri has outgrown the anger expressed in *The Continent of Circe*. The new mellow tone of his writing shows his desire to make a truce. Chaudhuri conceives happy living as "living to some purpose." (7) What he means by the phrase is "living in the light of an ideal, and with a sense of vocation" (35) based on self-criticism and "a searching and continuous examination, to bring about revalidation." (9) Chaudhuri believes that living directed towards the acquisition of wealth or mere survival is not living to any purpose.

A man, who was a combination of both Faust and Don Quixote,

escaped to England in 1970 with many expectations. If he admired Europe and England, it was one which was dead and buried with Mozart, Jane Austen, and Lord Patmerstone. He had to witness, in the 1970s, London still swinging in long hair and bellbottoms, remote from the refinements and graces of the Victorian/Edwardian High Culture. The disenchantment followed. *Three Horsemen of the New Apocalypse*[12] is the product of his bitterness, turning him into a decline-spotter and decadence-sniffer. He has raged against short skirts, America, English women wearing jewellery, abortion, and contraception. Predictably, the book could not find a publisher in either England or America. The Oxford University Press, India, has ultimately published his last book.

But this book is a worthy coda, its always relevant citations comprising an anthology of his immense reading, and the focus broadened into global range. And above all, while his prime subject is the decline of Western civilization under the hooves of "three horsemen," individualism, nationalism, and democracy, here are to be found Chaudhuri's *pensees* poignant, shining and, in the literal meaning, encouraging on death, which by then held him by the hand. He lived and died and beyond that, there was for him, as for us all, "the ectasy of having lived and been alive for a moment." In India, he was unIndian, in England, he was unEnglish.

NOTES

1. Nirad C. Chaudhuri, *The Autobiography of an Unknown Indian* (Bombay: Jaico, 1951; 1969), p. 192.
2. M.K. Naik, "Nirad C. Chaudhuri's First Publication," *The Journal of Commonwealth Literature*, Vol. XLX, No. 1, 1984, pp. 98-99.
3. Nirad C. Chaudhuri, "Between Anarchy and Freedom," *Encounter*, XXLX, No. 3, September 1967, p. 77.
4. Nirad C. Chaudhuri, *A Passage to England* (Delhi: Orient Paperbacks, 1959), p. 141.
5. C. Paul Verghese, *Nirad C. Chaudhuri* (New Delhi: Arnold Heinemann India, 1973).
6. Chetan Karnani, *Nirad C. Chaudhuri* (Twayne, 1980).
7. Nirad C. Chaudhuri, *The Intellectual in India* (New Delhi: Vir Pub-

lications, 1967), p. 27.
9. Edward Shils, *Intellectuals between Tradition and Modernity: The Indian Situation* (The Hague: Mouton, 1961), p. 50.
10. Doh Joon-Chien, *Eastern Intellectuals and Western Solutions*, (New Delhi: Vikas, 1986), p. 10.
11. Nirad C. Chaudhuri, *To Live or Not to Live* (Delhi: Orient Paperbacks, no date), p. 196.
12. Nirad C. Chaudhuri, *The Three Horsemen of the New Apocalypse* (Delhi: O.U.P., 1997).

Unknown Indian: An Obituary

MULK RAJ ANAND

Odd genius Nirad C. Chaudhuri was obviously a rebellious child who reacted against the mud and slush of his native village, in what is now Bangladesh. He went to school and later to college in Bengal Province, where Lord Macaulay had introduced the English language as the medium of instruction and knowledge in the education system. Thus young Nirad grew up to receive education in the English language.

Reform had been initiated by Rammohun Roy, in the mid-19th century, who favoured the English language to disperse the wealth of information and culture available in British publications. Roy, though a master of Sanskrit, Persian and Arabic, felt that all renaissance knowledge was in the European languages. Under the patronage of Lord William Bentick, he encouraged the nurturing of European culture in the English language.

Lord Macaulay propagated English at the Calcutta University, which was to become the model for the other universities of British India. Thus, the early novels in Bengali were inspired by British fiction. Young Nirad read English novels which were university text books. He also read Shakespeare's plays.

As novels came into Bengal earlier than elsewhere, Nirad Chaudhuri's admiration for English literature can be understood as being dominant in his make-up. Lonely and bereft in a corner of Bengal, he also became aware of how Clive had led the British Army against Siraj-ud-Daulat and defeated the Governor of Bengal in the Battle of Plassey. He was to write a book in honour of Clive, whom he seems to have regarded as a hero.

He was aware that British officials were interested in Indian culture. Sir William Jones translated Kalidasa's *Shakuntala*, Horace Hayman Wilson, *Little Clay Cart*, and Arthur Avalon (Sir John Woodroff) Tantra philosophical texts.

Nirad Chaudhuri never said so, but for a few years he served as secretary to Sarat Bose, the elder brother of Subash Bose, which shows that he was not unaware of the Indian urge for freedom.

It seems that his Master's degree from Calcutta University did not help him find a suitable job. This might have rankled. Unlike the usual post graduate, he was a voracious reader of European, especially British literature. Therefore, one can understand his life-long admiration for British intelligentsia and their culture. Tagore felt that the literary artist, in general, was conscious of the political domination of India—the cruelties inflicted on rebels in the Indian Mutiny of 1857, the shooting ordered by General Dyer at Jallianwala Bagh in 1919.

Nirad Chaudhuri seems never to have mentioned the atrocities of British in 1857. Nor did he notice the suppression of the National Movement for Freedom, in the fifty years of the twentieth century, even though he knew Subhash Bose was incarnated frequently.

What we suddenly saw was the dedication to "the British Empire" of his Autobiography. And he began to say, in an unbridled manner, that the whole of modern India was the creation of British rule. Soon after, he left India to settle in Oxford. The British Conservative Government honoured him with the title "Companion of Indian Empire."

It is possible that being the odd Indian with fullsome praise for the British Government and its education system, he sensed the contempt most members of Indian intelligentsia had for him. But this made him more childish in his petulant sarcastic dismissal of all those who dared express their doubts about his abiect loyalty to Imperial British.

There is an apt Hindustani phrase "*Badnam bhi honge to kya naam na hoga*—even if we get bad name, will not we be famous?" This seems to have been the childlike attitude of Nirad Chaudhuri throughout his adult years.

Five foot, five inches tall, lean and eloquent, Nirad Chaudhuri remained, until the hundredth year of his life, the devotee of Britain.

Of course, apart from his childlike attitude to the Imperial system, he had a profound respect for British, German and French interpreters of our ancient Indian cultures.

He considered Hinduism, as praised by Max Muller, Spengler and Walt Whitman, to be the perfect religion. He refused to notice the caste system of Brahmins which has relegated millions of outcastes to hell in life for centuries. And though he worshipped his own wife, he did not consider the reduction of woman to slavery by the Sage Manu, and subjugation of the Indian woman for centuries.

In his later Autobiography, he surpasses his earlier contempt for everything Indian as being vulgar. Except that he began to see, in his last book, *Three Horsemen of the New Apocalypse*, vulgarity in the lives of the British and the Americans and, eventually of course, in India.

Maybe one can guess that he loved India so much that he hated it for not being a Britain. All the same one cannot refrain from offering praise to Nirad Chaudhuri for his enormous knowledge and brilliant style of Indian English writing.